New York History Review
Annual Issue 2013

New York History Review Annual Issue 2013
Volume 7, Issue 1

Copyright © 2014 New York History Review
Published by New York History Review Press
Elmira, New York

ISBN: 978-0-9838487-2-1

Printed in the United States of America

Cover image, Sullivanville, New York photograph by Maude Ennick.

Table of Contents

From NYHR

Our mission is to provide readers with a multitude of New York State history articles, and provide New York history writers an online publishing venue with an annual hard copy. We are dedicated to exploring all aspects of New York State's rich and diverse history.

Welcome to the *New York History Review Annual Issue 2013* and please visit our online magazine.

NewYorkHistoryReview.com

Historical Connections: Homer, New York and Cornell University

by Martin A. Sweeney

Drawn by the author from his book *Lincoln's Gift From Homer, New York: A Painter, An Editor, and a Detective*

Twenty-four miles northeast of Ithaca, New York, in Cortland County is the Town of Homer with a village also bearing the name of the Greek poet of Antiquity. Those who have ventured down the Main Street of the village have noted the nineteenth century architecture, the stately trees between the curb and sidewalks, and the American flags patriotically fluttering in the breeze. More than once the comment has been made about the village's Norman Rockwell appearance, and one first-time visitor stated, "I thought I had driven onto the set of a Civil War era movie." Indeed, the community can boast of 220 structures posted in the National Register of Historic Places. One of those structures, a red brick residence built in the Federal style in 1819 and remodeled in the 1880s in the French Second Empire style, has a significant connection to Cornell University. Located at 81 South Main Street, with its distinctive steep Mansard roof, projecting dormer windows, and bracketed eaves, the edifice bears a plaque indicating it is the birthplace of Andrew Dickson White, the first president of the Ivy League university founded in Ithaca in 1868.

Being the geographical origin of Cornell's founding president would be enough of a claim to bragging rights by the proud caretakers of Homer's Historic District, but what seems to go overlooked are the

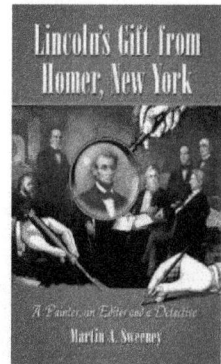

other significant connections the Town and Village of Homer have with the university. Two other native sons of Homer, William Osborn Stoddard and Francis Bicknell Carpenter, have historic ties with Andrew D. White and the university.

Just around the corner from where White was born on November 7, 1832, is another brick house at No. 5 Albany Street, which was built by Homer silversmith and farmer, John Osborn. In front is a blue and gold New York State historical marker proclaiming to the passing motorist that it is the place where Osborn's grandson, William Osborn Stoddard, was born on September 24, 1835. While Stoddard was a journalist, inventor, and author of a slew of adventure stories for boys, he is better known as the assistant personal secretary to President and Mrs. Lincoln at the Civil War White House.

Being neighbors and close in age, White and Stoddard became childhood chums. Together, the two lads explored the wildflower-covered banks of the nearby Tioughnioga (pronounced tie-off-ni-o-ga)

The photo of the author portraying Lincoln's personal secretary, William Stoddard, courtesy of Bob Ellis, photographer of *The Cortland Standard*

River and swam in the millponds at the opposite ends of the village. Their fathers, Horace White and Samuel Prentice Stoddard, were both clerks at The Great Western, the Wal-Mart of nineteenth century Central New York owned by Jedediah Barber. The three-storied emporium on Homer's Main

A. D. White birthplace on Main Street, Homer, courtesy of David Quinlan

Street claimed "no one could ask for an article which the Great Western Store could not produce." The store did manage to offer "everything a farmer could raise or a skilled worker could make."

Both Horace and Samuel gave up their clerking jobs at the Great Western in the 1840s and moved their families north to Syracuse, a village of some five thousand people that was becoming a thriving hub of commerce because of its location on the Erie Canal. Horace found employment at the Onondaga County Bank, and Samuel opened a bookstore and publishing firm on Salina Street. Since both men initially bought homes on Fayette Street, their sons were able to continue their childhood friendships and to come of age together in the expanding community on Onondaga Lake.

Both lads attended a private boys' school in the basement of the Congregational Church in Syracuse. Later in life, both of them extolled the fine instruction and modeling of Christian virtues offered by the "tall, handsome, pleasant-mannered" James W. Hoyt. Stoddard claimed Hoyt "possessed a rare talent for getting young brains at work to the best advantage." White concurred with his classmate: "We doubtless agree in thinking that the lack of grammatical drill [in studying Virgil, Horace, and Xenophon] was more than made up by the love of manliness, and the dislike of meanness, which was in those days our very atmosphere."

As a sign of their close camaraderie, young White presented Stoddard with a beautiful rifle with telescopic sights, which had been a gift from a friend of his father. He explained to Stoddard, "I haven't any use for a rifle. You take it and use it as long as you want to, just as if it were your own. Take it home with you, flask, pouch, and all." Stoddard did so. He kept it through several years and named the future president of Cornell University as the one deserving credit for his future reputation, even with President Lincoln, for being a crack shot with a rifle.

Under Hoyt, Stoddard showed great interest and ability in writing. Foreshadowing his future career, he printed a little weekly for school he called *The Frolic Manual*. In 1853 he went to New York City to see the first World's Fair in America. He wrote a long account of the sights and sent it to the Syracuse *Chronicle*, where he found "my story was a good one and it was printed in full." This increased his standing with his classmates at school.

Earlier, in October of 1851, Stoddard's classmates were presumably equally impressed by the bruises he had sustained in violating the Fugitive Slave Law of 1850 during the famous Jerry Rescue. A mob of Abolitionists forcibly removed runaway slave William "Jerry" Henry from federal authorities, and sixteen year old Stoddard "was lost in the rush but was close enough to see the axes and crowbars go up and down upon those wooden window bars" of the jail near Clinton Square. Stoddard's introduction to Abolitionist activity had already occurred in Homer. As a ten year old visiting at his Grandfather Osborn's farmhouse, he had stumbled upon a slave in the cellar and learned that Squire Osborn, pillar of the local Baptist Church, was participating in an anti-slavery organization called the Underground Railroad.

Through formal education and life experiences, White and Stoddard were ready to depart Syracuse for higher education. White left for Geneva College and then went off to Yale. There, he attended classes with another childhood friend from Homer, Theodore T. Munger. Munger went on to be a distinguished theologian and Abolitionist. Stoddard went off to the new university at nearby Rochester and then traveled out to Illinois, where he became co-editor of The *Central Illinois Gazette* and made the acquaintance of a politically ambitious circuit lawyer named Abraham Lincoln.

Stoddard worked for the nomination and election of Lincoln to the Presidency of the United States and landed a position as the assistant personal secretary to Lincoln and the First Lady from 1861 to 1865. In that capacity, and at Lincoln's bidding, Stoddard made two handwritten copies of the Emancipation Proclamation from the President's draft. Cornell University is in possession of a copy of the document written "by a secretary." Judging by the style of handwriting, it is one of the two copies made by the hand of Homer's native son, William O. Stoddard.

Another son of Homer was born August 6, 1830, a few miles north of the village. His name was Francis Bicknell Carpenter. He was a prominent portrait painter working in New York City in 1863 when he learned of Lincoln's document that would initiate the process of freeing slaves and would culminate later in the Thirteenth Amendment's abolition of slavery. Carpenter described the proclamation as "an act unparalleled for moral grandeur in the history of mankind." He determined that he would render a painting of Lincoln and his cabinet at the moment when the proclamation was first read that would "give freedom to a race." Furthermore, it was his desire that the painting should become "the standard authority for the portrait of each and all especially Mr. Lincoln." He got his wish. From February to July of 1864, the man who had already painted the visages of three sitting presidents – Tyler, Fillmore, and Pierce – was, in Lincoln's words, "turned in loose" at the White House and given "a good chance to work out your idea." The artistic skills that had begun in a one-room schoolhouse in Homer and had been encouraged by a benefactor, Jedediah Barber's son Paris Barber, came into full blossom with Carpenter's completion of "The First Reading of the Emancipation Proclamation before the Cabinet." Lincoln told Carpenter, "I believe I am about as glad over the success of this work as you are," and he deemed the portraiture to be "absolutely perfect."

After Lincoln's assassination, Carpenter hoped that the nine foot by fifteen foot oil painting would be purchased by the national legislature and placed in the Capitol Building. Much to his chagrin, Congress showed no interest in appropriating the $25,000 requested, and the tough economic times of the Panic of 1873 did not help. However, it was Stoddard who on behalf of "his warm personal friend of long standing" arranged for a wealthy philanthropist to pay the artist $25,000 and lobbied successfully for Congress to accept "the national picture" in 1878 and to have it displayed in the Capitol Building. Since then, the figure of Lincoln as "The Great Emancipator" with what Stoddard referred to as "the sad, far-seeing eyes" has become universally iconic.

The same artist that painted Lincoln has a direct tie to Cornell University. When Stoddard's friend, Andrew D. White, became the first President of the university – a land-grant college under the Morrill Act signed into law by President Lincoln -- Carpenter was present for the institution's opening in 1868. And it was Carpenter whom White commissioned to do the portraits for the university of Louis Agassiz, Goldwyn Smith, James Russell Lowell, and George William Curtis. Ezra Cornell posed, too. In the law school library, his image can be seen standing, with his hand upon a document bearing his time-honored wish of 1868: "I would found an institution where any person can find instruction in any study."

In 1869, when the progressive, co-educational Academy on Homer's Green celebrated its fiftieth anniversary, Carpenter was in attendance, and the gentleman selected to give the main oration was Andrew D. White. From 1871 to 1891, Carpenter worked on the only other painting he ever did on a grand scale. Depicting the signing of the Treaty of Washington on May 8, 1871, he called it his "Arbitration Painting." To celebrate its completion, a dinner in Carpenter's honor was held in New York. The Reverend Dr. Theodore Munger was one of the twenty-seven guests, and the toastmaster for this special occasion was none other than Andrew D. White.

White, Carpenter, and Stoddard, three sons of the same community in Central New York, lived through tumultuous times of civil strife and human bondage – times that the nation now recalls during its Sesquicentennial observance of the American Civil War. Each man left autobiographical writings and reminiscences as part of his legacy. These have served as primary sources for scholars of nineteenth century American history, politics, and culture. Through the life-long friendships and working bonds they formed with each other, these men of arts and letters forged a link between Homer and Cornell University based on more than geographic proximity. The connection is part of the rich fabric of history to be found in the Finger Lakes region of Central New York State.

About the author: Mr. Sweeney, a retired history teacher, writes mostly historical non-fiction. Besides the book on Homer's connection to Lincoln, he wrote *Death In The Winter Solstice: A Narrative Of A True Murder Mystery In Homer* (Cortland County Historical Society, 2012) and co-authored with David Quinlan "Lincoln's Empire State Bastion: Homer, New York," a scholarly article published in the Spring 2011 issue of The Lincoln Forum Bulletin. This scholarly article focused on the religious and secular forces in nineteenth century Homer that influenced Lincoln iconography.

"Stick to Your Guns!"
The Third United States Artillery
and the Battle of Oswego 1814

by Matthew MacVittie

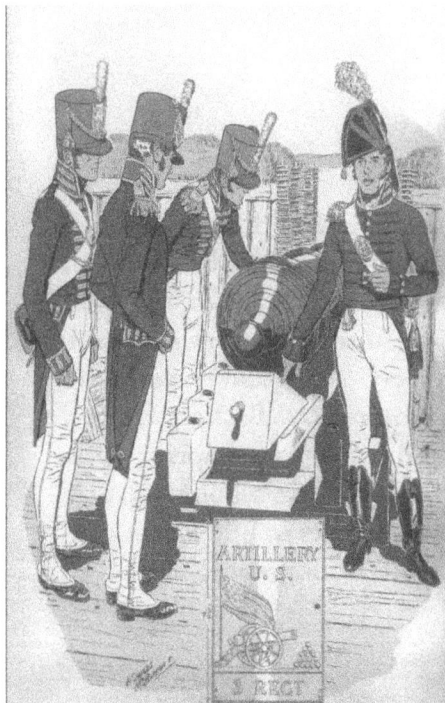

This year marks the beginning of a very significant event in American history, the bicentennial of The War of 1812. Many historians have called The War of 1812 "a funny little war" worthy of little note or academic study, a view that would have been contested by the roughly 18,000 individuals who lost their lives on both sides of the conflict.[1] Like most frontier counties in New York State, Oswego County saw its fair share of war time activity. It is important to remember that Oswego County did not exist until 1816 when it was formed from the northernmost territories of Onondaga County. Within those borders of then northern Onondaga County, a small but important fortification named Fort Ontario lay on the shore of Lake Ontario.

At that very fortification, late in the war, an under equipped and outnumbered American force would clash head on with the full force of the British Empire. Many have claimed the 1814 Battle of Oswego was a minor footnote in the war, and in a way they are correct, as no real major repercussions resulted from it. The goal, as told by many of the nineteenth century histories, was for Commodore Yeo of His Majesties Navy to capture cannon and naval stores intended for American Commodore Chauncey's fleet that was currently being built at Sackets Harbor. But, Commodore Yeo did not capture the majority of the cannon and only a moderate amount of naval supplies nor did he significantly delay Chauncey to any degree. Colonel Mitchell of the American Third United States Artillery, who was sent to Oswego in case of British attack, did not repel the British force and did little damage accept for perhaps, proving a small force fighting against an invader is capable of putting up quite a fight. But this battle is a perfect example of the strangeness and difficulties of the war, and almost echoes the entire war itself: supply problems, under manned and under equipped American forces trying to repel what was still the largest world power, and a handful of triumphs and disappointments for both sides.

In 1814 a ship building race between the British and American forces on Lake Ontario continued at a fever pitch. On April 14, 1814 Commodore Sir James Lucas Yeo of the Royal Navy was the first to complete his squadron of frigates based in Kingston. However, Commodore Isaac Chauncey of the United States Navy was dangerously close to completing his squadron of more powerful frigates at his ship building yard near Sackets Harbor. If Chauncey was allowed to complete his task, Lake Ontario would become an American Lake. Therefore Commodore Yeo knew that he must delay Commodore Chauncey if he was to maintain control of the lake, but what few realize is why he needed to maintain control of the lake. As previously mentioned the popular understanding of the Battle of Oswego 1814 was that Yeo wanted the guns, this is true but not for the guns alone. In order to understand why this battle took place one must first look to the actions on the Niagara Frontier.

In the spring of 1814 things were looking grim for everyone near the Canadian settlements at Niagara and York. The previous year the American forces led a large scale assault capturing British Forts George and Erie before being checked at Stony Creek and American Militia General McClure had burned Niagara. Afterward, Lieutenant General of Upper Canada Sir Gordon Drummond found himself with his army on the Niagara frontier facing severe food shortages. On April 22, 1814 Lieutenant General Sir Gordon Drummond, wrote to George Prevost, Governor in Chief of British North America of his dilemma that "the

Native Allies alone are receiving 1200 barrels of flour per month and this amount of flour does not exist in the country.[2] "Furthermore that the number of barrels needed to sustain the men not including the militia or the Garrison at York approached 2000 barrels per month, and that the right division would almost certainly lose its ground if they lost the native allies, flour must be send from Lower Canada immediately.[3] From a logistical standpoint George Prevost was in a tight spot, the road networks throughout both the Upstate New York and Canada were of retched quality. Stumps were often not removed and mudslides were a frequent occurrence after a rain storm. Furthermore, wagons could only carry a relatively small amount of supplies and due to the rough road conditions were prone to breaking down. The easiest and cheapest way to get flour to the British troops stationed at Niagara was the waterways of Lake Ontario and the St. Lawrence River.

Yet lack of flour was not the only problem that faced Drummond's army. How would the flour and other supplies arrive via the water route at York and Niagara? Records show that the British had only five merchant sloops (one mast) and schooners (two masts) left on Lake Ontario by the spring of 1814, The British Queen, Mary, Prince Edward, Elizabeth and Lady Washington, the last two having been captured American Vessels.[4] The six the British lost at one time in the fall of 1813 that were picked off by Chauncey after the Burlington Races on 28 September 1814 and off the Duck Islands[5] dealt a substantial blow. Although they varied in size, average was 50-60 tons burthen which was the standard size merchant vessel of the day.

Records from the Augustus Porter Papers at the Buffalo & Erie County Historical Society give information on the cargo capacity of these vessels but for barrels of salt, which were as heavy as, but much smaller than barrels of flour, salt being a much denser material. They show as many as 500+ barrels of salt carried but the average is less than 300.[6] Therefore a good estimate is 200 barrels of flour would fill one merchant schooner. At 200 pounds per barrel total weight, that equals roughly 40 tons. This would mean the merchant schooners would need to make ten round-trip voyages from Kingston to York or Niagara and return per month for the flour, assuming the locally provided flour would take care of the militia and residents. If there was a good easterly wind going from Kingston to York/Niagara and a good westerly wind coming back, the crews of the merchant schooners could do a round trip in three or four days, but Mother Nature was not often that kind. Many times it took Chauncey's squadron four or five days to go from Sackets to Niagara and sometimes as long coming back even with the prevailing westerly winds.[7] A bad storm could delay the voyage even more. A safe estimate may be one round trip per week with four round trips per Schooner per month. With the five merchant schooners available to the British that makes a total of 20 trips per month. Of those planned 20 merchant trips per month at least half of those would be taken up just moving flour. That would leave only ten trips for the other provisions (beef, peas, corn, and bread), the troops themselves (room for only about only about 50-60 per schooner. Transporting only one regiment would have used up the remaining ten trips that month. Plus ordnance, ammunition, gunpowder, camp equipment and civilian goods. The fact of the matter is there just were not enough merchant schooners available to the British by the spring of 1814.

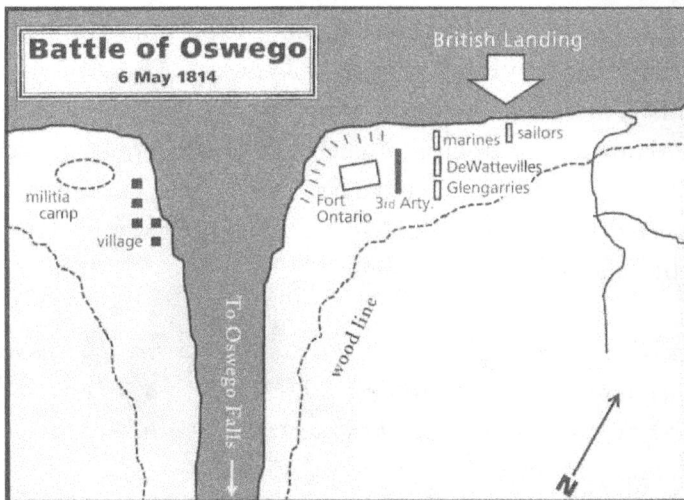

Battle of Oswego
6 May 1814

British Landing

marines sailors
DeWattevilles
Glengarries
Fort Ontario   3rd Arty.

militia camp
village

To Oswego Falls

wood line

N

Later in the war out of necessity the British began to use their brigs and schooners (Star, Magnet, Charwell and Netley) as troop and stores transports[8] and why Commodore Chauncey was able to pick off the Magnet with a load of gunpowder on her way from York to Niagara in early August 1814. Furthermore, the moment the British regained command of Lake Ontario in October 1814, after the 102-gun St. Lawrence was launched, Yeo began to use his squadron as merchant schooners and made two round trips from Kingston to Niagara transporting provisions and other badly needed supplies for Drummond's army.[9] By the time Yeo returned from the second trip it was well into November and the sailing season on the lake was over for that year. In the spring of 1814 the British loss of Lake Ontario would mean Drummonds army would be forced to fight on reduced rations, and as history has proven, hungry men do not fight well.In April 1814 Gordon Drummond, suggested using the next few weeks when Yeo's squadron was stronger than Chauncey's to attack the main American harbor and base at Sackets's Harbor, New York. Most of its garrison had marched off to the Niagara River, leaving only 1,000 regular troops as its garrison. Nevertheless, Drummond would require reinforcements to mount a successful attack on the strongly fortified town, and the Governor General of Canada, Lieutenant General Sir George Prevost, remembered the direct assault on Sackets Harbor the previous year had been a failure. Combined with reports from his spies that the Americans had substantially increased the fortifications around the town since then, he refused to provide the troops.[10] Therefore a plan had to be devised that would delay Chauncey, and quickly, as British Spies at Sackets Harbor had reported to Commodore Yeo that Chauncey would be ready to launch by June 1, 1814.

> *You will regret with me that the Enemy's preparations are so great, and yet so short a time back as the 20th January not a keel was laid at Sackets. Now they have 400 shipwrights and two of their new Ships nearly ready for launching, a third will be ready by the 1st of May and a fourth by the latter part of that month. The roads from Albany, Boston and New York are covered with Ordnance and Stores*

for these Vessels and which when added to their old Squadron, will be far superior to any thing I can bring against them. It therefore becomes my duty to acquaint you that unless I receive immediate reinforcements of Guns long 24 and 32 Pounders, men and Stores of every description Upper Canada will, in my opinion be lost to His Majesty.[11]

The situation at Oswego was known to Drummond who wrote Prevost:

I conceive that a successful attack on their great naval depot at Oswego would nearly, if not entirely circumscribe the proceedings of the enemy, because we would be so fortunate to destroy the stores ect. That are now collected there, for the use of the fleet, it is very improbable they could shew themselves on the lake for sometime at least. [12]

Therefore Drummond and Yeo decided to attack the smaller and less defended post of Fort Ontario at Oswego New York in the hopes they might capture naval supplies, guns and anything else that would sufficiently delay the launch of Chauncey's squadron. American General Brown learned of a possible attack, but it was not clear whether the British would strike Sackets Harbor or Oswego. Therefore he dispatched his closest troops, the battle-tested Third Regiment of U.S. Artillery.

With war on the horizon congress passed a bill authorizing two new regiments of artillery, the second & third, on January 11, 1812. A race to recruit and train officers and enlisted men for these new regiments began shortly thereafter. The artillery corps required a man to be part solider and part engineer; naturally it attracted a mixed lot of seasoned military men and the inexperienced alike. However, finding men that could meet both skills sets often proved problematic, and led to the all too common lack of qualified personnel that plagued the U.S. military throughout the war. However, even under staffed, the Third had served with distinction in the early days of the conflict, notably at the Battle of Queenston Heights and the first Battle of Sackets Harbor. Early in March 1814, the Third marched from Sackets Harbor to Batavia NY where they set up a temporary camp and waited for their tents and cannon to arrive. Once fully equipped they planned to meet the rest of their brigade which was being assembled near Buffalo in preparation for a renewed push on the Niagara Peninsula. However, before their equipment could rendezvous with them in Batavia, General Brown ordered the Third to Oswego to defend against a possible British attack at Fort Ontario. Consequently the Third was quickly dispatched to protect Fort Ontario and prevent the seizure of the naval supplies, which were stored near Oswego Falls (modern day Fulton) as well as the village of Oswego, which were intended for Chauncey's fleet at Sackets Harbor. Lieutenant Colonel George Mitchell took the 342 men of the Third on a forced march with only what they could carry to Oswego, to meet the British forces and prevent the course of events Commodore Yeo had set into action.

The Third arrived at Oswego on April 30, 1814, into a situation that was all but hopeless. The village of all but 40 warehouses and taverns lay on the west side of the mouth of the Oswego River. To the east, the remnants of Fort Ontario sat high upon the bluff. Fort Ontario had been all but abandoned until the beginning of the war and largely maintained its 18th century configuration, until this point the Fort had been left largely under the control of militia troops who were ill equipped and not up to the task of restoring a major military post. Captain Rufus McIntire of the Third wrote:

"The hand of time has destroyed every picket, we found five pieces of artillery in it, three 4 pounders, one 6 and one 9, all very old. Three without trunions and all miserably mounted. Indeed they were condemned pieces but had been mounted in case of necessity and we were compelled to use them for the same cause." [13]

Lieutenant Colonel George Fleming, commander of the militia at fort Ontario until 26 October 1812 had written Governor Tompkins on numerous occasions that local militia forces were suitable to repel a British attack. This opinion was further shared by Major Charles Moseley who concluded artillery would be ideal for Oswego, but that the detachment of militia present will be vigilant and prepared for anything that may happen. [14] That combined with the fact that the post was not constantly in use as a supply depot led the U.S. military to not leave a permanent garrison at the post, nor fixed shore batteries for naval defense.

Lieutenant Colonel Mitchell directed his men to repair the guns as best they could and start making cannon cartridges. Some men were picked to form gun crews while the rest would serve as infantry in case of a British landing. The gun crews constructed a battery of 3 guns outside the fort on the north side and a battery of two guns on the eastern wall, while others placed tents on the east side of the river to make their force seem larger than it was. On May 4 Mitchell received word from General Brown that "We have at this moment received word that the enemies fleet are out. Two ships, two Briggs and one schooner, is all that have as yet been seen, your post is as likely to be the object as any other place, and I rejoice to know that you are there." [15] The 342 Men of the Third U.S. Artillery, and approximately 200 undisciplined militia troops readied themselves for battle. Lt Col Mitchell determined to succeed, had a man climb the flag pole above the fort and nail the flag in place. The message was clear; there would be no surrender. [16]

On May 3, 1814 Yeo set sail from Kingston for Oswego with a landing force consisting of the 2nd battalion of Royal Marines (350), the light company of the Glengarry Light Infantry (50), six companies of the Regiment de Watteville (450) (a Swiss regiment in British service), a detachment of 200 sailors, a detachment from the Royal Artillery (24) with two field pieces and a detachment of the rocket company (6), roughly 1000 men total.[17] These troops were not only more experienced than the American troops that waited at Oswego, they also outnumbered the American force by roughly 2 to 1, not including the US militia force that did little during the assault. In the late morning of May 5 the British Flotilla arrived in the waters off Oswego. However, due to light winds they found themselves incapable of getting into a firing position until mid afternoon. Both sides exchanged cannon fire and the British attempted a landing, but were required to retreat due to an incoming storm. The British Flotilla withdrew for the evening; neither side had sustained much damage except for one of Lieutenant Colonel Mitchell's cannons, which burst while firing.[18] Both British and American Forces rested what little they could, and awaited the next day's events.

The next morning Mitchell ordered the 200 militia troops to the west side of the river to give the appearance that a larger force had arrived and provide the illusion of strength. The flotilla appeared, hauling landing boats filled with infantry, marines and sailors armed with boarding pikes. Yeo's ships than began to open with cannon fire upon Mitchells gun emplacements, the American guns soon returned with their own fire. With the deafening sound of artillery the undisciplined militia troops soon fled for the woods, leaving Mitchell and his men alone. The British force, over 1000 strong, began to land and advance toward the Fort. A number of British troops had gotten their powder wet while scurrying to evacuate their small landing boats, an advantage Mitchell desperately needed. The Third fired seven volleys of musket fire directly into the advancing British column, but numbers prevailed and the British still continued to advance.[19] Mitchell began to see the Third would be over run if they maintained their position. He quickly ordered a retreat and his men slowly began to leave their position, most of which were located in a ditch surrounding the fort, as Mitchell had not wanted to be trapped inside, fighting the whole way out. The gun crew upon the fort wall was said to have yelled "let us give them one more fire!" not realizing the British were mere feet away from them. The last man to leave the Fort was Colonel Mitchell himself. As he rode out, a wounded soldier begged for assistance. Mitchell was reported to dismount, and proceeded to place the man on his horse. Calmly, on foot, Mitchell walked at the rear of his men.[20]

The British entered the fort and attempted to seize the flag Mitchell had nailed to the tall post on the Fort bastion, but they were hit with light musket fire from the Americans. The man who eventually succeeded in removing it was Lieutenant John Hewett, whose ancestors still posses the flag in their collection, located in their ancestral castle in Scotland. The British reported casualties of 24 killed and 96 wounded, the American casualties are listed as 6 killed, 38 wounded and 25 missing, but reports vary.

Commodore Yeo had captured 1,045 barrels of flour, pork and salt, 70 coils of rope, three long 32 pound cannon, four 24 pound cannon, one 12 pound cannon and one six pound cannon, along with raising two schooners that had been scuttled.[21] Notably the Schooner Penelope was a serious prize as it had been sunk in shallow water and not only was easily raised but contained several of the large guns intended for Chauncey, as it had a large hatch and was apt for hauling bulky goods.[22] This was not only a victory in its cargo but lightened the burden, however small, on the lack of British merchant schooners.

After the battle Commodore Yeo set sail for Sackets Harbor in an attempt to blockade the harbor and prevent the stores he had not captured in making their way to Chauncey. This plan failed as the remaining supplies were taken up the road network from Oswego Falls to Sackets Harbor, a difficult feat as the road was hazardous at best. Through a cause and effect based argument we can see that the 1814 Battle of Oswego was based on the fact that Commodore Yeo needed to maintain control of Lake Ontario for the survival of the Niagara Frontier army. But, his attack on Oswego had mixed results. First, unknown to him, Chauncey would not have been able to launch on July 1 as Yeo's spies had reported. Chauncey claimed that the frigate Mohawk was not ready[23] and he became quite ill that month. In fact, Chauncey did not launch his Great Lakes Squadron until August 1, 1814. Therefore, if Yeo had not attacked he still would have maintained control of Lake Ontario until August 1814. Second, even if he had seized all the cannon intended for Chauncey, two months was more than enough time to replace them with new cannon from New York Naval Yard. Yeo's only real triumph was the seizure of the food and naval stores and the acquisition of the two schooners. The battle was technically a British victory, but that victory had a high cost for the victors, the most serious cost to the British was William Howe Mulcaster, Post Captain of the Frigate Prince Regent whose wound left him permanently disabled. Men on both sides of the engagement fought with valor on May 6, 1814. The Third United States Artillery certainly proved that a hopeless situation can still put a crimp in the enemy's plans. General Jacob Brown said it best when he stated "Mitchell's men have established themselves with a name in arms, worthy of the gallant nation whose cause they fight, and highly honorable to the army".[24] Men who prevented the British from capturing vital supplies that was essential to Chauncey's fleet, and earned The Third US Artillery notable status in the pages of American history.

About the Author: Matthew J. Mac Vittie serves as the Assistant Curator of History of the Onondaga Historical Association in Syracuse NY which will be celebrating its sesquicentennial as a historical organization in 2013. Previous positions include Executive Director of The Friends of History in Fulton NY INC (Fulton New York Historical Society) and various positions with New York State Parks Recreation and Historic Preservation. Matthew Mac Vittie has a Bachelors of Arts in American History from The State University of New York and is currently a Master of Arts candidate in the Military History program at Norwich University.

Endnotes

[1] Hickey, Donald R (2006). *Don't Give Up the Ship! Myths of The War of 1812.* Urbana: University of Illinois Press.
[2] Drummond To Prevost, April 26 1814, C Series 683, Public Archives Canada
[3] Drummond To Prevost, April 26 1814, C Series 683, Public Archives Canada
[4] Gary M Gibson, *Merchant Vessels on Lake Ontario 1812-1814.* Unpublished.
[5] Isaac Chauncey to William Jones #86, 6 October 1813, SNLRC, 1813 vol 6 item 126, M125 roll 31. SNLRC: Secretary of the Navy Letters Received from Captains ("Captain's Letters")
[6] Augustus Porter Papers, Folder 200, Buffalo and Erie County Historical Society, Buffalo NY.
[7] One such five-day trip from Sackets Harbor to Niagara is referenced in Isaac Chauncey to William Jones #132, 10 August 1814, SNLRC, 1814 vol 5 item 84, M125 roll 38.
[8] Transcript of court martial of Acting Lieutenant George Hawksworth for the

loss of HMS Magnet, 14 November 1814, NAUK, ADM 1/6447.

[9] James Lucas Yeo to John Wilson Croker #36, 24 October 1814, NAUK ADM 1/2737.

[10] Drummond to Prevost, April 28th 1814. C Series 683 Public Archives Canada

[11] Yeo to Admiral John Borlase Warren, 5 March 1814 NAUK, ADM 1/2737, NAC film roll B-2941.

[12] Drummond to Prevost, April 27 1814 NAC, RG8, C.683

[13] McIntire to Homes, 9 May 1814, found in Fredricksen, "Rufus McIntire": 321

[14] Moseley to Tompkins, July 21 1812, Military Papers of Daniel D Tompkins Vol 3, 49

[15] Brown to Mitchell, May 4 1814, *Long Range Guns, Close Quarter Combat: The Third United States Artillery Regiment in the War of 1812*

[16] Mitchell to Brown, May 4 1814, *Long Range Guns, Close Quarter Combat: The Third United States Artillery Regiment in the War of 1812*

[17] Drummond to Prevost May 3 1814. C Series 683 Public Archives Canada

[18] Mitchell to Brown, May 5 1814 *Long Range Guns, Close Quarter Combat: The Third United States Artillery Regiment in the War of 1812*

[19] Richard V. Barbuto, *Long Range Guns, Close Quarter Combat: The Third United States Artillery Regiment in the War of 1812*, 83

[20] Mcintire to Holmes, May 9 1814, Found in Fredrickson, "Rufus Mcintire": 314-5

[21] Return of Stores Captured at Oswego, May 7 1814. C Series 683 Public Archives Canada

[22] S. 16th Congress 1st Session H.Rep 81; U. S. 16th Congress 2nd Session, H.Rep 39.

[23] Isaac Chauncey to William Jones #132, 10 August 1814, SNLRC, 1814 vol 5 item 84, M125 roll 38.

[24] Macomb to Mitchell, 29 May 1814, Historical Society of Cecil County

Three Poetic Monologues from Redwing, New York

by Dr. Katharyn Howd Machan

TUBMAN GREENE: Redwing, 1888

My father traveled fast and traveled far,
away from warmer rivers, warmer land--
all time, he said, a single guiding star
and charity from one brave woman's hand.
My mother followed, praying that my name
could be my own when I was born, held free
of master's choices, master's whip, the same
as any baptized white child's days would be.
What hunger? What sharp terror must have torn
their breath as they ran hiding in the dark,
each cellar, church, and barn, each field of corn
or fog-swept swamp dark hell but for her spark?
They've raised me thanking God that their first son
has lived to honor her for what she's done.

HARRIET GREENE: Redwing, 1888

He loves me well, my brother. I'll defend
his words of loyalty and history
against the fools who sneer so mightily
at what he swears—the truth!—will finally end
the way life's river has been forced to bend
for those of us with color, who may be
the sanest creatures highest God can see,
but must endure the way the waters wend.
What can he ask of me? I'll gladly give
my breath the way the woman whose dear name
I hold in reverence helped our parents live
within a world of whitest deadly blame.
But who am I? A girl in love with life—
the one I'm making, free to be a wife.

IRIS BIRDWELL: Redwing, 1888

I see him all the time, the boy I loved.
His smile under the quickening oak tree
green leaves hiding gold, his hair
smooth upon his forehead, brown
as the deer we glimpsed one twilight
from a curving wooden bridge.

I hear him play piano again
midsummer where small bats flew close,
the moon as round as the watch on his vest
while his hands moved the polished keys
under the columned roof where a wedding
would join two souls next day.

I touch him, ten years, twenty gone:
my fingers light upon his brow, his palms
where I traced the lines I thought
we would share together. Chautauqua,
and the lake at sunrise, calls of ducks
on water black to blue.

Katharyn Howd Machan studied creative writing and literature at the College of Saint Rose and at the University of Iowa, taught college for five years, returned to graduate school for a Ph.D. in Interpretation at Northwestern University and, now as a full professor, has been teaching on the faculty of the Department of Writing at Ithaca College ever since. In 2002 she was named the first poet laureate of Tompkins County, New York. Her poems have appeared in numerous magazines (Nimrod, Yankee, The MacGuffin, Snake Nation Review, Hanging Loose, Dogwood, Runes, Slipstream, Beloit Poetry Journal, South Coast Poetry Journal, Hollins Critic, The Salmon, West Branch, Seneca Review, Louisiana Literature, etc.) and anthologies/textbooks (*The Bedford Introduction to Literature, Poetry: An Introduction, Early Ripening: American Women's Poetry Now, Sound and Sense, Writing Poems, Literature: Reading and Writing the Human Experience*, etc.), and in 30 collections, most recently *Belly Words: Poems of Dance* (Split Oak Press, 2009), *When She's Asked to Think of Colors* (Palettes & Quills Press, 2009), *The Professor Poems* (The Main Street Rag Publishing Company, 2008). In 2000 she was awarded the Ann Stanford Poetry Prize from the University of Southern California by judge Dana Gioia for her poem "Tess Clarion: Redwing, 1888" and in 2006 the Luna Negra Prize from Kent State University for her poem "Gingerbread." In 2012 she edited *Adrienne Rich: A Tribute Anthology* for Split Oak Press.

"The Architect and the Artist: FDR, Olin Dows, and the New Deal Post Office Program"

by Jim Blackburn

A happy coincidence brings to us today a unique opportunity. The cornerstone at Rhinebeck's new Post Office is about to be laid as a part of this ceremony of dedication. The Post Office has been built by the Secretary of the Treasury, who is with us. It has been turned over to the Postmaster General, who will use it and who is also with us. Their Royal Highnesses, the Crown Prince and Crown Princess of Denmark and Iceland have come to us, having voyaged from Denmark through the Panama Canal to San Francisco and back across the Continent.[1]

It is unknown if these royal guests were offered hot dogs during their stay with the Roosevelt's as they were, famously to the King and Queen of Great Britain later that same summer, but the dedication of the Rhinebeck post office on May 1, 1939 nearly overwhelmed the modest Hudson Valley river town. Novelist and Rhinebeck resident William Seabrook would state that the building's dedication was "without doubt the most thoroughly dedicated small-town post office in the Western Hemisphere." Seabrook would go on to describe celebrities, news reels, sound trucks, an army of metropolitan reporters and camera men, and the first female photojournalist for Life magazine, "Margaret Bourke-White thrown in for good measure!" The day began with a parade which included marching bands and mounted state-troopers, but also included, because of the royal presence the Danish Girls-Scandinavian-American Society. After a somber invocation, Treasury Secretary Henry Morgenthau Jr. was first to speak, an unusual choice if one did not know that the architecture and the mural artwork inside the post office were both the product of bureaus under the auspices of the Treasury Department. Morgenthau symbolically handed the post office over to postmaster general James A. Farley,[2] and then FDR himself gave the dedication address.[3]

FDR was photographed at the event standing behind a podium, the metal braces that supported his frame barely visible. He began his speech with his first memories of Rhinebeck:

> *Half a century ago—I do not feel that it was that long—a small boy was often driven through the town of Rhinebeck by his father and mother to visit his great-uncle and aunt at their home south of Barrytown.*
>
> *Then, as I grew older, I came to know something of the history of these river towns of Dutchess County, and to develop a great liking for the stone architecture which was indigenous to the Hudson Valley.[4]*

The president then went on to explain that buildings made of local stone in the Hudson Valley were generally called "early Dutch Colonial." He also pointed to the German settlers or Palatines who were invited to Rhinebeck by Judge Henry Beekman (1652–1716), a resident of Kingston who starting in 1697 held substantial land throughout Dutchess County. Beekman was FDR's fourth great-uncle, the brother of Dr. Gerardus Beekman (1653– 723) his paternal fourth great-grandfather. But of closer relation was Isaac Roosevelt (1726–1794), who would be featured in the Poughkeepsie post office murals, and was a favorite ancestor of FDR's because of his involvement in the Revolutionary War and as a member of the group that ratified the United States Constitution for the state of New York in 1788.[5]

> *Because through one line of my ancestry I am descended from the early Beekmans who settled Rhinebeck, and because on the Roosevelt side my great-great-grandfather lived in Rhinebeck for some time during the period of the Revolution and was not only a member of the State Senate, as his great-great-grandson was, but also a member of the Dutchess County Militia, I have a claim to kinship with this town that is second only to the town of Hyde Park.[6]*

FDR then explained why the post office had its unique architectural design. It, along with five others in the Hudson Valley, were built in a distinctive Dutch Colonial revival style during the Great Depression. The president himself had determined the Dutch Colonial architecture, asking that a historic building from each locale be used as a model. For Rhinebeck the Kip House, a structure which burnt to the ground in 1910, and is sometimes referred to as The Kip/Beekman/Livingston House (c.1700-1910), served as the model. The name mirrored the various families who resided on the river estate for over three centuries.[7]

You all know the inspiration for the design of the building which we are dedicating today. Fortunately, I am old enough to remember the old house on the River Road in which were entertained so many famous men before, during, and after the Revolutionary War.[8]

Earlier, when Roosevelt was championing the Kip House as the potential model for the Rhinebeck post office, he played on the importance of historical "firsts." The president claimed that the Kip House was the first house occupied by a white settler in the county, one of Washington's headquarters, and the place where Washington took the oath as President of the United States – none of which was true. But FDR's hyperbole was probably more of an attempt to use historical platitudes and inaccuracies for what was maybe the highest goal of the New Deal post office program, the re-creation of common links to an earlier time and place when Americans had encountered great obstacles and overcome them. The Rhinebeck dedication was a perfect setting for him to express the importance of a shared past by using his own heritage to connect the present to this idealized history.[9]

> *Soon, too, the old cornerstone will be on display in the lobby, together with the famous pane of glass which has been given by Mrs. Suckley and which was rescued from the fire by Colonel John Jacob Astor.*
> *Furthermore, within a short time, a most interesting painting, a frieze around the inside of the lobby, painted by Mr. Olin Dows, is going to grace this building.[10]*

Another aspect of the post office program was the involvement of the community to help the buildings architect and mural painter not only reflect the community historically and culturally, but to establish a community consensus favoring the federal art appearing in their locality as democratically possible. The idea of "taste" is highly individualistic but the economic strains of the 1930's brought together both reluctant artists, who sometimes thought their work was socially autonomous or that the ideal of "art for art's sake" inspired them, and a public who sometimes viewed the artist as a social alien unable to understand the sensibilities of the general populous. During the Great Depression very few escaped hardship and as Harry Hopkins stated "artists have got to eat just like other people," and in turn, the public would have its first fully funded public arts program.[11]

It is, I think, an interesting fact that during the past few years the government, in the designing of Post Office buildings, has been getting away from the sameness of pattern which characterized the past... We are seeking to follow the type of architecture which is good in the sense that it does not of necessity follow the whims of the moment but seeks an artistry that ought to be good, as far as we can tell, for all time to come. And we are trying to adapt the design to the historical background of the locality and to use, insofar as possible, the materials which are indigenous to the locality itself.[12]

Once an official document named Roosevelt as an architect, though this was a jest between the president and architect Henry J. Toombs. When Toombs was designing what would become Top Cottage in 1938 he let FDR sign the design "Franklin D. Roosevelt, Architect," as a joke between the two but also to point to the level of interest (or maybe interference) Roosevelt showed in buildings he commissioned – all of which were in the Dutch Colonial style. When these signed drawings appeared in Life magazine, they upset Frank Lloyd Wright's architect son, John Lloyd Wright,[13] who wrote a sharp reply to Life stating: "The moral breakdown and integrity of the architectural profession now seems complete." An overreaction for sure, but it would not be the first or last time Roosevelt would irk an architect, especially when one did not have the affinity for field stone as he did. The president was also featured in the New York *Times* Magazine article "F.D.R. As Architect" in 1940, in which the author took a more appreciate viewpoint in terms of preserving cultural heritage than Frank Lloyd Wright's son, but Roosevelt's love of indigenous field stone is similar in some aspects to Wright's famous father's philosophy of organic architecture.

The president then ended his speech by putting the Rhinebeck post office in a historical context, but also finished with the humor and charm that is legendary in the remembrances of FDR as a man who could be jovial even with the weight of the world upon him. No doubt, his struggles with polio during the 1920's would have maybe completely laid low a person who could not accept the cure of laughter, especially in a time period when it truly was the best and only medicine:

> During all the years to come—during the long life, in spite of what the Postmaster General says, which lies ahead of our new Post Office—generations which will live here will always remember that the cornerstone was laid by our distinguished guest.
>
> The Crown Prince used the trowel on the cornerstone and, upon the completion of this ceremony, the President said:
>
> I now announce this very historic cornerstone has been well and truly laid and also that His Royal Highness is an honorary member of the Union, in good standing.[15]

If anyone could joke to royalty about being a member of a union, with a big smile on his face, and get away with both the crowd and the royals laughing together – it was Roosevelt. But through the dedication of this building in the small town of Rhinebeck and the short but sincere speech of the president, we can find the New Deal writ large.

To understand much of the architecture during the New Deal, and the post office program in particular, is to understand the workings of the Office of the Supervising Architect a bureau within the Treasury Department. And to understand the Office of the Supervising Architect is to understand from where FDR found inspiration and aesthetic value: from his genealogical ancestors and their place in local Hudson Valley history, the houses they inhabited, and the American spirit that both represented to him. This is reflected in the choice of the Kip House to serve as the model both architecturally and artistically through the post office murals. In the same manner, the argument FDR makes (though false) of the "firsts" in regards to the Kip House offers an exploration of the process of creating federal public murals.

The Treasury's art programs completed 1,205 murals across a divergent country with sectionalized tastes. From rural to urban areas, to regions with distinct cultures and social values, the problems of public mural art were hypothetically many yet actual controversies rare. The Treasury's mural program was as a whole a success, and a closer look through the perspective of Olin Dows, who was both a mural artist and New Deal art programs administrator, offers an opportunity to see both the artistic stage and the workings behind the curtain. The questions raised by the Rhinebeck post office and the president's speech then are ones at the heart of the journalistic approach: who, what, and why. The who is FDR and Olin Dows, the what is the Treasury's architecture and arts programs, and the why is the Great Depression. The results of this synthesis can still be seen at 6383 Mill Street just south of the intersection with New York 308 at the center of Rhinebeck village, though all the actors who brought the stage to life have entered into history themselves.

Who then was Franklin Delano Roosevelt as architecture and local historian? FDR's interest in architecture grew from an early appreciation of the local history of the Hudson Valley through the influence of his parents as he was home schooled till his early teens. The place where he grew up was Springwood in Hyde Park, an area close to where his ancestors first settled Dutch New York. His family's genealogy was the subject of his history thesis at Harvard in 1901 titled "The Roosevelt Family in New Amsterdam before the Revolution," which was for the most part a reconstruction of the information found in his family's Dutch Bible (on which he would take the oath of office). FDR would be involved in the Hudson-Fulton Celebration of 1909, serving as one of the 805 committee members of what could be described as a collection of New York state gentry. New York Governor Charles Evans Hughes[16] would say at a speech in Catskill that the heart of the

Hudson-Fulton Celebration was that –

> *...the leading events in our history should be better known; the struggles of the early days better appreciated; and that we may be equipped to meet the exigencies of the present and to solve the problems of the future.*[17]

Hughes language was very much in keeping with the New Deal's philosophical approach to the post office program over thirty years later. It could be interpreted that FDR's federal policy during the New Deal could have been an extension of what he was exposed to on a local and state level.[18]

The post office in many areas was the only physical manifestation of the federal government, and Roosevelt through the post office program wanted the American populace to reimagine what the role of government could be in people's lives. In that way he reflected the progressive ideals he had admired in his relative Theodore Roosevelt. Historians have noted the influence Teddy Roosevelt had on FDR though at the time it was taken for granted and not much commented on. FDR emerged from the shadow of his famous kinsman while juggling the Great Depression and WWII, events unprecedented in American history (as well as FDR's four terms in office). But the progressive movement's concern over the rise of immigration in the late nineteenth and early twentieth century in which Roosevelt came of age, did have both positive and negative attributes. On the one hand progressives tended to believe immigrants needed to assimilate into mainstream culture more quickly, though it should be noted their concern was more pragmatic, wanting to promote citizenship and good government, rather than a symptom of prejudice. It should be noted too, that Dutch was the predominate language of the Hudson Valley well into the nineteenth century, as the eighth president of the United States Martin Van Buren (1782–1862), who was a Hudson Valley native, spoke fluent Dutch and English as a second uncomfortable language. It took generations not years for many to assimilate in America yet history, and local history in particular, was seen as a social cohesive in both the Hudson-Fulton Celebration and the New Deal Treasury programs. Historian Roger Panetta states that the Hudson-Fulton Celebration:

...was a great embrace of diversity of class and ethnicity, which he [Governor Hughes] hoped would be deepened. He believed it would reconnect citizens with neglected local history and bind diverse Americans to place and country.[19]

Ultimately, the new mass media such as radio and motion pictures would unite Americans culturally in the 1930's where civic festivities and governmental programs failed. Roosevelt would have one foot firmly in the realm of radio with his famous Fireside Chats, but his other was located in the Progressivism of Teddy Roosevelt and Woodrow Wilson, as policies concerning the Treasury's architect and art programs would look to provide a sense of social cohesion that was in many ways an invention or secular myth of an idealized American past.[20]

Franklin Roosevelt would continue his whole life to be interested in local history. A few years after the Hudson-Fulton Celebration he would become a founding member of the Dutchess County Historical Society in 1914, and when he was planning his presidential library he had one room set apart for the county historical society itself. During what could be considered his "Polio Years," FDR became most active in local history. From 1926 to 1931 he was the town historian of Hyde Park and had published in 1928 the Records of the Town of Hyde Park: 1821 – 1875. Roosevelt was also an avid collector and the many books, maritime themed memorabilia, and pieces of artwork reflected his interest in the Hudson Valley and his colonial Dutch forbearers. His presidential library holds almost nine hundred titles on the Hudson Valley. One of these book in particular, John Lothrop Motley's[21] *History of the United Netherlands from the Death of William the Silent to the Twelve Year's Truce 1609* published in 1867, would help start what art historian Annette Stott has termed "Holland Mania."[22]

Stott writes that in 1903 the *Ladies Home Journal* proclaimed Holland the new Motherland of the United States, and the source of America's political and cultural roots. The journal's editor Edward Bok was a proponent of this theory as shown in this excerpt from his article

> *...the men who founded New York were not Englishmen, but largely Hollanders: that the Puritans who settled Plymouth had lived twelve years in Holland: that the Puritans who settled elsewhere in Massachusetts had all their lives been exposed to a Dutch influence: that New Jersey, as well as New York, was settled by the Dutch West India Company: That Connecticut was given life by Thomas Hooker, who came from a long residence in Holland: that Roger Williams, who founded Rhode Island, was a Dutch scholar: and that William Penn, the founder of Pennsylvania, came of a Dutch mother.[23]*

One could imagine this was music to the ears of the Roosevelts, and especially to an up and coming FDR. In fact, Holland Mania occurred roughly between 1890 and 1920, a time when he was moving from adolescents to mature adult. The two primary ingredients of Holland Mania were revisionist history and visual images, both pertinent in context with the Treasury's art and building programs.

Another work by Motley entitled *The Rise of the Dutch Republic* was considered the seminal work on Dutch History until the twentieth century and is the text from which the revisionist aspect of Holland Mania is drawn. Motley had a romantic style and his work describes a Dutch Republic declaring its independence from an evil and oppressive Spain – "Was it necessary that many generations should wade through this blood in order to acquire for their descendants the blessings of civil and religious freedom?" Throughout the text Motley writes from an American perspective, outlining the history of Holland from the times of the Romans to the sixteenth century with an undercurrent that "we have seen it ever marked by one prevailing characteristic, one master passion—the love of liberty, the instinct of self-government." The Dutch interpretation of American history did not completely replace the British version, but it did alter concepts of American identity and methods of portraying it. In essence, Dutch ancestry became more patriotic. Collecting Dutch artifacts and Dutch paintings became fashionable. FDR's art collection included works of Dutch themes by American artists such as John Sartain, who worked in the Netherlands during the height of Holland Mania. At its heart, behind the painting of windmills and the high stakes investment in Dutch masters, what Americans were drawn to most was the celebration of small-town life, the neighborliness, and a simplicity of a sentimentalized preindustrial Holland. The idyllic setting of tradesman and yeoman farmers of northern European protestant stock, contrasted sharply with the rampant industrialization and the tenement dwelling immigrants of the present. The love of all things Dutch also included genealogical societies, organizations whose pursuits fitted that of the Dutch proud Roosevelt family perfectly.[24]

Theodore Roosevelt would make a pilgrimage after his presidency to the Netherlands in 1909, visiting Delft and paying his respects to the martyr of Dutch independence, William the Silent. TR would state that "I come from a great free Republic to the home of my forefathers, of which it may be said, that they were among the very first, to establish freedom as we now understand the word." But this idealized heritage would be reflected across America from different perspectives through the Treasury programs under FDR, forgetting the negative and embracing an unreal narrative of American history. As Cynthia Koch, former director of the Franklin D. Roosevelt Presidential Library and Museum writes:

> *Nineteenth-century Americans who admired the Dutch found it easy to overlook that the wealth of the great Dutch merchants derived from the African slave trade and brutal colonization in Asia and South America. Instead, they saw antecedents for their own burgeoning middle class society. Even better, as a source for American cultural identity, the Netherlands' worldwide empire augured well—this being the era of Manifest Destiny—for an eventual empire for the United States.[25]*

Both Teddy Roosevelt and FDR would join the Holland Society, the hereditary genealogical society of male descendants of early Dutch New Yorkers. The Holland Society acted as a vehicle for a few projects FDR would see through to publication in the 1920's and 30's. Roosevelt had first started to write a screenplay on John Paul Jones and a history of the United States in 1924, neither of which were completed but fragments of these works give us an insight into a historian who challenged the status quo. Writing about "firsts" such as Henry Hudson and the settling of the east coast in general, Roosevelt would write –

What a ridiculous assumption to teach that Henry Hudson in 1609 was the first to enter the river that bears his name; or that Chesapeake Bay was first seen by the Virginia colonists in 1607; or that the Pilgrims were the first to see Cape Cod in 1620.[26]

Roosevelt would hypothesize that French and Spanish traders were in the areas earlier. This observation shows an individual with a grasp of historiography beyond what is represented in the New Deal policies concerning architecture and art, highlighting that he was a politician first and a historian second. But during this time period when he was unable to participate in politics he proposed a two volume project to The Holland Society, in which he wanted to document the vanishing heritage of the Hudson Valley. The results were two books: *Dutch Houses in the Hudson Valley before 1776* (1929) by Helen Wilkinson Reynolds, and *Pre-Revolutionary Dutch Houses and Families in Northern New Jersey and Southern New York* (1936) by Rosalie Fellows Bailey.[27]

Franklin Roosevelt would write the introduction to both texts and in Dutch Houses in the Hudson Valley before 1776 his introduction is dated 1928 from Hyde Park, and begins again as in the Rhinebeck speech harking back to his childhood:

The Genesis of my interest in Dutch Houses in the Hudson Valley before 1776 lies in the destruction of a delightful old house in Dutchess County, New York, when I was a small boy; for, many years later, in searching vainly for some photograph or drawing of that house, I came to realize that such dwellings of the colonial period in New York as had stood until the twentieth century were fast disappearing before the march of modern civilization and that soon most of them would be gone.[28]

The house mentioned by Roosevelt may well be the Kip House, for which a photograph was eventually found but not easily. A history of the Kip House was included in *Dutch Houses in the Hudson Valley before 1776* along with the only known photograph of the river estate as seen below:

Rudolph Stanley-Brown, pencil and ink drawing, Rhinebeck Post Office, gift for FDR (FDRL).[30]

The southern (right) end of the house here shown was built in 1701 (widely dated as c.1700) by Hendrick Kip at Kipsbergen (now part of Rhinebeck), Dutchess County. The central and northern portions were additions made probably in the eighteenth century, while roofs, doors, windows and shutters were alterations of still later date. In recent years the house was burned (c.1910), and only ruined walls are   now standing. The plate was made from a photograph obtained through the courtesy of Mrs. Theodore de Laporte of Rhinebeck, NY. The property is variously known as the Kip and Beekman house (sometimes as the Heermance house).[29]

The Rhinebeck post office has been described as the most "picturesque" of the New Deal Hudson Valley buildings. The president wanted only to reproduce the original section of the Kip House, which led to some windows being reproduced sixteen-by-sixteen pane with wooden sashes. He was willing to change the sloping front porch roof so that it covered the entire porch, adding to the unique roof with clipped gabled ends. The roof is composed of asphalt shingles which gives the impression of the original wooden shingles. The main ingredient of Dutch Colonial architecture is also prevalent in the use of natural Hudson Valley field stone. Concerning the interior, FDR wanted the building to resemble as closely as possible an eighteenth century style. This included paneled walls to look like a colonial parlor, and hand hewn beamed ceilings.[31]

Roosevelt was also interested in the architecture as a way to understand his cultural heritage, writing "that which has interested me in this survey even more than the collection of architectural data has been the information as to the manners and customs of the settlers of the valley." He noted that people tended to think of "our forebears" as livings a life of ease in large houses, but that the truth of the matter was "that the mode of life of the first settlers of New Netherlands and of their immediate descendants was extremely simple." This simplicity of design, in combination with the natural field stone of the Hudson Valley would be the common denominator in all of FDR's building projects.[32]

Roosevelt's first building project would also be his first experiment with Dutch Colonial architecture. Springwood, the family's Hyde Park country house had been built around 1826, and completed remodeled into an Italian villa when James Roosevelt purchased the property in 1867. This style did not suit FDR's taste, as he was already planning to redesign the home as early as 1903. Additions and alterations to Springwood took place in 1915 and continued throughout 1916. In a rare disagreement between mother and son, Sara Roosevelt wanted a brick and stucco exterior, but Roosevelt won the debate and his mother paid the extra costs of having the wings built of native fieldstone. Springwood after the remodeling was a hybrid of both Georgian and Hudson River Dutch. The next project would be Eleanor Roosevelt's Val-Kill. According to Marion Dickerman, one of the women along with Eleanor and Nancy Cook who would stay there, it was FDR's idea to build a cottage by a stream a mile and a half east of Springwood. An argument over the design of Val-Kill highlights Roosevelt's attitude toward revivalist structures. On a sheet of elevation studies FDR penciled in "flat top window! Please!" concerning the arching of windows, as Roosevelt was adamant that no "Italian" feature should dilute that of his Dutch Colonial design.[33]

He was then involved in his mother's project to build the James Roosevelt Memorial Library. She had purchased a lot in Hyde Park in 1926 and the library was completed with field stone from properties FDR owned. Field stone was important to him in his Hudson Valley projects, and trouble developed over this in the construction of the Rhinebeck post office. When architect Rudolph Stanley-Brown and two engineers visited the Kip House site and found insufficient material to construct the building, word leaked back to FDR that they planned to quarry new stone. Thus, on April 25, 1938 Treasury Secretary Morgenthau called the Supervising Architect of the Office of the Supervising Architect Louis A. Simon.[34]

> *Morgenthau: The President of the United states is very much disturbed because he hears that the Rhinebeck Post Office—they're not going to use old stone wall, that they're planning to open up some stone quarries. And his instructions are that they should use old stone wall.*
>
> *Simon: Well, Mr. Secretary, here's what the situation is. We sent Stanley-Brown up there and he found that we could get quite a little stone from the old building that...*
>
> *Morgenthau: Well, listen, you better write me a memo on it. And the President wants old stone wall.*
>
> *Simon: Yes, I see how the thing came about. Mr. Shipley (Arthur Suckley)[35] who is the owner of the place, said that he'd rather not use the old French wall off his place, but there are plenty of more old stone walls all over Dutchess County.*
>
> *Morgenthau: Well, are you going to use old stone wall?*
>
> *Simon: Sure we are.*
>
> *Morgenthau: Well, for God's sake do, please.*
>
> *Simon: Yes, we certainly are.*
>
> *Morgenthau: And no new stone.*
>
> *Simon: No.*
>
> *Morgenthau: Well, the country is saved. O.K.*
>
> *Simon: All right.[36]*

Roosevelt would end his introduction to Dutch Houses in the Hudson Valley before 1776 by praising where houses were placed geographically in early Dutch New York, "in cosy places, back from the highway, down below a hill, far from a neighbor," and most importantly "happy in their isolation."[37]

For a person struggling to recover from polio, before the Great Crash of 1929, isolation on a social and governmental scale probably did reflect some aspects of FDR at the time of composition in 1928. Isolationism and individualism were two strongly embedded currents in American thought, against which he would have to fight in order to bring about the social cohesion needed to confront both the economic collapse of the 1930's, and a world at war in the first half of the 1940's. But in 1928, the prospect that he would never recover the ability to walk was maybe setting in and Republican control of the White House seemed seamless through the 1920's. Herbert Hoover would be elected as one of the most popular presidents in recent history. Everything changed in October of 1929 with the beginning of the Great Depression, and as the days of the week were given the adjective "black" Hoover steadily fell from grace. When his administration needed public works construction to ease unemployment they looked to the one department with an infrastructure already in place to start projects immediately - the Office of the Supervising Architect.[38]

The Office of the Supervising Architect (1852–1939) was responsible for erecting thousands of federal structures, which, along with the post offices, included customs houses, federal courthouses, marine hospitals, mints, and many large federal offices. The United States Constitution included two provisions that established a legal basis for a federal building program. Article 1, Section 8 states that Congress had the authority "to establish Post Offices and post Roads," as well as "to exercise like Authority over all Places purchased by the Consent of the Legislature of the State in which the Same shall be, for the Erection of Forts, Magazines, Arsenals, dock yards, and other needful buildings." The responsibility for federal design and composition fell to the Treasury Department because of collection and administrative tasks related to the new nation's customs houses and marine hospitals, which required federal revenues. The Office of the Supervising Architect itself would eventually emerge under the auspices of the Treasury Department to carrying out post office and non-military federal construction during the rapid growth of the nation's urban and governmental institutions in the 1850's.[39]

The Hoover administration first faced the tremendous economic and social problems created by the Great Depression with trepidation, as it truly was a "first" in its magnitude and its length. America had in the past considerable economic panics and downturns, but nothing on the scale which now faced a country where every citizen was somehow affected. President Hoover early in his administration imagined some sort of voluntary action on the part of the private sector, where corporations and the wealthy would help the suffering and starving public. He named this unsuccessful synthesis "volunteerism." Eventually, Hoover did initiate both public works efforts and federal programs to curtail the 20% unemployment found in the last year of his presidency. Under Hoover, the Supervising Architect would change from its function in the 1920's as a bureau providing accommodations for a federal government indifferent to public relief into a vehicle for providing jobs to unemployed workers in an attempt to lift the dire economic conditions prior to the 1932 election. In January of 1930, Treasury Secretary Andrew W. Mellon wrote that every effort was being made to comply with Hoover's wishes to expedite the construction work under the Supervising Architect. As an example Mellon wrote "for smaller buildings standard sets of drawings are being utilized with such modifications as are required by topography of sites and service facilities," with the intention that standardized designs would speed up construction contracts. The results were not as grand as Mellon's vocabulary. Everything would change when Roosevelt took office. He immediately instructed all expenditures stopped for public building projects until his administration had formulated a national program for public works and unemployment relief.[40]

After his inauguration in 1933 FDR looked to ease unemployment, and to alleviate unemployment among American architects in particular with the post office building program. Treasury Secretary Morgenthau and Postmaster General Farley vigorously worked with the president to build over eleven-hundred post offices. Since the inception of federal buildings in the early Republic there had always been a conversation concerning architectural symbolism, a discussion revolving around what was suitable architecture for a federal building. Architectural styles would change with different periods, but when FDR took office an outline was drafted to guide the Office of Supervising Architecture in its design process, which was a complete break from Hoover's assembly line approach. It stated that all federal buildings should be:

> (1) of simple governmental character in consonance with the region in which they are located and the surroundings of the specific sites; (2) materials shall be such as to require no excessive maintenance; and (3) the building shall be of sufficient capacity to reasonably meet the needs of the Federal Government as may be anticipated for a ten- year period.[41]

This initial general policy would be elaborated on later given the decision to reject formulaic design types; rather the architects would design buildings that reflected the personality of the locality –

> Architectural traditions, as well as the utilization of natural or manufactured products of the vicinity, are given every practicable consideration. Thus, in New England will be found examples of Colonial architecture with exterior facing of brick or stone; in the Southwest, many of the buildings designed for that locality will reflect the Spanish influence in elevation and materials; and in sections of more recent traditions, buildings of contemporary character have been designed.[42]

It can be assumed that FDR's personal architectural credo did shine through in the philosophy of the post office building program. Roosevelt is unmistakably present in the wording; his passion for local history and his preference for localized architectural design were the foundation of the New Deal post office building program.[43]

In his Rhinebeck speech Roosevelt mentioned that he wanted to construct buildings "that ought to be good, as far as we can tell, for all time to come." In a sense this line of thought could apply to many of the New Deal programs such as Social Security, The Fair Labor Standards

Act 1938 (creating for the first time a federal minimum wage and pro-hibited the exploitation of minors), the Federal Deposit Insurance Corporation (FDIC), the Federal Crop Insurance Corporation (FCIC), the Federal Housing Administration (FHA), the Tennessee Valley Authority (TVA), the Securities and Exchange Commission (SEC), all of which are in existence today, though they came from the effort to provide relief and reform during the Great Depression. FDR looked to the past and the conditions of the present, in which to create a federal government that has been good, as far as American citizens can tell, and should be for as long as they followed the blue print of the political architect who revolutionized a government while preserving its democratic essence.

The symbolism of a building though is limited in its ability to tell a detailed historical narrative, but an old adage tells us a picture or painting is worth a thousand words. Frances V. O'Connor writes in the introduction to her essay collection *The New Deal Art Projects: An Anthology of Memoirs* –

> *Art in America did not always flourish as it appears to do today. Indigenous artistic expression was incredibly narrow and conservative at the time the market crashed in 1929. Whether one listens to Mrs. McMahon describe the purile contents of provincial museums, or Jacob Kainen the repressive hegemony of the etching societies, or Mrs. Gavert the essential irrelevance of art at the early 20th Century Fairs, one cannot escape the reality that something very vital—indeed, something revolutionary—happened to American culture during the 1930's.*[44]

To be sure, America did not have a sustained tradition of public investment in fine art. Social art, such as murals, were generally commissioned as a form of mass media. The success of a few industries in the 1920's led to a mural revival, which lost its steam as funds for unique advertising evaporated in the early years of the Great Depression. The corporate artist was completely bound to the whims and demands in the style and subject matter of their murals by the private patron. This paradigm was not overly attractive to many artists, who felt commissioned mural art was at odds with the modern philosophy of fine arts in general, especially since the rise of the avant-garde as church and state arts had declined in patronage since the nineteenth century. It is an interesting question then, how the Treasury Arts programs and the WPA's Federal Art Project managed to produce over 200,000 pieces of art collectively by 1943? The formulation and administration of these programs can be traced back to three individuals who helped FDR create the New Deal arts programs: George Biddle,[45] Edward Bruce,[46] and Eleanor Roosevelt.[47]

Not everyone was completely pessimistic about the condition of the art world early in the Great Depression; George Biddle was one artist who viewed a silver lining in the economic collapse's impact on fine arts – an erosion of artistic elitism. Art historian Karal Ann Marling relates masterfully the details of two separate events on May 9, 1933 that directly affected the Treasury's art programs, and in effect, shaped what would be featured in the Rhinebeck post office murals. Marling writes, "the promise of cultural rebirth from the ashes of despair—the promise of a democratic, public, people's art of mural painting—glimmered before the eyes of George Biddle." Biddle, who was more of an acquaintance than confidant of Roosevelt, since they attended the Groton School and Harvard College together, would write a letter on a May day in 1933 hoping to create a new revolutionary partnership between artists and government. His letter marks a real "first" in the process of New Deal art patronage. Biddle began his letter to FDR:

> There is a matter which I have long considered and which some day might interest your administration. The Mexican artists have produced the greatest national school of mural painting since the Italian Renaissance. Diego Rivera tells me that it was only possible because Obregon allowed Mexican artists to work at plumber's wages in order to express on the walls of the government buildings the social ideals of the Mexican revolution. The younger artists of America are conscious as they never have been of the social revolution that our country and civilization are going through; and they would be very eager to express these ideals in a permanent art form if they were given the governments cooperation. They would be contributing to and expressing in living monuments the social ideals that you are

*struggling to achieve. And I am convinced that our mural art with
a little impetus can soon result, for the first time in our history, in a
vital national expression.*[48]

Roosevelt was interested in his old friend's suggestion, but understandably hesitant. Starting in 1920 Alvaro Obregon, the president of Mexico from 1920 to 1924, funded public murals that were predominantly Marxist interpretations of contemporary events. The question of subject matter was of the highest concern to FDR when considering launching a public art program in America. He did not want revolutionary themes painted across the country, when the county itself was perilously ripe for radical politics. Roosevelt only had to look to the other event on the day dated on Biddle's letter to reaffirm his trepidation.[49]

May 9, 1933 was the day John D. Rockefeller Jr. ordered the destruction of Diego Rivera's mural for the newly constructed Rockefeller Center. Rockefeller was concerned by a portrait of Lenin in the work prominently "guiding the exploited masses toward a new social order based on the suppression of classes...in contrast to the war, unemployment, starvation, and denigration of capitalist disorder." Nelson Rockefeller's words of regret concerning Rivera's mural mirrored the concerns of the Roosevelt administration, that the "piece is beautifully painted... if it were in a private house, it would be one thing, but this mural is in a public building and the situation, therefore, is quite different." In the 1930's governments under fascist and communist control, and even Marxist leaning countries like Mexico, would portray through mural art the contemporary conditions and ideologies of the present to persuade the populace to follow them into the future. There was also the mural school of Thomas Hart Benson, called Regionalism or social realism, which looked to portray contemporary subjects, but there was concern in the mural program to not focus on the conditions of flux and confusion which were the overriding realities of the time. In contrast, the federal arts program in general, notes Olin Dows, would look to local history for a way to imagine a better future in spite of present conditions. The Treasury art programs then, reflected what we have already seen with the Supervising Architects building program: a president firmly at the helm of his country, leading a dedicated crew through the rough waters of the Great Depression, confidently raising moral as they all entered into the uncharted waters of the New Deal government, guided by the light of his Hudson Valley heritage and personal philosophy as a local historian.[50]

Roosevelt, who loved the sea and was an avid collector of all things naval, would have heard the ancient sailor's proverb "a captain is only as good as his crew." Olin Dows, a New Deal administrator, the mural artist who completed the paintings in the Rhinebeck post office, was most importantly, in an attempt to gain insight into FDR and the New Deal, a native son of the Hudson Valley. Dows grew up in the idyllic lifestyle of the privileged Hudson Valley "River Family." Dows' father, Tracy Dows, was the son of a wealthy New York grain merchant and his mother, Alice Olin, was a descendant of Judge Robert R. Livingston (1718 – 1775), who lived with her family at "Glenburn" a river-family estate in Rhinebeck. Glenburn had been handed down though marriage since the Beekman Patent of 1697. Dows' father bought 500 acres around the Glenburn estate's 60 acres and constructed Fox Hollow, "his grander version of Washington's Mount Vernon" built in an "imposing" colonial style.[51]

Dows was exposed to painting at a young age as his family inherited, commissioned, and collected artwork. In addition, Dows was tutored in drawing by C.K. Chatterton of Vassar College, who is known as a figure in the twentieth century realist movement. Dows attended St. Mark's School outside Boston at twelve and was committed to painting as a vocation already at this time; he then enrolled at Harvard in 1922 where he stayed for only two years before transferring to Yale Art School for another two years of training. At Yale Dows studied under Eugene Savage, a "then renowned mural painter," that could be seen as leading to Dows' enthusiasm to paint murals himself a decade later. Graduating in 1927 Dows then completed his formal study with a year at the Student League in New York. Teaching at the Student League in New York at this time was Thomas Hart Benton, who would be at the forefront of the social realism mural movement, and would look to the usable present in his work. Jackson Pollack would be Benton's most famous student, and like Dows, worked as an artist for the federal arts program during the late 1930's. In 1930, Dows "like many artists of his generation was attracted to the culture and art of modern Mexico, and his paintings, prints, and screens on Mexican themes were favorably reviewed." Dows was an artist concerned "with visual properties of line, form, and color, but he was also an educator." Politically, he was not an extremist, and did not join the school of left-wing leaning social realism. The famous author Thomas Wolfe, who portrayed a young Dows as the character Joel Pierce in *Of Time and the River*, would describe his political thought in 1927 as "a Bertrand Russell Socialist." Dows thought of Roosevelt as being like "the great Americans of the eighteenth century," with a strong sense of social consciousness and sense of community. When Dows heard of the New Deal arts program, he did not hesitate to go to work for a family friend he had known since childhood – Franklin Delano Roosevelt. But like many Hudson River estate families they were more than just friendly neighbors, they were in many instances related. In fact, FDR, Eleanor Roosevelt, Olin Dows, and Margaret "Daisy" Suckley (a personal friend to the president and resident of Rhinebeck who played a role in the post office's design) were all related to each other from ancestors depicted in Dows' Rhinebeck murals.[52]

A question is often raised as to why these individuals, such as FDR and Olin Dows who were never in want for anything money could buy, were so committed to ending the suffering of the poor in America. To put it simply – they were the children of privilege, they went to elite colleges, they were at the top of the social order, yet they dedicated their lives to helping others through the unprofitable career choice of the public servant. Historian Robert S. McElvaine titles one of his chapters "The Lord of the Manor: FDR." It is appropriate in the context of Roosevelt's Dutch New York ancestry, but also in trying to define how the president and public viewed the paradox of his wealth and politics. McElvaine states that one of the main differences between America and Europe was that America lacked an ancient influential landed aristocracy. He points to this European nobility as acting as a check between the industrialists' exploitation of the common people. Citing a "sense of noblesse oblige led to a degree of paternalistic care," and that the social welfare laws of Europe pre-dated those in America by thirty to fifty years because of the efforts of this aristocracy to check the power of the new rich, and to provide through government the care for the common people they were unable to supply themselves. McElvaine make the point that it is important in the study of FDR to understand that:

Although the United States lacked a powerful class of aristocrats, it did possess certain individual patricians of great influence. The Roosevelt family is, perhaps, the best example of this limited American aristocratic paternalism. Theodore Roosevelt was a leading figure in the new paternalistic, nationalistic liberalism of the Progressive era. His relative, Franklin, brought those ideas to fruition.[53]

This paternalistic and compassionate worldview in addition to his able stewardship of the Republic through the Great Depression and WWII, may explain why FDR has been both one of the most fondly remembered and respected of past presidents,. Since he did not consider himself one of America's new rich, like the Vanderbilts for example, he was able to criticize this class without hesitation, as in this letter dated from 1939 –

These millionaires, are a funny crowd. They are perfectly willing to go along with lip service to broad objectives, but when you ask them to help put them into effect by any form of practical means, they howl in opposition and decline to suggest any other course.[54]

Another factor that may have played into FDR's governing style was the challenges of the paralysis from polio which changed him in many ways. Up through the 1920's Roosevelt had succeeded in his pursuits almost effortlessly, after his illness his aristocratic stoicism in the face of hardship was put to the test. Ultimately, Roosevelt's suffering may have broadened his sense of stewardship into a place of "a more genuine sense of compassion." Frances Perkins would write of the metamorphosis which occurred in the future president during his attempts at recovery, "the man emerged, completely warmhearted, with humility of spirit, and a deeper philosophy. Having been to the depth of trouble, he understood the problems of people in trouble." Roosevelt would recruit those who shared his belief that to be American was not only to profit from the system, but to give back more in citizenship than to take. His choice of Olin Dows and Edward Bruce are examples of why the Treasury's art program was so successful, in that many of those working for the New Deal were in many ways selfless and passionate about the New Deal themselves.[55]

Dows states in his memoir, "I find it difficult here, as elsewhere in this article, to convey the sense of hope, excitement, and enthusiasm that the early New Deal days inspired," but a look at the Treasury's various arts programs reveals that the results of this initiative produced tangible public relief. There were four major art programs implemented during the Roosevelt Administration, and "human economic relief was the motive behind all the New Deal's art programs." Dows would work for three programs which could be termed Treasury programs because they were administered by the Treasury Department: the Public Works of Art Program or PWAP (1933 – 1934), the Treasury Relief Art Project or TRAP (1935 – 1939), and the Section of Painting and Sculpture which was later renamed the Section of Fine Arts or just the Section (1934 – 1943). The fourth New Deal arts program was the Work Progress Administrations Federal Art Project, the largest arts programs but one not under the auspices of the Treasury.[56]

Employed first with the short lived PWAP and then the Section; Dows would work closely in the early to mid-1930's with the director of both programs, Edward Bruce. Bruce in Dows' opinion personified the spirit of the New Deal. A former Columbia football star and an honor graduate from that University's Law School, Bruce though did not settle on law and instead pursued a variety of interests including owning the Manila Times in the Philippines. He would finally settle in as an artist and was making a comfortable living from his art work when he came to Washington to become involved in the art programs. Dows became friendly with Bruce when they met visiting the former Secretary of the Treasury Andrew Mellon's apartment to view the art collection. Dows also writes of the first meeting of the Treasury art program in 1933, which included many museum directors and important people in the field of art, as well as Eleanor Roosevelt sitting at the table from which Bruce was directing the meeting, "knitting steadily," and every once in a while adding to a remark or question. In 1935 Dows was appointed Chief of the Treasury Relief Art Program or TRAP, and would stay in this position till 1938.[57]

TRAP was by far the smallest New Deal artist relief program, employing about 446 people of whom 75% were on relief. But a smaller department had some benefits to the artists it employed as Dows states that "ours was considered a privileged program... being small, it could afford to be considerate and flexible." Many of the jobs done by TRAP were similar to those of the Section, primarily post office murals. Dows as director would search out buildings either new or old that possessed optimal spaces for murals and sculptures, but lacked the funding for building decoration.[58]

In only one instance did Dows meet with the "old friend of my family" in a professional manner as a New Deal administrator. When the funding for TRAP was in jeopardy in 1936 Dows met with FDR:

I called Mrs. Roosevelt and explained to her what was disturbing me. She asked me to lunch the next day and said she would try and let me see the President. When I went into his oval office, I showed him a dozen photographs of work that was under way. Marvin Mc-Intyre, his secretary hovered nervously in the background, fearing, I expect, that I would waste the President's time. FDR obviously had other things on his mind, but he looked through the photographs and listened to what I had to say. He asked a few questions, nodded his head and said, 'I see.' Scrawled an undecipherable hieroglyphic on a chit of paper about the size of a hat check, he told me to give it to the Director of the Budget. The matter was settled, the job completed as planned; our program kept unspent funds, and we even got supplementary appropriations later without much difficulty.[59]

Eleanor Roosevelt, as can be seen was the best ally a person could have on issues that concerned FDR and his administration. After five busy years Dows would step down from his government position and take an extended vacation visiting his sister in Egypt in 1938; on returning he would trade the trappings of the bureaucrat and pick up again his calling as an artist in the form of the post offices murals he had so recently been in charge of commissioning.

The federal arts program, Dows writes, "favored subjects that would be intelligible and inspiring to the people who daily used the buildings," and would also focus on local history and scenery but above all should avoid "controversy." Dows felt that "our knowledge of history comes largely through art," and that art "helps form and shape our beliefs" to "help us to understand our past, to integrate our belief in the present, and to strengthen our faith in the future." He stated in 1938 that "one of the social problems confronting the U.S. is an undigested mixture of races." In an attempt to highlight the process of "Americanization," Dows would highlight the various origins of Rhinebeck's population through periods of colonial and American history. Each perceived ethnic group was assimilated seamlessly from the original Native American residents through various periods of immigration, representing people of Dutch, English, Huguenot, Palatine, African, Scottish, Italian, Irish, and Walloon origin. But it should be noted that during the colonial period of America "all the participants came from regions where boundaries were in negotiation and definitions were in progress" and that "(the colonist's) own identifications was with their locality or with some larger, more amorphous entity." In essence, Dows strove to show his version of humanity, the colonial and more modern, the poorest and the richest, but not in division or strife. They are depicted in their work, worship, and leisure, in what Dows described as "those simple activities which bind our lives to the past and to each other." Slavery is also represented when many murals did not include the institution, especially in the northeast where its existence in colonial America was often overlooked. Dows wanted to include details about the slavery depicted in his mural, but he was ultimately overruled on this uncomfortable subject which did not fit into the mold of Dutch New York nostalgia. It is a small but telling testament, to both Dows and Roosevelt as local historians, that slavery was included in these murals when it just of easily could have been excluded.[60]

One does not have to search far to realize that Olin Dows' viewpoints on society, in conjunction with the New Deal post office project, mirror almost identically FDR's belief that public architecture and artwork should reflect the re-creation of common links to an earlier time and place when Americans had encountered great obstacles and overcome them. Or the Progressive ideals that influenced Roosevelt, as in Governor Hughes speech in Catskill during the Hudson-Fulton Celebration that public events and local history in general would "bind diverse Americans to place and country."

But as mass media would create social hegemony more effectively than any New Deal program, so too would World War II solidify the place of federal government in the lives of Americans. Everything changed with the coming of WWII: Eleanor lost the favor she used to have with the president as he focused all his remaining energies on the war effort, the Treasury's art programs would die with their creator and caretaker in 1943 when Edward Bruce passed away, the Office of the Supervising Architect would be moved out of the Treasury Department in 1939 and slowly cease to exist as it was reconfigured and folded into other programs, Olin Dows would serve during WWII as a sergeant in the European war theater as an artist for the Army Engineers and would return to live out a long life in the town he loved, and Franklin Delano Roosevelt would become as has been said often – the greatest casualty of the war.

The Rhinebeck post office is a curious building in the town of Rhinebeck, which for one day was the center of the New Deal movement. It stands today as a testament to the herculean effort Roosevelt and his administration put forth to relieve the nation of the heavy burden of the Great Depression through art and architecture. Finally, the post office also represents the masses of American citizens who helped the president shoulder the burden of an unprecedented economic collapse, while at the same time guiding an isolationist leaning country into the inevitability of a world war of unimaginable proportion. In the end, FDR, with the citizens he cared for so deeply, and them him – would not allow Atlas to shrug. Though their troubled times were of a colossal weight.

Works Cited

Bok, Edward. "The Mother of America." *Ladies Home Journal*, October 1903: 3.

Dows, Olin. *Murals in the Rhinebeck Post Office, with maps, a description of the murals and notes on the town*. Rhinebeck: The Civic Club of Rhinebeck, 1940.

Dows, Olin. "The New Deal's Treasury Art Program: A Memoir." In The New Deal Art Projects: An Anthology of Memoirs, edited by Frances V. O'Connor, 11-49. Washington: Smithsonian Institution Press, 1972.

Kennedy, David M. *Freedom From Fear: Tha American People in Depression and War 1929-1945*. Oxford: Oxford University Press, 1999.

Koch, Cynthia. "Franklin Roosevelt's "Dutchness"." In Dutch New York: The Roots of

Hudson Valley Culture, edited by Roger Panetta, 339 - 376. New York: Hudson River Museum, 2009.

Kupperman, Karen Ordahl. "International at the Creation: Early Modern American History." In Rethinking American History in a Global Age, edited by Thomas Bender, 103-122. Berkeley: University of California Press, 2002.

Lee, Antoinette J. *Architects to the Nation: The Rise and Decline of the Supervising Architect's Office.* Oxford: Oxford University Press, 2000.

Marling, Karal Ann. *Wall-to-wall America : A Cultural History of Post-Office Murals in the Great Depression.* Minneapolis: University of Minnesota Press, 1982.

McElvaine, Robert S. *The Great Depression: America, 1929-1941.* New York: Three Rivers Press, 2009.

Morgenthau, Henry. "Diary." Vol. Morgenthau Papers. Franklin D. Roosevelt Presidential Library and Museum, 1938.

O'Connor, Frances V., ed. The New Deal Art Projects: An Anthology of Memoirs. Washington: Smithsonian Institution Press, 1972.

Panetta, Roger. "The Hudson-Fulton Celebration of 1909." In Dutch New York: The Roots of Hudson Valley Culture, edited by Roger Panetta, 301-338. New York: Hudson River Museum, 2009.

Reynolds, Helen Wilkenson. *Dutch Houses in the Hudson Valley before 1776.* New York: Dover Publications, 1965.

Rhoads, William B. "Franklin D. Roosevelt and Dutch Colonial Architecture." New York History, 1978: 430-464.

Rhoads, William B. "Olin Dows: Art, History, and a Usable Past." In The Livingston Legacy, edited by Richard T. Wiles, 427-440. Annandale-on-Hudson: Bard College, 1987.

Roosevelt, Franklin Delano. "History of the U.S." Vols. Family, Business, and Personal Affairs. Franklin D. Roosevelt Presidential Library and Museum, 1924.

—. "Presidential Address at the Dedication of the New Deal Post Office in Rhinebeck." Poughkeepsie Star-Enterprise, 1 1939, May.

—. "The Roosevelt Family in New Amsterdam before the Revolution." Vols. Family, Business, and Personal Affairs. Franklin D. Roosevelt Presidential Library and Museum, n.d.

Schaefer, Paul. "Tracy Dows, Community Organizer." About Town, Winter 2009.

Stott, Annette. *Holland Mania: The Unknown Dutch Period in American Art & Culture.* Woodstock: Overlook Press, 1998.

Thomas, Bernice L. The Stamp of FDR: New Deal Post Offices in the Mid-Hudson Valley. New York: Purple Mountain Press, 2002.

White, Philip L. *The Beekmans of New York in politics and commerce, 1647-1877.* New

York: New-York Historical Society under a grant from the Beekman Family Association, 1956.

Endnotes

[1] Presidential Address at the Dedication of the New Deal Post Office in Rhinebeck, Poughkeepsie Star-Enterprise, May 1, 1939.

[2] Farley would resign in 1940 in protest of FDR's unprecedented third term as president and would head Coca-Cola International for over thirty years.

[3] Bernice L. Thomas, *The Stamp of FDR: New Deal Post Offices in the Mid-Hudson Valley* (Fleischmanns: Purple Mountain Press, 2002), 7 & 64; Olin Dows, *William Seabrook, and Chanler A. Chapman, Murals in the Rhinebeck Post Office* (Rhinebeck: The Civic Club of Rhinebeck, 1940), unpaged.

[4] Presidential Address, Poughkeepsie *Star-Enterprise*, May 1, 1939.

[5] Philip L. White, *The Beekmans of New York In Politics and Commerce: 1647 – 1877* (New York: The New-York Historical Society, 1956) 73 & 122.

[6] Presidential Address, Poughkeepsie *Star-Enterprise*, May 1, 1939.

[7] Helen Wilkinson Reynolds, Dutch Houses in the Hudson Valley before 1776 (New York: Dover Publications, 1965), 419.

[8] Presidential Address, Poughkeepsie *Star-Enterprise*, May 1, 1939.

[9] Cynthia Koch, "Franklin Roosevelt's 'Dutchness,'" in Dutch New York: The Roots of Hudson Valley Culture, ed. Roger Panetta (New York: Hudson River Museum, 2009), 359; William B. Rhoads, "Franklin D. Roosevelt and Dutch Colonial Architecture," in New York History (October, 1978), 446.

[10] Presidential Address, Poughkeepsie *Star-Enterprise*, May 1, 1939.

[11] Karal Ann Marling, *Wall-to-Wall America: A Cultural History of Post-Office Murals in the Great Depression* (Minneapolis: University of Minnesota Press, 1982), 7.

[12] Presidential Address, Poughkeepsie *Star-Enterprise*, May 1, 1939.

[13] John Lloyd Wright (1892 – 1972) – besides being born to a famous father Wright invented Lincoln Logs in 1916.

[14] Thomas, *The Stamp of FDR: New Deal Post Offices in the Mid-Hudson Valley*, 8.

[15] Presidential Address, Poughkeepsie *Star-Enterprise*, May 1, 1939.

[16] Charles Evans Hughes (1862 – 1948) is an interesting character in New York and national politics, and as well his connection to the young Roosevelt during the celebration he would also be a prominent force during his presidency. Hughes was governor of New York, secretary of state, and chief justice of the U.S. Supreme Court. As the Republican candidate for governor of New York in 1906, he narrowly beat the Demo-

cratic candidate, William Randolph Hearst. An unconventional politician, Hughes never actively sought office for himself. His nominations for governor of New York in both 1906 and 1908 were pushed upon him reluctantly at Republican conventions by President Theodore Roosevelt.

In 1916 Hughes was an obvious choice for the Republican presidential nomination, and he was nominated once again without any effort on his part. Hughes resigned from the Supreme Court only after the nomination had been secured. He lost a close election to Woodrow Wilson, being defeated by 13 electoral votes. In 1930 President Herbert Hoover nominated Hughes to serve as chief justice of the U.S. Supreme Court. During Roosevelt's presidency, starting in May 1935 Hughes led a unanimous court in striking down three New Deal measures: the National Industrial Recovery Act (Schechter Poultry Corp. v. United States), the Frazier-Lemke Act providing for relief of farm debtors (Louisville Joint Stock Land Bank v. Radford), and the Federal Home Owner's Loan Act of 1933 (Hopkins Federal Savings & Loan Assn. v. Cleary).

Hughes also played a role in the defeat of Franklin Roosevelt's Court Reorganization Plan of 1937. He wrote a letter to the Senate Judiciary Committee indicating that the Court was not behind in its work. It was a devastating blow to the Roosevelt proposal. Robert H. Jackson, one of the president's aides in the Court fight, later noted that Hughes's letter "did more than any one thing to turn the tide in the Court struggle." But something did come of FDR's efforts to shake up the Court, because in the next three years Hughes voted with the majority to uphold the constitutionality of other New Deal measures such as the Social Security Act of 1935, the Public Utilities Act of 1935, the Bituminous Coal Act of 1937, the revised Agricultural Adjustment Act, and the Fair Labor Standards Act of 1938. Hughes resigned from the Supreme Court in July 1941. He died in Cape Cod, Massachusetts.

Note from: Betty Glad, "Hughes, Charles Evans," American National Biography Online (Feb. 2000).

[17] Roger Panetta, "The Hudson-Fulton Celebration of 1909," in Dutch New York: The Roots of Hudson Valley Culture, ed. Roger Panetta (New York: Hudson River Museum, 2009), 334.

[18] Franklin D. Roosevelt, "The Roosevelt Family in New Amsterdam before the Revolution," (December 1901, FDRL), Family, Business, and Personal Affairs.

[19] Panetta, "The Hudson-Fulton Celebration of 1909," 335.

[20] David M. Kennedy, Freedom From Fear: The American People in Depression and War 1929 – 1945 (Oxford: Oxford University Press, 1999), for Theodore Roosevelts influence on FDR 3-4, 115, and 248, for Radio and Culture 228-230.

[21] John Lothrop Motley (1814 – 1877) was a historian and diplomat, he was also a member of the Brahmin caste of New England. Motley entered Harvard in 1827. He was bright and had a facility for languages, especially German, but he was negligent in his studies and had to be suspended. Upon returning to Harvard he applied himself and was elected to Phi Beta Kappa before graduating with an A.B. in 1831.

In 1850 he chose for his historical subject the early Dutch Republic. Similarities between the struggles of the Dutch provinces against Catholic Spain and those of the American colonies against Britain influenced his theme. A memorable visit to another Brahmin historian, William Hickling Prescott, who was writing a history of the reign of Philip II of Spain, encouraged Motley to undertake his project and to make use of Prescott's library.

The three-volume *The Rise of the Dutch Republic* (1856) received immediate popular and critical acclaim (by 1857 15,000 copies had been sold in London). Praised by scholars on the Continent and soon translated into Dutch, German, and Russian, the history was commended by important historical writers in America, including Washington Irving, Bancroft, and Prescott.

Motley enjoyed the social life of Boston and his membership in the Saturday Club with Oliver Wendell Holmes (later his biographer), Nathaniel Hawthorne, Louis Agassiz, James Russell Lowell, Henry Wadsworth Longfellow, and Prescott. His newly won fame, according to Holmes, made Motley a citizen of the world. Although he would return to America for brief visits, Motley spent his mature years abroad. He died near Dorchester, England in 1877.

Note from: Donald Darnell, "Motley, John Lothrop," American National Biography Online (Feb. 2000).

[22] Koch, "Franklin Roosevelt's 'Dutchness,'" 348-349; Annette Stott, Holland Mania: The Unknown Dutch Period in American Art & Culture (Woodstock: Overlook Press, 1998), 11.

[23] Edward Bok, "The Mother of America," *Ladies Home Journal* (October, 1903) 3.

[24] Koch, "Franklin Roosevelt's 'Dutchness,'" 344-345, 349; Annette Stott, Holland Mania: The Unknown Dutch Period in American Art & Culture, 78-80, 100.

[25] Koch, "Franklin Roosevelt's 'Dutchness,'" 344.

[26] FDR, "History of the U.S.," (1924, FDRL), Family, Business, and Personal Affairs.

[27] Koch, "Franklin Roosevelt's 'Dutchness,'" 345-346, 350.

[28] Helen Wilkenson Reynolds, *Dutch Houses in the Hudson Valley before 1776* (New York: The Holland Society of New York, 1929), unpaged.

[29] Reynolds, *Dutch Houses in the Hudson Valley before 1776*, 419.

[30] Thomas, The Stamp of FDR: New Deal Post Offices in the Mid-Hudson Valley, 56.

[31] Ibid., 57-59.

[32] Reynolds, *Dutch Houses in the Hudson Valley before 1776*, unpaged.

[33] Rhoads, "Franklin D. Roosevelt and Dutch Colonial Architecture," 431-432

[34] Ibid., 436-439.

[35] Daisy Suckley proposed to her brother that he donate the stone, but he wished to be paid fifty cents per cubic yard. In her possession she had the stone lintel and the pane of glass saved from the fire, and she lent them to the post office asking only that they be kept inside rather than displayed outside the building.

Note from: Thomas, *The Stamp of FDR: New Deal Post Offices in the Mid-Hudson Valley*, 61.

[36] Henry Morgenthau, Jr., Diary (1938, FDRL) Morgenthau Papers.

[37] Reynolds, *Dutch Houses in the Hudson Valley before 1776*, unpaged.

[38] Antoinette J. Lee, *Architects to the Nation: The Rise and Decline of the Supervising Architect's Office* (Oxford: Oxford University Press, 2000), 238.

[39] Ibid., 5-6, 12, & 39.

[40] Kennedy, *Freedom From Fear: The American People in Depression and War 1929 – 1945*, 82 & 87; Lee, *Architects to the Nation: The Rise and Decline of the Supervising Architect's Office*, 238, 248, 252-253.

[41] Lee, *Architects to the Nation: The Rise and Decline of the Supervising Architect's Office* 262.

[42] Ibid., 263.

[43] Thomas, *The Stamp of FDR: New Deal Post Offices in the Mid-Hudson Valley*, 7 & 11; Lee, *Architects to the Nation: The Rise and Decline of the Supervising Architect's Office*, 12.

[44] Frances V. O'Connor, *The New Deal Art Projects: An Anthology of Memoirs* (Washington: Smithsonian Institution Press, 1972), 4.

[45] George Biddle (1885–1973), a member of the famous Biddle family of Philadelphia, was an artist who attended the Groton School in Massachusetts and Harvard College with FDR. Biddle's artistic development was interrupted by World War I, in which he fought in many battles, including that of the Marne, and was mustered out with the rank of captain in 1919.

From 1923 to 1926 he mingled with members of the art world's avant-garde and attended Gertrude Stein's famed salons. His close contact with French modernism and such movements as cubism, dada, and surrealism reinforced his inherent "Americanism" and his belief in the primacy of realism in art.

In 1928 Biddle traveled with Mexican artist Diego Rivera on a sketching tour of Mexico. After his Mexican trip, Biddle's work began to reflect a deeper interest in the social and political aspects of American life. In 1930 he constructed a house and studio at Croton-on-Hudson, where he lived for the rest of his life.

Note from: Martin R. Kalfatovic, "Biddle, George," American National Biography Online (Feb. 2000).

[46] Edward Bruce (1879–1943), though he enjoyed painting at a young age, he pursued a career in law and graduated from Columbia Law School in 1904. In 1923 Bruce gave up his career in law and business and began to paint, particularly landscapes.

In 1933 Bruce was appointed Chief of the newly established Public Works of Art Project, a federal government New Deal program within the U.S. Treasury Department, which employed artists to decorate numerous public buildings and parks. Though this federal program lasted less than a year, Bruce worked with Secretary of the Treasury Henry Morgenthau, Jr., to establish the Treasury Department's Section of Painting and Sculpture in 1934 - later renamed the Section of Fine Arts in 1938. Bruce was appointed Director of the department and played a primary role in securing federal government support for American artists. In 1940 he was appointed to the Commission of Fine Arts by President Franklin Delano Roosevelt.

Note from: Biographical Note, "Edward Bruce" Smithsonian Archive of American Art (research collections), Edward Bruce papers, 1902-1960.

[47] Marling, *Wall-to-Wall America: A Cultural History of Post-Office Murals in the Great Depression*, 5-9; Olin Dows, "The New Deal's Treasury Art Program: A Memoir," in The New Deal Art Projects: An Anthology of Memoirs, ed. Frances V. O'Connor (Washington: Smithsonian Institution Press, 1972), 12.
[48] Marling, *Wall-to-Wall America: A Cultural History of Post-Office Murals in the Great Depression*, 31.
[49] Ibid., 30-31.
[50] Marling, *Wall-to-Wall America: A Cultural History of Post-Office Murals in the Great Depression*, 31, 91-92; Dows, "The New Deal's Treasury Art Program: A Memoir," 36.
[51] William B. Rhoads, "Olin Dows: Art, History, and a Usable Past," in The Livingston

Legacy, ed. Richard T. Wiles (Annandale-on-Hudson: Bard College, 1987), 427-428; Paul Schaefer, "Tracy Dows, Community Organizer," About Town (Red Hook, NY) Winter 2009; Tracy Dows (1871 – 1937) passed away in London before the Rhinebeck post office project. After losing much of his fortune in the Great Depression he spent his last years remodeling and running the Beekman Arms, which is adjacent to the post office property.

[52] Rhoads, "Olin Dows: Art, History, and a Usable Past," 428, 432-433.

[53] Robert S. McElvaine, *The Great Depression: 1929-1941*, (New York: Three Rivers Press, 2009), 95-96, 106.

[54] Ibid., 96.

[55] Ibid., 104-106.

[56] Dows, "The New Deal's Treasury Art Program: A Memoir," 11-12, 16.

[57] Ibid., 26.

[58] Ibid., 10, 12, 14-15, & 26.

[59] Ibid., 27-28.

[60] Karen Ordahl Kupperman, "International at the Creation: Early Modern American History," in Rethinking American History in a Global Age, ed. Thomas Bender (Berkeley: University of California Press, 2002), 106; Rhoads, "Olin Dows: Art, History, and a Usable Past," 431.

About the author: Jim Blackburn is a non-traditional student majoring in history at Bard College. He is an editor for Cyberwit and is the founder of South Jersey Underground magazine. He currently lives in Saugerties, NY.

The *Vin Fiz* leaving Sheepshead Bay, NY on September 17, 1911. Image property of the author.

The Vin Fiz Lands in Elmira, New York

by Diane Janowski

O n September 11, 1911, the Elmira *Star-Gazette* reported:

> *C. F. Rodgers, the young aviator backed by Ogden Armour [of hot dog fame], will pass over Elmira the last of this week on his record-breaking aeroplane flight from New York to Chicago. If things go right, Rodgers should reach this city the second or third day out of New York. In all probability he will make a stop in Elmira, whether or not he spends the night here.*

"Vin Fiz" was the name of a new grape-flavored soft drink that sold for a nickel and was hailed by the Vin Fiz Company [a division of the Armour Company of Chicago, Illinois] as "refreshing and invigorating." The new product, however, presented one large marketing problem –it tasted terrible. The company, knowing that it needed a very special scheme if they were to sell their product, came up with a novel idea to boost its popularity. The marketing team chose an aviation stunt to promote their soda pop. The Vin Fiz people decided that a good way to spread the word of their product was to endorse and financially support an aviator in this effort.

About eleven months earlier, publishing magnate William Randolph Hearst offered $50,000 to the fastest aviator to cross the country coast-to-coast within thirty days. Teaming with Hearst's contest, Vin Fiz had its gimmick. Early in Hearst's contest, several aviators tried, but the task proved too difficult. Even nine years after the Wright brothers first successfully flew airplanes, the public still considered impractical and were reserved for novelty flights at county fairs and flying exhibitions. These airplanes flew at levels lower than the tops of our hills, had no radios, could only fly in good weather, and broke down on almost every flight.

In September 1911, three aviators said that they were ready to try. Hearst set no specific route –just fly ocean to ocean. Pilot Robert Fowler intended to fly from California to New York, while pilots Jimmy Ward and Vin Fiz's Calbraith Rodgers were to fly from New York to California. Fowler took off in California on September 11, Ward left Governor's Island, New York on September 13, and Rodgers left Sheepshead Bay, New York on September 17. His aircraft was decorated with the Vin Fiz trademark, and aside from the prize money, should he win it, Rodgers was to receive $5 from Armour for every mile flown with his aircraft so lettered.

Robert Fowler crashed on his first day in the California mountains, but he vowed to continue. After a week of crashes, he finally became utterly discouraged and quit the challenge. Meanwhile, Jimmy Ward planned to follow the Erie Railroad line through New York, but at Jersey City, New Jersey, got confused and started following the Lehigh

Valley Railroad line. When he realized his mistake, he retraced his route to Jersey City and found the correct railroad line and headed to Middletown, New York where 6,000 fans were waiting. On his second day, the wire service out of Port Jervis, New York reported, "Never before in the history of Neversink and the Delaware River valley has any single event caused as much excitement and interest as the flight of Aviator Ward, who is bound from the Atlantic to the Pacific coast." Here, the weather turned bad and he was stuck in Callicoon for two days, missing his "fly over" at the fair in Owego, New York. On the fourth day, Ward flew over Binghamton at 2:45 PM, but soon developed mechanical difficulties and landed at Owego. When he left Owego on the fifth day, someone was supposed to telephone Elmira to say that he was coming, but before the call was made, Ward was already here. A few people reported seeing him fly over Elmira at 11:15AM, and shortly thereafter his bearings burned out and he was forced to land on Rose Hill in Corning, New York. Repairs took almost three days. On the eighth day, he took off, but soon crashed in farmer Benjamin Lynch's cornfield near Addison, New York. Farmer Lynch threatened to sue for his damaged corn, but changed his mind the next day. Ward claimed he had a "jinx" on his plane. Ward eventually had to abandon the challenge because his money ran out. Thirty-two-year old Calbraith Perry Rodgers (1879-1912) had less than sixty hours of flying experience when he left New York in a Wright brothers type EX spruce, wire, and fabric biplane with a 35-horsepower 4 cylinder engine. "Cal's plane followed a special train operated by the Vin Fiz Company. The passenger car, with its top painted white, served as his beacon. Rodger's wife, Mabel, his cousin, Lt. John Rodgers, Crew Chief Charles Taylor and other members of the crew occupied the other cars. The special car was dubbed the "white hanger" and provided a first aid center and a machine shop with spare parts and tools. A rumor suggested a coffin too, just in case.

Elmiran Joyce Van Curen's grandmother lived in Middletown, New York and she was "visited" by Rodgers when, on his takeoff form Middletown, he crashed into her chicken coop killing her chickens. Joyce said her grandmother had never seen and airplane before, and she was mad. "She went out and gave him the devil." That crash put Cal's plane out of commission for three days.

Spotters on the Lake Street bridge first saw the *Vin Fiz* after 5:00PM on September 22. First, he was just a speck in the southern sky, but as he neared, he was flying so low that the words, "Vin Fiz" were clearly readable.

When Rodgers got to Elmira, he flew over the city looking for the Chemung County fairgrounds. He saw nothing that looked like it, and doubled back. He found his train near the Elmira Bridge Works plant (between Miller and Home Streets). It had been side-swiped by a freight train, but sustained no serious damage. To get to his train, he landed in the first field that he came to – farmer Edmund Miller's open meadow (now McNaught Field near Miller's Pond) at 5:55PM. Both the Elmira *Star-Gazette* and the Elmira *Advertiser* said that his landing was "graceful." Youngster Lucy Leveridge, whose home was across the street, was the first one to run and greet the aviator. Rodgers was then taken "to the city" in an automobile to the Rathbun Hotel on East Water Street where his crew had gathered.

The airplane was roped off for the night. The next morning, spectators began gathering early, and by 8:30AM the meadow "looked like a county fair." After making some minor repairs to the plane, several thousand Elmirans watched Rodgers leave the Southside at 2:15PM.

Rodgers continued his journey across New York State, west to Illinois, south to Texas, and finally west to California. Eventually, weather and machinery failure cost him any hope of winning the prize. He was in Oklahoma when the prize date expired, but he continued on to fulfill his contract with the sponsor. Rodgers had his share of problems in Texas where he admitted spending more time on the ground than in the air. He said, "I am the only aviator on earth who had a tire punctured by a cactus spine."

The *Vin Fiz* was the first airplane ever seen in many of his stops or crashes. (Elmira was slightly more sophisticated than the rest of the country because two months earlier the city witnessed Lincoln Beachey's biplane.) In Austin, Texas, 3,000 spectators came out to see their first airplane. On October 17, 1911, the *Vin Fiz* became the first airplane seen in Denison, Texas. Rodgers landed in a field near Denison to refuel his plane after dropping little pink leaflets advertising Vin Fiz. He then lost his way and went nearly to Wichita Falls before he corrected his direction and headed for Fort Worth. He did continue to finish his contract with Armour and became the first man to fly across the continent. Cal Rodgers used forty-nine days to travel 3,350 miles. He made sixty-nine stops and crash-landed nineteen times, and the *Vin Fiz* had to be rebuilt four times. He ended the first transcontinental flight by landing in Tournament Park (now on the CalTech campus) in Pasadena, California.

Although Cal made it to California, he felt his journey was not finished until the *Vin Fiz* actually touched the Pacific Ocean. On November 12 he left Long Beach, but was forced to land on the beach and taxied into the water. A few days later, Rodgers was "chasing sea gulls" when one became caught in the rudder wire, and while trying to extricated the bird, the wire broke and the plane crashed into the Pacific Ocean killing Rodgers. In 1934, the rebuilt *Vin Fiz* joined the collection of Smithsonian Institute in Washington, D. C. Calbraith Perry Rodgers posthumously received his induction into the National Aviation Hall of Fame in 1964.

Sources:

Elmira *Advertiser,* September 11-30, 1911.
Elmira *Star-Gazette*, September 11-30, 1911.
http://caltech.edu.matchi/pasadena.html
http://www.150.si.edu/150trav/discover/d515a/html http://nasm.edu.nasm/aero/wroghtes/htm
    Personal interview. Joyce Van Curen. December 1999.

About the author: Diane Janowski is an author of New York history books, editor/publisher of the *New York History Review,* an artist, and a musician. She lives in Elmira, NY and is the Elmira City Historian.

Remembering Olympia Brown: Pioneer Minister and Advocate for Equal Rights for Women

by Herbert C. Hallas

Olympia Brown. 1919. Library of Congress

One hundred and fifty years ago this summer in the North Country, Olympia Brown became the first woman in U.S. history to become a fully ordained minister with a degree from a regularly established theological school.[1] She was ordained by the St. Lawrence Association of Universalists in the Universalist Church of Malone, New York on June 25, 1863, and graduated from the St. Lawrence University Theological School in Canton, New York two weeks later.[2]

For the rest of her 91-year-old life, she doubled as an outspoken Universalist preacher and a fearless campaigner for suffrage and equal rights for women. Of the original pioneer crusaders for women's rights with whom Olympia worked closely—Susan B. Anthony, Lucy Stone, Isabella Beecher Hooker, Matilda Joslyn Gage, and Elizabeth Cady Stanton – only Olympia lived long enough to vote after the Nineteenth Amendment was added to the U.S. Constitution in 1920.

Olympia was born in a one-room log cabin in Schoolcraft, Michigan, a small settlement in the southern part of the state, on January 5, 1835. She was the oldest of four children born to her parents, Lephia Olympia and Asa, who had migrated to Michigan from Plymouth, Vermont.[3]

Olympia grew up in a "strong anti-slavery" family. Her uncle's house nearby was part of the Underground Railroad system and she often traveled there to visit with runaway slaves. For seven years, one of the fugitives worked for her father as a hired hand on the family farm.[4]

According to Olympia, her mother was a "very zealous" Universalist and "the earliest reformer I ever knew." She taught her daughter about universal salvation, the brotherhood of man, and the importance of equal rights for women.[5]

The radical views concerning women's rights, anti-slavery, and dress reform in Horace Greeley's New York *Weekly Tribune* also helped shape Olympia's value system. When she was a teenager, family discussion of the Tribune's coverage of speeches given by Anthony, Stanton and Stone at a women's rights convention in Worcester, Massachusetts "stirred her soul." The three women promptly became "great heroes" to her.[6]

After high school, she attended Mount Holyoke Female Seminary, an all-girls school in Massachusetts. She left after one year to go to another college after being crushed by Mt. Holyoke's "strict rules" and repulsed by the weekly prayer meetings which bombarded her with threatening talk of hellfire and brimstone.[7]

Olympia's choices to obtain a higher education after leaving Mount Holyoke were slim. Almost every college in America at that time was exclusively for men. She considered Oberlin, the nation's first co-educational college located in nearby Ohio but she rejected the school because it would not allow women to participate in public exercises. Instead, she chose Antioch, also in Ohio, because the college's president, Horace Mann, promised incoming students the opportunity to take part in "a great experiment"—the education of women on the same terms as men.[8]

As a student at Antioch, she wore clothing popularized by women's rights advocate, Amelia Bloomer. Olympia found the long baggy pants, worn under a skirt, "convenient and comfortable." In keeping with the spirit of her new garb, she challenged the college's practice of only inviting men to be visiting lecturers and arranged for Antoinette Brown Blackwell, a well-known women's rights activist and lay preacher, to come to Antioch and speak. It was the first time Olympia had heard a woman preacher and Olympia said she felt as though "the Kingdom of Heaven were at hand."[9]

Greatly influenced by Blackwell's appearance, Olympia decided that after she graduated from Antioch in 1860, she wanted to go to theological school and become a fully ordained minister. She knew of no other woman in America who had done that and she wanted to be the first.[10]

Like most of the undergraduate colleges in the U.S. at this time, theological schools were also almost entirely for men, not women. She applied to the Unitarian Theological School at Meadville, Pennsylvania but it turned her down because of her sex. Oberlin's theological school said it would accept her but Olympia chose not to go there because Oberlin's acceptance, once again, was on the condition that she not participate in any public exercises.[11]

Olympia ended up applying to the only other theological school open to her—the Theological School of St. Lawrence University, a Universalist seminary which had opened in 1858 in Canton, New York. The school's president, Ebenezer Fisher, told her she could come to the school but should not expect to be ordained as a minister. He said he did not think women were called to the ministry but added, "I leave that between you and the Great Head of Church." Olympia thought that was "just where it should be left" and arrived in Canton for classes in the fall of 1861.[12]

She was the only female student on campus. Faculty wives were either cool to her at first or outright hostile. During her first year, male students derided her by standing outside her windows at night and mimicking her soft, high-pitched voice.[13]

Olympia spent her vacations between classes getting experience preaching. She took assignments at Universalist churches in Vermont, and in and around Canton, including those in nearby Ogdensburg and Heuvelton. The congregation in Heuvelton liked her so much, they offered her a full-time job to be their pastor after she graduated. However, first she had to become officially ordained by a governing body of the Universalist church.[14]

The governing body closest to Olympia's school was the St. Lawrence Association of Universalists. It had been officially organized in 1839 and represented the Universalist churches in St. Lawrence, Franklin and Clinton Counties. Every June each of the Association's churches sent their minister and two delegates to an annual meeting where they would transact ecclesiastical business, which included ordaining ministers.[15] The Association's next meeting was scheduled for June 24, 1863 in Malone, New York, about 50 miles east of Canton, in Franklin County.[16]

Olympia was on track to graduate from theological school on July 9, 1863 and once again discussed ordination with President Fisher. He told her he was opposed to her ordination and would speak against it in Malone if she sought it at the Association meeting. She knew that the representatives from the Heuvelton Universalist Church would support her bid for ordination at the meeting, so whether the president of her school supported her or not, she decided to go to Malone and seek ordination by herself.[17]

In June 1863, Malone was bustling with Civil War news and activity. Newspapers were filled with stories about Robert E. Lee's invasion of Maryland and Pennsylvania and speculation that Confederate forces might continue their advance into western New York State and attack Buffalo.[18] A train carrying the Sixteenth Regiment, a unit organized in 1861 with men recruited from Clinton, Franklin and St. Lawrence Counties, had recently pulled into the Malone railroad station. The men's term of service had expired and the regiment's 350 men had returned home from the fighting.[19] Ulysses S. Grant had tightened his siege of Vicksburg and the Provost Marshal's office in Malone was busy registering men under the newly enacted draft law.[20]

Families in Malone were also excited by the fact that on the same day that the St. Lawrence Association of Universalists planned to open their annual two-day conclave, A.P. Ball's Great Collosseum [sic] would be in Malone to put on a show in a two-center-pole tent that was said to hold 2,000 people. Ticket holders had been promised that they would see "gymnastic feats, acrobatic performances, antique Olympic games, grotesque dances, comic scenes, pantomimes and plays."[21]

If Olympia had read the local newspapers as she waited for the Association's meeting to open, she would have been encouraged to see that three women in Malone were advertising their own businesses—a music and drawing teacher, a "fashionable" clothing store operator, and a bonnet and dress trimmings store owner. However, Olympia probably would have been appalled by two other articles about women that were in the newspapers. The first, entitled, "The Art of Wife-Preserving," provided women with advice about what wives should do to keep their husbands happy.

Cartoon by Henry Mayer entitled, "When our national guard is feminized." In the center, is a woman selecting colors of fabric for a military uniform. Surrounding this, are a number of scenes showing women in military uniforms. Illus. in: Puck, v. 75, no. 1943 (1914 May 30), centerfold (p. 12-13). Library of Congress.

The tips ranged from "be fresh, fair and fascinating" to "bring him slippers and coffee, care and courtesy" to "acquire cultivation."[22] The second article, entitled "'Woman's Rights' Which Have Been Overlooked," listed ten of such "rights." The number one "right" was "to have her home in order whenever her husband returns from business." Number two was "to be kind and forebearing whenever her husband is annoyed." It is highly unlikely that Olympia read the remaining eight "rights."[23]

Universalist preachers had begun coming to Malone as early as 1824. In 1846, the First Universalist Society of Malone was incorporated and a church building was erected on Main Street.[24] On June 24, 1863, the doors to that church swung open for the first session of the St. Lawrence Universalist Association's annual meeting, and Olympia walked in to make an argument for her ordination.

Her request to be ordained was "bitterly contested." Behind the scenes, she learned that one of the most potent arguments brought up against her ordination was that it would "bring down the price of preaching" because it would encourage women to "flock to the ministry." Nevertheless, the ordaining council voted in favor of ordaining Olympia and the official ceremonies were held on the next day, June 25, 1863.[25] Two weeks later, on July 9, 1863, Olympia became the first woman in U.S. history to become a fully ordained minister with a degree from a recognized theological school, when President Fisher handed Olympia her diploma.[26]

The Reverend Olympia Brown believed that it was her duty as a minister to candidly preach a "living religion" that made war on "the great social and political evils" of her day. She planned to wage battle for the weak and powerless not only in churches, but also in the nation's streets, homes, lecture halls, government offices and places of business.[27] One of the greatest evils Olympia planned to confront was the subjugation of women. She said, "The United States is an aristocracy of sex. It is the meanest aristocracy on the face of the earth."[28]

Life for women in America's "aristocracy of sex" was similar in many ways to life for women living today under Taliban rule in Afghanistan. Women's speech and participation in public events was proscribed. Their physical movement was limited by the restrictive clothing they were expected to wear. They were not allowed to control property they inherited or money they earned if they were married. Their access to higher education was practically non-existent. And they did not have the right to vote. Olympia dedicated her life to changing all of that.

Olympia felt that, for the most part, American women were "feeble abject beings, mere butterflies" overly devoted to the "frivolities of fashion, needlework and novels." In order to become free and strong, women had to have the opportunity to obtain a higher education and the vote—the two keys to self-respect and independence.[29]

The caption reads: "'Queen of the Home,' say the Anti-Suffragists. Yes; Queen of a Cook-Stove Throne." The cartoon shows a woman wearing a crown, slumped over, sitting on a chair atop a stove, holding a broom in her right hand, with pots and pans steaming around her. Illus. in: *Puck*, v. 76, no. 1970 (1914 December 5), p. 4. Library of Congress.

According to Olympia, women were being fed an education consisting of "broken bits of knowledge, half-truths and make-believes" that were all "crumbs from the rich man's table." She said that the female seminaries were "miserable farces" that cheated women out of any semblance of learning. Olympia demanded higher education for women that would give them "the executive ability of the business man, the intellectual acumen of the scholar, the comprehensive thought of the philosopher, and the prophetic vision of the seer." This kind of higher education would enable a woman to forge armor for herself "to do battle with the world," to learn how to support herself independently, and to realize "the power and beauty of true womanhood."[30]

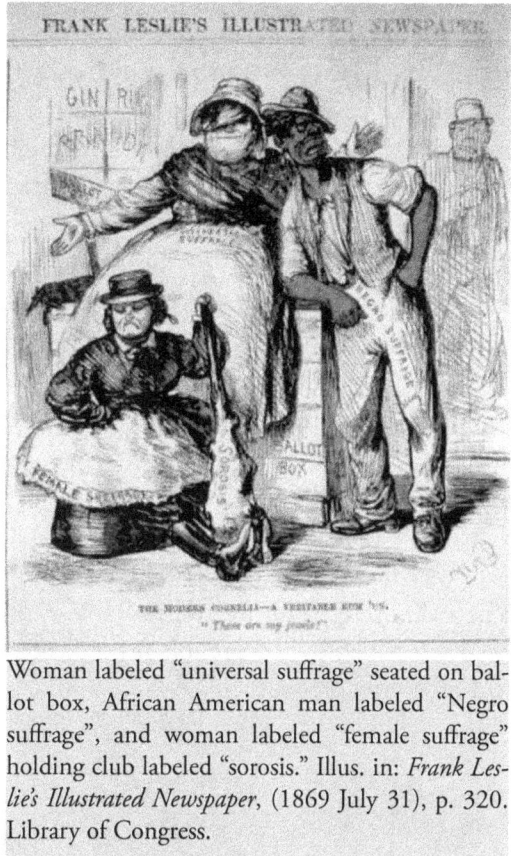

Woman labeled "universal suffrage" seated on ballot box, African American man labeled "Negro suffrage", and woman labeled "female suffrage" holding club labeled "sorosis." Illus. in: *Frank Leslie's Illustrated Newspaper*, (1869 July 31), p. 320. Library of Congress.

Olympia's demand for suffrage, the second key women needed to gain self-respect and independence, was couched in religious terms. She said that woman's suffrage not only involved the principles of democratic government, but also the doctrine of justice taught in the Golden Rule.[31] She contended that God had given women an interest in their government and had intended men and women to rule "side by side."[32] Paraphrasing words from the Bible, she argued that the founding fathers wanted to create a republic in which there should be "neither Jew nor Greek, nor bond nor free, nor male nor female."[33]

From the beginning to the end of her career, Olympia fought fearlessly for equal rights for women, never forgetting the biblical exhortation, "Let no man despise you."[34] She marched, lectured, testified, published, protested and picketed thousands of times from coast to coast.

Olympia was a woman of action. Her small, slim, delicate looking appearance was deceiving. Weighing in at barely 90 pounds, she may not have looked very formidable to bystanders[35], but she had no fear for her personal safety when she went into action. In 1867, at the age of 32, she campaigned for universal suffrage in the heat of Kansas during the months of July and August. Working alone, she traveled the length and breadth of the state speaking two or three times a day at meetings that were often 50 miles apart. She slept on floors, or in lofts in log cabins, or shared a bed in a dugout or sod house. In one town, by herself, she had to face down a howling mob of men that threw rocks and other debris at the school house where she was speaking.[36]

Fifty years later in Washington D.C., when she was 82, Olympia could still be found courageously demanding equal rights for women. Ignoring the risk of being attacked by gangs of hooting and jeering men as the police looked on, she picketed the White House to protest President Woodrow Wilson's failure to speak out in favor of woman's suffrage. A year later in 1918, she joined a protest demonstration in Lafayette Park, across the street from the White House, on the day Wilson was to be officially received by the French at the peace talks being held in Paris at the end of World War I.

Woman suffrage demonstrators at Lafayette Park in 1918. Library of Congress.

Woman suffrage pickets at the White House in 1917. Library of Congress.

About 400 women gathered to burn all of Wilson's speeches and books on freedom and democracy. A rowdy group of men also gathered to heckle the protesters. When Olympia stepped forward and threw the speech Wilson gave when he arrived in France, into the fire, the catcalling stopped. Her speech castigating Wilson brought applause and cheers.[37]

Olympia did not censure men only, she had plenty to say about women too. She told them that their indifference and inertia were the greatest obstacles to women's rights, especially suffrage.[38] She said that sometimes, women just did not fully understand what the women's movement was all about.[39] At a tea once, the poet and philosopher, Ralph Waldo Emerson, told Olympia that the women whose opinions he admired did not favor suffrage for women. She bluntly responded by telling Emerson, "I should not value the opinion of any woman who was opposed to woman's suffrage.[40]

When Olympia's battle for suffrage took her to Washington, D.C. to testify before congressional committees, she often had to joust with women who were opposed to suffrage. At the age of 78, Olympia rebutted the testimony of the treasurer of a national woman's anti-suffrage association who had charged that woman's suffrage was a "political disease" and that two-thirds of the suffrage leaders were out and out socialists.[41]

The most serious disputes Olympia had with women took place when she was in her 80's and was marching and picketing the White House as a member of the militant Woman's Party. The leaders of the National American Woman Suffrage Association, Carrie Chapman Catt and Anna Howard Shaw, condemned the marching and picketing as "disgusting and reprehensible." Olympia's state organization in Wisconsin agreed with Catt and Howard and shunned Olympia, describing her activity as "improper." Olympia answered by accusing her detractors of cowardice and being more interested in receiving publicity than working for principles. In a speech to her association's board of directors, she asserted that although the U.S. may have entered World War I to make the world safe for democracy, "we cannot say that the United States is a democracy as long as women cannot vote." To the criticism that it was improper and disgusting for women to march and picket, she declared that women had been dignified and proper for over 60 years and "we still do not have the vote."[42]

In her personal and religious life, she relentlessly challenged the status quo whenever she believed that it contributed to the subjugation of women. Nothing was sacrosanct—not marriage customs, her fellow ministers, or even the Bible.

After falling in love with John Henry Willis, a member of her first church's board of trustees in Weymouth, Massachusetts, and then marrying him after taking on a new job preaching in Bridgeport, Connecticut in 1873, she did not change her name to either Mrs. John Henry Willis or the Reverend Olympia Brown Willis. Following a trail blazed by Lucy Stone, Olympia kept her own name. She and her husband were in agreement not to take part in a custom that they felt had originated when women were "mere chattel" and marriages were financial arrangements between families.[43]

Belva Lockwood. left, and Olympia Brown, in 1913. An attorney, Lockwood was the first woman allowed to practice before the U.S. Supreme Court and was a candidate for president in 1884 and 1888. Library of Congress.

In 1915, When Olympia was president of the Federal Suffrage Association, an organization she had helped found in 1892, she criticized the fact that there were so many male preachers. She said that too many of them were "influenced by rich men in their districts" and were "afraid to attack child labor, white slavery, and other evils." Olympia's solution? More women should become ministers.[44]

When it came to the Bible, Olympia agreed with Elizabeth Cady Stanton that it was a document that had been written by men for men and that it was largely responsible for the subservient state women found themselves in. To help change that, Olympia worked with a committee that provided commentary for Stanton to use in writing her new book, *The Woman's Bible*. It assailed the rampant sexism she ascertained was prevalent in the recently revised King James version of the Bible. Stanton's book became a best seller.[45]

Olympia was an outspoken advocate for women's rights who lived by the motto, "Let the chips fall where they may!"[46] She took uncompromising positions which often alienated wealthy business interests, immigrant groups and blacks.

Shortly after she began organizing and speaking out for suffrage forwomen and black men, she crossed swords with abolitionists, black activists and Republican political leaders who were demanding that black men should get the vote before women did. Her first inkling that women were about to be pushed to the end of the voting rights line behind black men took place at a universal suffrage rally in Kansas in 1867 when she heard Charles Henry Langston, a well-known black activist and educator, ask the audience if they "wanted every old maid to vote?"[47]

Matters came to an ugly head on this issue at a subsequent meeting of the American Equal Rights Association at Cooper Union in New York City where she got into a bitter dispute with another nationally prominent black civil rights leader—Frederick Douglass. After listening to speaker after speaker discuss strategy for winning voting rights for black men, she questioned why no one was speaking up for women, only for black men. Olympia was promptly rebuked by the six-foot tall Douglass who said he championed the right of black men to vote because it was a matter of life and death for them, unlike women. Seething with anger, Olympia stood up and interrupted Douglass asking, "Do you really believe that it is more important for two million Negro men to vote than it is for seventeen million women?" He refused to specifically answer her question but continued to argue that the black man needed the vote to protect his life and property. Olympia responded stating that what Douglass had said about black men, applied equally to black women.[48]

During her career, Olympia refused to defer to wealth and she did not hesitate to tell her parishioners how she felt. In one sermon she said, "There are those today who are worshipping Mammon rather than God... [who] would sell their birthright in God's kingdom for a miserable mess of pottage in bank stocks and government bonds; and yet they attend church, sit in cushioned pews, and talk about enjoying religion."[49]

The title of this cartoon by Oscar Edward Cesare reads, "The genii of intolerance. A dangerous ally for the cause of women suffrage." It shows a genii "Prohibition" rising from a bottle labeled "Injustice Intolera[nce] Hypocr[isy]" tearing at a woman's banner reading "Votes for Women" as the woman flees from his clutches. Illus. in: *Puck*, v. 78, no. 2012 (1915 Sept. 25), p. 6. Library of Congress.

She ultimately paid a price for being so forthright. Shortly after she was hired to be a minister in Bridgeport, wealthy and influential members of her new church began work to oust her because they were angry the church had hired a woman. They called in ministers from neighboring churches to go among her parishioners telling them "what you need here is a good man."[50] In the end, she was driven out of her job and she left Bridgeport to become a minister in Racine, Wisconsin in 1878.[51]

Olympia also had a curious duel with the American liquor industry. She supported temperance because she believed the liquor interests were "destroying body and mind" with "the poisons" they were selling—"a great and manifest evil."[52] However, she was opposed to connecting temperance with woman's suffrage, as other organizations had done. She had seen in Kansas how the liquor industry fought woman's suffrage with newspaper ads, posters and speakers which warned voters that if women got the vote, they would shut down all the saloons.[53] Olympia was convinced that identifying prohibition with woman's suffrage was a political error. She said doing so "put us back twenty-five years."[54]

In the 1880's, when vast numbers of "new" immigrants from central and southern Europe arrived in the United States and became eligible to vote, Olympia made some of the most acrimonious statements of her career. She said it was "unbearable" that American women were "the political inferiors of all the riffraff of Europe that is poured upon our shores." Olympia stated that it was an "enormous injustice to women" that "we enfranchise the saloon and the poorhouse, the irresponsible classes" and "make the daughters of America subject to the serfs and slaves from the old world." She was infuriated that political leaders gave the vote to "aliens, paupers, tramps and drunkards" while refusing to give it to "teachers, church members, preachers, and mothers."[55]

Olympia did not expect to see "complete victory" for women's rights in her lifetime. She believed that "each generation must be content to do its part, leaving it for others" to do theirs.[56] Recognizing that woman's suffrage, in and of itself, would not grant women equal rights, Olympia called for Congress to introduce an equal rights amendment, immediately after it adopted the woman's suffrage amendment.[57] She could foresee that an equal rights amendment would not only help women make additional gains, it would also prevent Congress from passing laws to take rights away from women.[58]

As pressure on Congress to enact a constitutional guarantee of equality for women builds again, and debate in Albany about new legislation to protect and expand women's rights heats up, words on a bronze tablet installed by St. Lawrence University to honor the centennial of Olympia's graduation and ordination are more meaningful than ever on this, the sesquicentennial, of her history-making accomplishments. The last sentence on the tablet proclaims, "The Flame of her Spirit Still Burns Today."

NOTES

[1] There are a few historians who believe that Lydia Ann Jenkins may have been ordained several years before Olympia, however, most historians doubt this because records documenting Lydia's ordination have not been found. Antoinette Brown Blackwell's ordination in 1853 was not conducted by an official body of her church, only by the congregation of her local church. In any case, unlike Olympia, neither Lydia nor Antoinette were granted diplomas from a recognized theological school. Bidlack, "Olympia Brown," 129n22; Howe, "Lydia Ann Jenkins"; Zink-Sawyer, From Preachers to Suffragists, 52n70.

[2] Brown, Acquaintances, 59–60.

[3] Ibid., 9, 11–12.

[4] Willis, Autobiography, 17.

[5] Neu, "Woman's Suffrage," 278; Coté, *Olympia Brown*, 31; Brown, Acquaintances, 7.

[6] Brown, Acquaintances, 8–10.

[7] Willis, Autobiography, 20, 22, 38; Coté, Olympia Brown, 31–34.

[8] Willis, Autobiography, 27.

[9] Ibid., 32, 33, 35.

[10] Ibid., 32, 37.

[11] Brown, Acquaintances, 27; Willis, Autobiography, 38.

[12] Willis, Autobiography, 39; Brown, Acquaintances, 28; Black, Sixty-years of Saint Lawrence, 17.

[13] Willis, Autobiography, 39; Coté, *Olympia Brown*, 54.

[14] Willis, Autobiography, 41–42.

[15] Hough, *A History of St. Lawrence and Franklin Counties, New York*, 523–524; Today, the St. Lawrence District is made up of 34 Unitarian Universalist congregations in upstate New York and northern Pennsylvania with a central office in Buffalo. "Congregations of the St. Lawrence District of the UUA."

[16] "St. Law. Universalist Association."

[17] Coté, *Olympia Brown*, 60; Willis, Autobiography, 42.

[18] "Late War News."

[19] "The 16th Regiment"; "The Welcome to the 16th Regiment."

[20] "The Situation at Vicksburgh"; "The Provost Marshal."

[21] "Advertisement."

[22] "The Art of Wife-Preserving."

[23] "'Woman's Rights' Which Have Been Overlooked."

[24] Seaver, Historical Sketches of Franklin County, 486.

[25] Willis, Autobiography, 42; Brown, Acquaintances, 30, 59.

[26] Coté, *Olympia Brown*, 60.

[27] Brown, "Installation Sermon," 45, 49.

[28] Coté, *Olympia Brown*, 164.

[29] Neu, "Woman's Suffrage," 279; Brown, "The Higher Education of Women," 250.

[30] Brown, "The Higher Education of Women," 248–251.

[31] Brown, Acquaintances, 51.

[32] "Women in Council," 8.

[33] Bidlack, "Olympia Brown," 138.

[34] Brown, "Hand of Fellowship," 29–30.

[35] However, one newspaper described her as "a weather beaten, cross-grained, sour, snappish, fanatical, crabbed, skinny, smoked-looking old beldame." "Personal," 3.

[36] Brown, Acquaintances, 55–58, 62–64; Coté, Olympia Brown, 53, 81.

[37] Coté, *Olympia Brown*, 157–159, 163–164; Neu, "Woman's Suffrage," 285.

[38] Neu, "Woman's Suffrage," 286.

[39] "National Woman's Suffrage Society," 7.

[40] Brown, Acquaintances, 50–51.

[41] "Suffragists and Antis in Word War," 1.

[42] Coté, *Olympia Brown*, 159–161.

[43] Brown, Acquaintances, 37–38; Willis, Autobiography, 55; The couple had two children. Henry Parker Willis was born at a "water cure sanitarium" in Elmira, New York in 1874 because Olympia "did not approve of any of the Bridgeport doctors." Henry became a professor, editor and federal government official. Gwendolen Brown Willis was born in Bridgeport in 1876. She became a teacher of classics. Graves, "Notable American Women, 1607-1950," 257; Willis, Autobiography, 55–56.

[44] "'Pastoress' Scores 'Ping Pong' Pastors," 1; Coté, Olympia Brown, 133–134.

[45] Coté, *Olympia Brown*, 141.

[46] Brown, "Hand of Fellowship," 29.

[47] Brown, Acquaintances, 69.

[48] Coté, *Olympia Brown*, 98–100. This incident influenced Olympia to help found a national organization devoted exclusively to obtaining woman's suffrage.

[49] Brown, "Installation Sermon," 45.

[50] Willis, Autobiography, 55; Hart, "Encyclopedia of Connecticut Biography," 223.

[51] Coté, *Olympia Brown*, 112–113. She worked in Racine until 1887 when she resigned to work full time for woman's suffrage. Ibid., 125–126.

[52] Brown, "Installation Sermon," 45.

[53] Coté, *Olympia Brown*, 91.

[54] Neu, "Woman's Suffrage," 286.

[55] Coté, *Olympia Brown*, 130; Neu, "Woman's Suffrage," 281.

[56] Brown, "Installation Sermon," 49.

[57] Coté, *Olympia Brown*, 165.

[58] An Equal Rights Amendment was introduced in Congress in 1923, and 49 years later, in 1972, it was adopted. However, because it failed to win the approval of the necessary 38 states by a 1982 congressional deadline, the amendment was not ratified and therefore not added to the Constitution.

BIBLIOGRAPHY

"Advertisement." Frontier Palladium, June 18, 1863.

Bidlack, Beth. "Olympia Brown: Reading the Bible as a Universalist Minister and Pragmatic Suffragist." In Breaking Boundaries: Female Biblical Interpreters Who Challenged the Status Quo, edited by Nancy Calvert-Koyzis and Heather Weir. London: Continuum International Publishing Group, 2010.

Black, Malcolm S., ed. Sixty-years of Saint Lawrence. Norwood, MA: Plimpton Press, 1916.

Brown, Olympia. *Acquaintances, Old and New, Among Reformers*. Milwaukee: S.E. Tate, 1911.

————. "Hand of Fellowship." In Services at the Ordination and Installation of Rev. Phebe A. Hanaford, edited by Rev. Wm. Haskell. C.C. Roberts, 1870.

————. "Installation Sermon." In Services at the Ordination and Installation of Rev. Phebe A. Hanaford, edited by Rev. Wm. Haskell. C.C. Roberts, 1870.

————. "The Higher Education of Women." In Standing Before Us: Unitarian Universalist Women and Social Reform, 1776-1936, edited by Dorothy May Emerson. Boston: Skinner House Books, 2000.

"Congregations of the St. Lawrence District of the UUA." The St. Lawrence District of the Unitarian Universalist Association. Accessed February 5, 2013. http://www.sld.uua. org/congregations.html.

Coté, Charlotte. *Olympia Brown*. Racine, WI: Mother Courage Press, 1988.

Graves, Lawrence L. "Brown, Olympia." In Notable American Women, 1607–1950: A Biographical Dictionary, edited by Edward T. James. Harvard University Press, 1971.

Hart, Samuel, ed. "Staples, Frank Trubee." Encyclopedia of Connecticut Biography. Boston, New York and Chicago: The American Historical Society, 1917.

Hough, Franklin B. *A History of St. Lawrence and Franklin Counties, New York*. Albany, NY: Little, 1853.

Howe, Charles A. "Lydia Ann Jenkins." Dictionary of Unitarian & Universalist Biography. Accessed February 25, 2013. http://www25.uua.org/uuhs/duub/articles/lydiaannjenkins.html.

"Late War News." *Frontier Palladium*, June 18, 1863.

"National Woman's Suffrage Society." New York *Times*, May 12, 1875.

Neu, Charles E. "Olympia Brown and the Woman's Suffrage Movement." The Wisconsin Magazine of History, July 1, 1960.

"'Pastoress' Scores 'Ping Pong' Pastors." The Milwaukee *Sentinel*, July 16, 1915.

"Personal." Troy Weekly Times, August 3, 1867.

Seaver, Frederick J. *Historical Sketches of Franklin County. Albany, NY*: J.B. Lyon, 1918.

"St. Law. Universalist Association." *Frontier Palladium*, June 18, 1863.

"Suffragists and Antis in Word War." The Mansfield (Ohio) *Shield*, February 1, 1913.

"The 16th Regiment." *Frontier Palladium*, May 28, 1863.

"The Art of Wife-Preserving." *Frontier Palladium*, June 25, 1863.

"The Provost Marshal." *Frontier Palladium*, June 4, 1863.

"The Situation at Vicksburgh." *Frontier Palladium*, June 4, 1863.

"The Welcome to the 16th Regiment." *Frontier Palladium*, May 21, 1863.

Willis, Gwendolen B., ed. *Olympia Brown: An Autobiography*. harvardsquarelibrary, 1960. http://www.scribd.com/doc/47729286/Olympia-Brown-An-Autobiogrpahy. PDF e-book.

"'Woman's Rights' Which Have Been Overlooked." *Frontier Palladium*, May 28, 1863.

"Women in Council." *New York Times,* May 15, 1874.

Zink-Sawyer, Beverly Ann. *From Preachers to Suffragists: Woman's Rights and Religious Conviction in the Lives of Three Nineteenth-Century American Clergywomen*. Louisville, KY: Westminster John Knox Press, 2003.

About the author: Herbert C. Hallas is a retired history teacher and attorney and the author of *William Almon Wheeler: Political Star of the North Country* (Albany, NY: State University of New York Press, in press). He has contributed articles to the Franklin Historical Review and publishes a blog about New York State and North Country history at herberthallas.com.

Dutch Women in Seventeenth-Century New Netherland

by Maria Vann

On 6 March 1663, Altjen Sybrants appeared before the Honorable Council of War and the Honorable Court at Wildwyck, New Netherland in search of vindication from accusations of slander. Schout Swarthout, a member of the council, lodged the complaint after a previous visitation to Sybrants' home to notify her about a new order from the Council of War. Upon hearing the order prohibiting strong drink to be sold to militia or Indians, a frustrated Sybrants suggested the Schout "might cleanse his anus!"[1] Such slanderous words from anyone- no less a woman in New Netherland was a serious matter for the courts and Schout wanted restitution for his honor. Denying the accusation, Sybrants challenged male authority by arguing that, "he [the Schout] must prove this."[2] The case continued on subsequent days as witnesses were brought to testify in support of the defendant's guilt. Throughout the process, Sybrants never confirmed she had said such slanderous words; instead she declared that Schout treated her "in a manner out of spite," for what is not clear.[3] Eventually, after several testimonies against her, the defendant was sentenced and condemned as a public example for her "vile and foul language."[4] Altejen Sybrants was ordered to pay a fine of one hundred Caroulus guilders of which two-thirds was to be paid to the prosecutor Schout and one-third to the Church at Wildwyck.[5] Though Sybrandts lost her defense, much can be gleaned from her testimony, or lack thereof. She demonstrated a bold and unwavering will, capable of confronting the male establishment, signifying she knew full well her rights as a citizen with a voice in the Dutch Empire.

Such cases offer a glimpse into the lives of colonial Dutch women in New Netherland, which ran counter to the lives of other American colonial women. Dutch women were more active and engaged participants in society unlike their more submissive and hindered English counterparts. During the period beginning in 1624 to just prior to English takeover in 1664, New Netherlander women were involved in all aspects of society whether philanthropic, legal, business or religious endeavors.[6] They had a keen understanding of personal rights under Roman-Dutch law and they functioned within a landscape of some legal equity. A leveling affect from life on the borderland thus reinforced their pseudo-independent status in the colony.[7]

As a commercial society far from the crown, court records indicate New Netherland's people (only 50% of Dutch origin) held significant autonomy.[8] Dutch control may have disappeared after 1664, but the influence of the culture remained for many years as citizens struggled to resist assimilation of English ways. Additionally, as a trade-centered colony, New Netherland demographics, which included a large proportion of non-Dutch peoples, allowed for a more diverse and open society. Due to this diversity, women's roles within society highlighted existing social freedoms. Though women did hold lesser legal status than men did, many took advantage of one of the less restrictive societies in the seventeenth-century Atlantic world. The women of New Netherland were unique in their time and space because their social status enabled them semi-equitable civic, legal, and social involvement.

Consolidated through the Union of Utrecht in 1579, making the Netherlands one of the earliest republics in Europe, Dutch society afforded individual rights to all citizens, including women. The traditions of freedoms of conscience, speech and, in practice, the press were foundational ideals of Dutch society. These concepts were manifested in a variety of ways in the broader Dutch empire. The Union of Utrecht, Netherlands constitutive charter obliged the signing provinces to maintain the privilege and liberties of all the signators.[9] Individual freedoms were safeguarded to a greater degree than in other European nations because of an exceedingly decentralized political system. Local jurisdictions often protected rights of individuals against the central institutions of the Dutch Republic.[10]

Although certain rights were foundational, laws could vary from area to area in the Republic making for differences in how courts dealt with defendants. In 1659, the Dutch West India Company sent a booklet to New Netherland entitled *Ordinances and Code of Procedure Before the Courts of the City of Amsterdam* for additional guidance, and if questions arose local courts were to refer to the law of their homeland. New Netherland was governed by social norms in the Dutch republic but because of distance, variations existed.[11]

Prior to the emergence of women's studies, historians placed New Netherlander women in a similar position to that of other well studied colonial societies, such as New England, despite variations between them.[12] Early Dutch scholarship also faced obstacles that English scholars did not including a lack of translated documents and few oral histories. Historians of New Netherland mainly relied upon Anglo-focused narratives as opposed to accurate translations of Dutch documentation. Furthermore, the concentration of Dutch culture focused primarily on role of males in society, dealing little if at all with women. In his 1912 essay, "Wiltwyck Under the Dutch," historian Augustus H. Van Buren rendered only a partial portrait of colonial Dutch women when he stated, "she was what God Almighty designed a woman to be-the noblest, the holiest thing on earth-the helpmate of her husband and the mother of mankind."[13] Such writings placed women in a subservient, domestic and secondary role to men. Recently translated records challenge these assumptions revealing the actions of women who stood firm under masculine authority.

Additionally, limited accurate Dutch translations hindered early historical analysis of documents containing women's social activities and rights. Historical perspectives about New Netherland shifted, as bilingual scholars like Charles T. Gehring, of the New Netherland Institute and others translated nearly 65% of Dutch colonial documents.[14] Gehring's and native speaking scholars' translations enable more precise understanding of Dutch colonization. Utilizing research that embraces social history with these newly translated documents, Joyce D. Goodfriend analyzed and uncovered inadequate assumptions about women and their inactive roles in public society.[15] These analyses offer a greater understanding of the nature of women's roles in business and beyond the domestic sphere. Goodfriend suggests that with the emergence of the new social history, historians grasp a greater and more comprehensive understanding of colonial Dutch society as never before.[16] Goodfriend contends that new studies considered the whole of Dutch society as opposed to past methodologies that took a top-down approach, focusing more on history of the elite.[17] These new studies emerged in the 1970s following the Women's Liberation Movement, and gave great insight into the uniqueness of Dutch society through increased awareness of women's roles as an important aspect of history.[18]

Additionally, native Dutch historians are producing significant research. Native speaking historians offer new depths to Dutch study because of their ability to understand the culture and subtle qualities of which others may not recognize. This new trend is taking colonial Dutch studies in a fresh direction as "a means to uncover gender roles in the Atlantic world."[19] Applied to these studies are concepts of gender, which analyze how cultural and historical processes shape social differences between the sexes.[20] When viewed through this new lens, New Netherland's borderland provides a leveling effect allowing women a vital role as citizens in the Dutch colony.

New Netherland Settlement

Henry Hudson, an Englishman in service of the Dutch East India Company, discovered the region, which became known as New Netherland, in search of a trade route to the Indies in 1609.[21] Hudson's discovery of the area known, now as New York, thus began Dutch colonization by Amsterdam merchants in 1614.[22] Initially, the founding members colonized for the purpose of trade and private production.[23]

As early as 1659, New Netherland propaganda presented the colony as a haven for poor families, farmers, and craftsmen.[24] Additionally, the Dutch encouraged the formation of overseas households in order to establish solid familial ties for stability and enhanced productivity. To promote colonization of New Netherlands, the Dutch West India Company issued a Charter of Freedoms and Exemptions in 1629.[25] The charter required patroons, large land grant owners such as Kilian VanRensselaer, "within the space of four years" to "undertake to plant a colony there of fifty souls, upwards of fifteen years old," who "would be free from customs, taxes, excise, imposts and any other contributions for the space of ten years."[26] Based on this charter, many people traveled to the colony, most of whom planned to make a fortune and return to their homeland. Many of these initial immigrants remained. Approximately 9,000 were in the colony at

English conquest, most of who resided in New Amsterdam, now Manhattan.[27]

Settlers came as early as 1623 to the area later known as Beverwijck (modern day Albany) and 1658 to settle Wiltwyck (later called Esopus), now Kingston, New York.[28] In 1658, the population of Esopus, a settlement along the Hudson River was "now about seventy, men, women and children, with thirty of the former sex."[29] Likewise, Petrus Stuyvesant, Director General of New Netherland for the Dutch West India Company, surveyed the village of Beverwijck on April 10, 1652 by dividing land patents to settlers.[30] By the end of Dutch rule in 1664, New Netherland's population of about 9,000 contrasted the more populated New England colony that had 33,200 by 1660.[31]

For women, colonizing in an area with so few people was a courageous endeavor. In addition to a low number of inhabitants, disease decreased the population from time to time. For instance, in 1662, 19 adults and 17 children were killed by a chicken pox epidemic in Fort Orange.[32] Though disease was a continual threat to all societies, the effects appeared greater in a small colonial settlement because the depletion of citizens had a negative effect on population function and social morale. For colonists, especially women, life was difficult and required courage to endure all that accompanied settlement in New Netherland. Being away from the Netherlands, threats by Native Americans, adapting to a new geography, and making the Trans-Atlantic crossing required fortitude. Without question, the adventurous attitude needed for life on a borderland contributed to emboldening women in New Netherland.

One important contributing factor to the overall social framework of New Netherland was its existence as a borderland. Borderlands, or "a place that transcends national boundaries and the meeting place and fusing place of two streams of European civilizations," describe New Netherland and its structure.[33] Foundational characteristics, such as wilderness living and neighboring cultures, contributed to New Netherland's borderland environment and offered greater mobility for women in colonial settlements. Some historians define New Netherland as a frontier, yet the colony only shares frontier attributes.[34] As Elizabeth Shaw suggests, "New Netherland existed in a transatlantic, transfrontier and multicultural context."[35] This description more accurately reflects New Netherland as a borderland settlement. New Netherland as a borderland held many dangers, challenges to settlers, and some isolation from urban areas, while remaining well connected to the Atlantic World. A far cry from urban Amsterdam or even Amersfoort, the small settlements of New Amsterdam and Beverwijck were fine examples of colonial borderlands because of tension with neighboring Native Americans, a diverse population that included African slaves and Europeans, and a population intimately connected to the Atlantic World through trade and merchant activities. The investigation of Dutch borderland communities cannot be alienated from the study of the larger Atlantic World systems.[36]

As a region with racial, ethnic and religious diversity, New Netherland provided opportunity for conflict.[37] Women were often the recipients of both opportunity and conflict. Diversity and conflict manifested itself not only in the immigrant populations in the colony but also in the Native Americans whom settlers came in contact. New Netherlanders interacted with neighboring Algonquin and Iroquoian bands. These encounters sparked clashes, as well as resulted in the formation of important trade relations based on sewant and beaver pelts.[38] As in other colonial societies, neighboring Native Americans posed a great challenge for inhabitants of New Netherland.

Native Americans were often at war with the Dutch in response to the imposing Europeans, failed trade relations and hostility toward native tribes. Known as the Dutch Indian wars, or the Esopus Wars, the two groups battled on an off from 1641-1664.[39] Unlike New Amsterdam and Fort Orange, the village of Esopus was unique in that it was established as a farming community due to its land and distance from trading routes.[40] The stress over settlement of farmland that infringed upon Native Americans' land eventually caused tension.

By 1626, the Dutch built flourishing trade relations with Mahicans and Raritans and expanded trade with the Mohawks, a warring rival of the Mahicans.[41] Relations between the Dutch and Esopus Indians deteriorated due to Dutch aggression and trading with clan enemies.[42] The acquisition of firearms by Native Americans additionally contributed to vicious war with the Dutch.[43] Under the leadership of Director General William Kieft, relations were further damaged as he offered a bounty on Raritan Indian scalps, plunging the Dutch into years of attacks.[44]

After continually playing tribe against tribe and then turning on supposed allies, the Dutch found themselves in all out war. This directly affected the citizens of New Netherland. On 7 June 1663, the local Esopus Indians raided the New Village of Esopus. Women and children were taken into captivity and rescued months later.[45] Slaughter ensued on both sides as farms were burnt and women and children were murdered. When Petrus Stuyvesant assumed leadership as Director-General in New Netherland, the murders of Indians continued until the conclusion of the Esopus Wars finally came in 1664; the same year the English took over the colony. The conflicts with native peoples were one ingredient of colonial life and women responded with tenacity, economic know how and courage. Disdain for native peoples was evident as women engaged in trade relations with them.

The accusation against a woman of selling brandy to Indians in Fort Orange demonstrates the sensitivity of Dutch-Indian relations. On 3 November 1654, Maria Jans was brought to court by Jacob van Loosdrecht who testified as having witnessed an alcohol sale taken place.[46] The decision was postponed until June 8, 1655 when Jans, was "ordered to pay a fine of 300 guilders and prohibited from coming into this place for a year and six weeks, and by way of pardon and intercession in her behalf on part of the magistrates."[47] This hefty punishment demonstrated the severity in which sale of alcohol to Natives Americans was viewed, most likely due to trading restrictions or concern over possible aggressions caused by over consumption by Indians.[48] Dealing with Indians was not the only challenge in the Dutch colonies as citizens were also in constant contact with African slaves.

In New Netherland, as in other North American colonies, slavery was a reality of life and a factor that contributed to the Dutch colony's social character. The Dutch introduced African slaves in order to fulfill labor needs; however, slavery in New Netherland existed differently than in other European colonies.[49] In New Netherland as elsewhere, economic profit facilitated by persistent labor shortages justified the use of slavery, but other colonial societies instituted slavery also because of a sense of superiority.[50] This distinction is a direct result of New Netherland as a society with slaves as opposed to a slave society.[51] Though the Dutch enslaved African people, there existed practices and legal representation that implied a greater sense of slaves' humanity that seemed void in other European empires. As historian Joyce Goodfriend asserts, "African slaves' lives were defined by an impermeable color line that sharply limited their chances for individual autonomy and communal action" even though they were not "totally lacking in resources to define their identity and improve their daily existence."[52]

There is no doubt that the Dutch view associated black with that of slave but because of varied social structures, some slaves had prospects much different than that of others in European colonies.[53] The status held by slaves was a mixed lot, in that a minority within the Company opposed human ownership and they failed to define chattel bondage.[54] This lack of unity in the social stature of black slavery was due to insufficiently defined statutory basis causing slavery to vary throughout the Dutch colonies.[55] Dutch slavery was of a corporate nature and the West India Company rather than private owners owned most slaves. Although slaves were sometimes personally owned, the West India Company existed as the largest slave-owning corporation in the colony.[56]

As early as one year after Dutch settlement in North America came the arrival of the first group of Africans. During their Golden Age, the Dutch were responsible for the great expansion of black labor, though some historians feel perhaps the numbers were greatly exaggerated.[57] Captured from the Spanish ships, it is estimated that some twenty-three hundred slaves were seized between 1623 and 1626.[58] The Dutch viewed attaining slave in this manner as financially sound because they would lose less money by avoiding the voyage to Africa.

In addition to financially based decisions, the Dutch often preferred to hold slaves who had already had experience in European societies.[59] In fact, the first New Netherland slaves were a combination of both men and women who remained in service to the company as more of an employee. The company extended them certain basic rights, benefits, and privileges that were not granted to slaves owned by private colonists.[60] The nature of slaves' rights illustrates the overall function of New Netherland as a business venture as well as understanding how the Dutch dealt with the weakest members of society, including slaves and women.

Admittance to the Dutch Reformed Church (with all its benefits) emerged as a distinctive Dutch practice. Being a member of the church afforded slaves some rights in New Netherland including the ability to take part in legal transactions, earn personal wealth, and gain freedom.[61] One such benefit was the validation of slaves' marriages, similar to the treatment found in Brazilian slave society.[62] Interestingly, between 1640-1664, the New Amsterdam marriage book recorded twenty-six marriages in which one or both of the people were black.[63] Racial intermarriage points to the legal and social freedoms that both slaves and women held. These freedoms imply a society with varied opportunities despite constraints and prejudices.

Instances of interracial sexual activity also points to Dutch women's uncommon autonomy in the Atlantic world. On 6 October 6 1638, a midwife, Lysbet Dircks, testified to the paternity of a newborn.[64] Court records state that Dircks was asked, "Greitje Reyniers asked the midwife whom did the child resemble, was it like Andries Hudde, or her husband, Anthony Jansen?"; she replied, "If you do not know who the father is, how should I know? However, the child is somewhat brown."[65] Various individuals viewed interracial sexual activity as negative and as positive.

Eventually, there was a decline in African marriages likely attributed to the death of minister Reverend Everardus Bogardus in a shipwreck off the coast of England in 1647.[66] Bogardus, who replaced Domine Michaelius in 1636, was sympathetic to blacks not only concerning marriage, but he was responsible for supporting the presence of a schoolmaster to educate both Dutch and blacks.[67] His experiences in outposts on West Africa before coming to New Netherland, as well as rumors of possible personal involvement with an African woman may have contributed to his acceptance of interracial unions.[68] Interracial marriage considered socially unacceptable by some was mirrored in a poem by Jacob Steendam, written for a racially mixed boy suspected to be his son.[69] He wrote, "Since two bloods course within your veins, Both Ham and Japhet's intermingling; One race forever doomed to serve, the other bearing freedom's likeness, I wish you (in this human form) Japhet's freedom long foretold."[70] The fair treatment of slaves by people such as Domine Bogardus was not the norm within society as many rejected blacks. Klooster asserts that, "tolerance was never a matter of policy either at home or in America," and it can be argued that discussions between political and religious entities enabled greater flexibility in treatment toward people, including black and women, in varied locals.[71] The policies of tolerance were often cultural rather than legal. In the era of the Atlantic slave trade and based on tolerant cultural attitudes, slaves were awarded some rights in Dutch society so it is reasonable that white women were afforded greater mobility.

Table 1.2: All cases Involving Females as Plaintiffs or Defendants

Albany		New Amsterdam	
1648-52	7	1648-52	-----------
1653-57	48	1653-57*	184
1658-60	50	1658-60	164
1660-68	Records destroyed in 1911 Albany Fire	1660-64	383
		1665-67	105
1668-72	64	1668-72	178
1675-80	69	1673-74	55

*Most of the 1657 records are missing

SOURCE: *Slavery in New York*, edited by Ira Berlin and Leslie M. Harris (New York: The New Press, 2005), 43.

*This is an excerpt of a statistical table. The total number of black landowners listed was 28, owning 170 acres, 4 black women listed.

Lastly, black landowners existed in New Netherland as in other colonies. In response to the repeated attacks by native Indians, blacks served as soldiers and in return, the Council of New Amsterdam awarded these slaves freedom and given land in the buffer zone area north. Several freed black landowners, between 1643-1664, owned over 130 acres or what is now 100 square city blocks of property.[72] Though these landowners were placed as a buffer in harm's way from hostile Native Americans, these actions demonstrate their opportunities in Dutch New Netherland.

Who is the Boss?

Familial ties in the borderland environment appeared to be of great importance to the Dutch. The "household" or family ties were foundational to continued success and the arena in which women were irreplaceable. The importance of women's role in the borderland household was another means in which mobility was possible. The household became a metaphor for family relationships, those who necessitated women's activity in spheres commonly known to men.[73] In short, women of the borderland were counted on to negotiate the economic, legal and sometimes political realms of which their husbands took part within the broader Atlantic World.[74] Women in a Dutch home were jointly responsible with their husbands for debt, proper handling of not only household accounts, but also of their husband's businesses.[75] In addition to legal privilege warranted to women, the household served as a conduit through which movement and status were achieved.[76] The brazen reputation attributed to Dutch women was a characteristic that supported women's extended activities.

To outsiders, Dutch women were often said to be bossy and uncouth, ignoring common social conventions throughout other European cultures. Girls in the Netherlands were reported to give orders to their older brothers, treating them as oafs and further acting "unnaturally domineering over their husbands."[77] As portrayed in the English play, *The Tragedy of Sir John van Olden Barnevelt*, Dutch women stated, "We ourselves, our own diposers, masters, And those that you call husbands, are our servants," thus demonstrating their independent nature.[78] It was also common for women in the Netherlands to work outside of the home and travel while men stayed home.[79] English travelers to the Netherlands commonly described the reverse gender roles of the Dutch by stating, "Nor would I be a Dutchman/To have my wife, my sovereign, to command me."[80] Although women demonstrated verbal confidence and strong attitudes in Dutch society, it must not be misconstrued that women were in charge, as the Netherlands remained patriarchal.

Despite women's purported bossiness, there were other less positive aspects of New Netherland that Dutch women endured. As in most societies, there was abuse. Occupying a subservient role to men, women were often the victims of verbal and physical abuse. Few court cases of women's attempts to seek help were recorded, but there were likely many abuse cases never recorded. In one case, Elsje Gerrits pleaded before the court to have her incarcerated husband released in order to work for her, despite his having beaten both herself and her child.[81] Illuminating the hardships this woman had faced, in an act of desperation she appealed for her husband's freedom despite his abusive past. A violent occurrence was recalled as plaintiff Geertruyd de Witt accused another woman, Anneke Kocks of verbally abusing against both her and her husband in addition to kicking her while she was pregnant and biting her ear.[82] The case concluded eight months later on 3 October 1662, when the defendant, Kocks was "condemned to pay the Deaconry of this City as a fine, the sum of two hundred guilders for the injurious assault perpetrated on her (de Witt) by beating, kicking, and trampling her, and dragging the hair from her head."[83]

Fines for assaults toward others outside one's family unit were taken more seriously than internal matters. Though a few cases were recorded of women beating women, most cases of abuse involved men beating their wives suggesting women's submissive position. Some cases involved severe beatings and the courts handed out lesser punishments within marital cases as opposed to those of unrelated people. This suggests that within marriage or family units the idea that a man "owning" his wife or daughter existed. To reinforce this point, a woman, Judith Verleth, was attacked by Wolfert Webber, who "berated her for a whore and a strumpet, threatened to strike her with a whip, as he daily does his wife; that he assaulted her, bruising and dragging her arm, and kicked her sister so that her hip was blue."[84] The case was settled with monetary punishment for the defendant even though the man was known to beat his own wife daily. No court actions were recorded against him for any household occurrences.

Women in the Legal Domain

Women were active as plaintiffs and defendants in court records attaining similar legal outcomes as men of that era. Between 1648- 1700 in Albany, women were involved in three hundred and two cases as either plaintiff or defendant.[85] Women were in court for varied reasons such as slander, business transactions, paternity issues, and settlement of debts. Though women constituted 16.5% of all civil cases in the New Amsterdam records from 1653-1674, very few were involved in any criminal activity.[86] In violent cases where women were convicted, they were punished with leniency- usually fined.[87] Exceptions were women who beat men. They were told to beg for forgiveness of the court and warned of banishment if the crime were to occur again.[88] The testimony and rights of women were safeguarded and satisfied at a surprising rate, which underscored their status in society. One case illustrating women's position as acceptable court witnesses took place between 17 October 1662 through 29 January 1663. Grietjen Hendricks Westercamp brought Pieter Jacobsen to court claiming that he was her baby's father.[89] Jacobsen denied being the father and rejected the idea of marrying her without proof of paternity.[90] A deposition was taken by seven women who were present at the birth thus certifying that Westercamp swore three times that Jacobsen was the father.[91] During this period, it was the custom to question the pregnant woman while in the throes of childbirth as to the identity of the father.[92] At the point of birth, they reasoned a woman was in such a state that she was unable to lie. These women were accepted as authentic witnesses in court reflecting the level of female rights within society and the important role of women as midwives.[93] Women's regard as compelling witnesses coupled with their ability to support other women and the court's desire for the child's financial support by naming a father demonstrates women social relevance. The case was eventually settled in favor of Jacobsen, who was allowed to marry as he wished but was ordered to pay a fine for having lain with Westercamp.[94] Though Westercamp failed to win the case, she utilized the courts to seek civic restitution.

Table: 1.3 Numbers of Female Traders

	Albany		New Amsterdam
1654-64	46	1653-63	134
1665-74	10	1664-74	43
1675-84	13	---------	
1685-94	6		
1695-1700	0		

Source: Women and Property in Colonial New York: The Transition from Dutch to English Law, 1643-1727 by Linda Briggs Biemer (Ann Arbor: UMI, 1983), 7.

Table 1.4: Numbers of Female Proprietors

	Albany		New Amsterdam
1654-64	13	1653-63	50
1665-74	17	1664-74	17
1675-84	9	---------	
1685-94	8		
1695-1700	3		

Source: Women and Property in Colonial New York: The Transition from Dutch to English Law, 1643-1727 by Linda Briggs Biemer (Ann Arbor: UMI, 1983), 7.

Source: *Women and Property in Colonial New York: The Transition from Dutch to English Law, 1643-1727* by Linda Briggs Biemer (Ann Arbor: UMI Press, 1983), 8.

Women's testimonies also included cases regarding financial issues. On 1 December 1654, Maria Jans of Fort Orange (now Albany) stood before the court as plaintiff against Abraham Crabaet, and she was awarded victory in a debt case against the defendant who was to pay, "in pain of imprisonment for debt."[95] Favorable settlements for women were common as was their self-representation in court appearances. Another case in Wiltwyck (Esopus, now Kingston) on 28 September 1661, involved a woman named Gritedgen Hillebrants who demanded that her master provide a reason for her dismissal and payment of her full wages.[96] The case was delayed as the defendant Juriaen Westgaer, denied all charges and ordered her to produce a witness.[97] Court appearances spanned over a forty-nine day period and concluded with the woman's victory as two witnesses attested and Westgaer agreed to their statements. The court ordered him to pay Hillibrants a quarter year's wages.

Such occurrences were not isolated to any specific area of New Netherland. In Beverwijck, after acknowledging his debt of thirteen beavers, Teunis Slingerlant had to give as security, the mortgage on his house to Johanna de Hulter.[98] An award of thirteen beavers was significant as each beaver held a worth of eight guilders. This debt illustrated the handling of goods by women in New Netherland.[99] Women commonly collected debts in a variety of forms. One New Amsterdam woman, Maria Verlett, widow of Paulus Schrick, appeared before the court on 22 January 1664, to find satisfaction when Metje Wessels paid three beavers to resolve an outstanding debt.[100] Likewise, Mary Peeck brought Marten Clazen to court testifying that she had paid him money to build her a house, of which he had not.[101] She demanded compensation and the carpenter was ordered to build the house and deposit the money with this city.[102] Numerous cases including women are scattered throughout the extant records.[103]

In court, women used strong language and appeared fearless, both pertaining to monetary issues and in confronting religious authorities. Trepidation about repercussions from the town Domine appeared legitimate and thus standing up to church authorities might have seemed futile in most colonial societies.[104] New Netherlander did not appear to fear religious figures or personal harm if confronted. In addition to some political rights, women were well aware of the freedom of religion which governed the Dutch Republic, "without hindrance on part of whosoever, in order that each individual shall remain free in his religion and that no one shall suffer any tribulation on account of his religion," in accordance with the Pacification of Ghent."[105] The seventeenth century Dutch were unlike other European powers regarding religion and the Netherlands had become a haven for varied faiths such as Portuguese Jews, English sectarians and French Huguenots.[106] In 1657, Fort Orange's minister, Gideon Schaets wrote, "some six hundred people attended church services (in Fort Orange); he added, "not including seventy to eighty Lutheran families."[107] This serves as a fine example of the mixing of diverse religious backgrounds.

Since some religious tolerance was present in Dutch society, it is not surprising to find examples of a woman standing up boldly to the authorities regarding religious choice. One case involved a Fort Orange woman named Marretie, wife of Cornelis Teunissen. Teunissen was taken to court for charges of slander as it was asserted that she had "seen the minister drink at times."[108] An accusation such as this toward a man of the cloth was slanderous and the defendant did not deny having said, things such as, "Those who are willing to revel and feast with the Domine are his friends and because I do not want to do it, I am a child of the devil."[109] She continued by stating that is if she could she would not sit in church as the hypocritical others do with their Bibles and pretend to be righteous. Teunissen continued, saying that because she refused to be a hypocrite she is seen as, "a child of the devil." To this accusation she defiantly exclaimed,- "But let me be a child of the devil."[110] Not to be construed as a woman acting up, Teunissen's actions were an example of a woman taking a stand. Her audacity was reinforced by the fact that she was not regularly in court as other inflammatory women who repeatedly made appearances.

Powerful words from a woman about a religious figure and the congregation that followed him, demonstrated the freedom of religion, rights and fearlessness that females held. New Netherland's public liberties were thus a direct result of Dutch philosophy and served to level their culture. Nevertheless, degrading stereotypes toward women were also evident in court records. Grietje Reyniers, who had given birth in the aforementioned suit, was called a "whore" by the defendant.[111] Reyniers and her husband appeared as plaintiffs in March 1639 and listened as the defendant testified when "her mistress went away and saw through a hole in the door that Grietje above named had her petticoat upon her knees...she is a nasty whore."[112] Several other paternity cases corroborate such slanderous and degrading terms toward women; thus reinforcing a double standard. When the paternity of Grietjen Westercamp's child came into question, the defendant Pieter Jacobsen responded by saying the plaintiff, "did not behave as a decent girl should...she lay under one blanket with Jan van Breeman, with his daughter between them...he admits having lain with the plaintiff, gave her no money for it."[113] These types of accusations infer the double standard that existed between men and women about sexual practices.

Women in Business

The considerable presence of women in business in New Nether-land and their roles as deputy husbands was not unlike those of neighbor-ing Englishwomen.[114] Women not only took part in businesses opera-tions, but also represented their business interests before the courts. An intriguing case found in Esopus, on 3 April 1663, suggests that a woman had trained a man in a trade. Johanna Ebbingh sued Pieter van Boohee-men for, "four beavers, two and one-half of which had been loaned and one and one-half of which were for goods furnished." While the defen-dant admitted to having received the goods said, "he [did] not owe the plaintiff anything, as the latter did not keep her promise to let him learn a trade."[115] The court entered a ruling in favor of the plaintiff, Johanna Ebbingh. This case suggests that a woman was indeed teaching a trade to a man and demonstrated how some women attained positions typically held by men. The implication that to teach a man was to hold a position of power reversed typical patriarchal gender roles.

Though married women were restricted in some legal matters, single women held the ability of full control over their own legal interests. For married women, their husbands acted as guardians and gained full control over their property, including businesses and land.[116] Under the law, when a women married she could do so in two ways. One option was according to usus, namely an ante-nuptial agreement took place in which she rejected the marital power, thus renouncing community property.[117]

The second option was according to manus, in which she was subject to her husband.[118] Manus became the law in the Netherlands as well as New Netherland. However, it was still common for women to enter into business transactions and legal proceedings without the consent of their husbands. Similar to those in the Dutch Republic, women existed under a husband's guardianship but she was,"a partner rather than a servant within marriage."[119] Often with a properly notarized prenuptial agreement a women who was a trader merchant acted independently of their husbands.[120] This was not a departure from the cultural norm of the Netherlands.[121]

One Margaret Hardenbroeck, an Atlantic trader, was recorded to be periodically working independently as well as in partnership with her husbands.[122] First Hardenbroeck had married Pieter Rudolphus DeVries, a fellow merchant, and when he died she inherited his property and business.[123] In fact, Hardenbroeck not only owned ships but also land in New York, New Jersey, the Netherlands and Barbados.[124] Her second marriage to Frederick Philipsen was entered by the terms of usus, and she was able to keep her own business and property.[125] Hardenbroeck was the epitome of a business-woman in colonial America, who managed all aspects of trade and the Dutch legal system as it existed, did not require a choice between marriage and the marketplace; but enabled her to find success in both."[126]

Margaret was not alone in her business activity. Several other women under the pseudo-equitable Dutch legal system held positions as traders and proprietors. After English Rule, the numbers decreased and eventually disappeared. This may be a direct result of varied social attitudes about women and their usefulness in all areas of society, including business, as well as very distinct gender roles. Female Traders numbered 46 and Female Proprietors numbered 13 whereas by 1695-1700 the number is recorded as 0 Female Traders and only 3 Female Proprietors.[127]

Table: 1.3 Numbers of Female Traders

	Albany		New Amsterdam	
1654-64	46	1653-63	134
1665-74	10	1664-74	43
1675-84	13	---------	
1685-94	6		
1695-1700	0		

Source: Women and Property in Colonial New York: The Transition from Dutch to English Law, 1643-1727 by Linda Briggs Biemer (Ann Arbor: UMI, 1983), 7.

Table 1.4: Numbers of Female Proprietors

	Albany		New Amsterdam	
1654-64	13	1653-63	50
1665-74	17	1664-74	17
1675-84	9	---------	
1685-94	8		
1695-1700	3		

Source: Women and Property in Colonial New York: The Transition from Dutch to English Law, 1643-1727 by Linda Briggs Biemer (Ann Arbor: UMI, 1983), 7.

Statistical data suggests that under Dutch authority, females attained positions outside the domestic sphere more so than under later English rule.[128] Numbers of female traders and proprietors dropped off significantly, though the decline was more rapid in New Amsterdam as opposed to the outlying settlement of Albany.[129] These trends suggest the leveling effect of borderland living represented in the slower change in more rural areas.

Women in New Netherland had privileges such as the ability to own land and the right to inheritance. As in Hardenbroeck's case, as well as others, women demanded restitution in court with payment of land. On 1 April 1664, Johanna de Laet, wife of Jeronimus Ebbingh, stood as plaintiff in Esopus to collect payment from Cornelis Barentsen Slecht. De Laet requested that, "the estate and possessions of defendant be inventoried and that she may be paid in full, " adding, "she requests that the purchase made yesterday by Frederick Philipsen, of a lot in Wildwyck, be annulled," because he purchased it from the defendant.[130] The courts decided that her payment would come from Slecht's goods but suggested that she bring suit against Philipsen for the purchase money.[131] Johanna de Laet is the aforementioned Johanna Ebbingh was identified as wife of Jeronimus Ebbingh in that document. This distinction is because the plaintiff most likely was standing in on behalf of her husband's interests.[132]

In New Netherland, women were awarded equal property rights because of the traditional Roman-Dutch law of their homeland. In marriage, women were considered equal and afforded the opportunity of community property.[133] This Dutch practice dated back to the early middle ages and remained part of New Netherland law until English rule. The will of Matthew Blanchan and Magdalen Goore dated 30 July 1688 illustrates one instance.[134] "If Matthew Blanchan happens to dye first," the document decreed," his wife shall continue in possession of all the property so long as she lives."[135] Jan Jacobsen's and Marritje Pieters' marriage contract stated that, "First, in regard to the property which he, the bridegroom, shall leave behind in case of his death, whether movable or immovable, or such as may rightfully belong to him, it shall belong in free ownership to Marritje Pieters aforesaid, without any of Jan Jacobsen's blood relations having claim thereto."[136] In contrast, generally under English law women were unable to own land. In the English Colonies, land ownership was the prerequisite for the right to vote and this right was never achieved for women in the American colonies.

Table 1.5: Distribution of Testators' Real Property among Sons and

Daughters, New York City, 1664-1750

	EQUAL OR NEAR EQUAL	ALL OR BULK TO SONS	OTHER
1664-1695	88.2%	9.8%	2%
1696-1725	80.6	18.3	1.1
1726-1750	65.7	30.4	3.9

SOURCE: Taken from *A Dutch Family in the Middle Colonies, 1660-1800*, by Firth Haring Fabend (New Brunswick: 1991), table 6.2, 118.

Unlike the English who practiced the concept of primogeniture, in which the oldest male in a family was the recipient of a father's property, the Dutch system allowed women the right of inheritance and joints wills.[137] At least half of the wills drawn up and filed before 1700 were joint.[138] One such example was that of Jan Tysen and his wife, Madelena Blansjan who filed jointly in Ulster County, New York dated 25 September 1676.[139] Another example was filed naming Tryntie Barentse, wife of Cornelius Barentsen as "co-testastor" with her husband who both desired the whole estate to "be inherited by the survivor," and divided equally among their children in case of both their deaths.[140] The practice demonstrated the equity under the law of men and women in inheritance issues.

Women's legal status extended their ability to attain power of attorney for husbands, sons, and others. Maritien Jans, mother of Dirck Dircksz, was awarded power of attorney by her son "with full power in the principal's name and on his behalf to demand and receive from their honors at the Chamber in Amsterdam, all such money," which was due to his father for service rendered.[141] Jans, an inhabitant of Fort Orange was not an isolated example as less than a month later on August 1, 1658; Johanna de Hulter received power of attorney from Poulus Martensen.[142] Often women represented men in court by holding power of attorney.

Philanthropic Needs as Sign of Societal Care

Dutch benevolence was replicated in New Netherland and offers insight into the philanthropic attitudes and care that their society expounded. Munificent practices were a combination of religious observance as well as economic necessity. In a society where philanthropic activity exists, so too are women as administrators and recipients of such aid and opportunity.

One such example, where women were incorporated in a necessary role, was that of care for the poor and sick in Fort Orange. Unique civic duty to aid the needy rather than imposed compulsory taxes was the manner in which the poor were helped in New Netherland. Preventative poor relief was realized through voluntary donations, poor boxes, and church services, both by deacons and local women.[143] For instance, a Rensselaerswijck poorhouse building was completed in 1655 followed by a poor farm in 1657 in order to meet the needs of the society.[144] In the second half of the seventeenth century, a total of 193 people depended on charity for varied amounts of time and was based on unknown standards by deacons.[145] It appears that many who lived on the edge of poverty in Beverwijck were not recorded as receiving aid.

In 1657, Susanna Jansen never received aid and was illegally selling brandy to Indians because "poverty pushed her to it."[146] Her level of poverty coupled with personal actions considered improper, possibly laziness or drunkenness, may have constituted rejection of the deacon's aid. Assistance was not distributed to just anyone who requested it. In New Netherland, deacons were guided by the rendementsprincipe, or efficiency principle, which was that the smallest amounts of funds were used to ensure the highest possible level of poor relief.[147] Deacons were required to safeguard those who they determined were most deserving of aid. Aid was given based upon need, but citizens were required to live up to a standard in order to continue to receive. One recorded case of Poulijin Jansen's family in Fort Orange states that the deacon requested Jansen's children to be boarded with another family due to improper care, and when the family refused; his aid was cut off after twelve years of collections.[148]

Assistance was also awarded in the form of care for the sick of which women were the primary caregivers. The area of knowledge has limited information and its affect on women's lives is a point of speculation. Women who nursed the sick were given payments of meat or other necessities. The church provided awards to such women who ensured that the ill were properly taken care of. Church was another outlet for females to work beyond their domestic sphere and their presence to ensure the health of society was irreplaceable.

Another mandated institution that served the social needs of New Netherland was the existence of orphan masters. According to the law, "every person under twenty-five years of age as well as persons above that age, who on account of mental or other disability were deemed incompetent to manage their own affairs, had to be provided with a guardian."[149] Women often administered the colony's incompetent and disabled citizens. The benevolent practices brought over to the colony were replicated in these small communities and women held a key role in aiding those in need.

Sex in the Colony

In New Netherland instances of the sexual activity or, lack of punishment for pre-marital acts was commonplace, and varied from that of their Puritan neighbors. Surprisingly, sexual activity among colonial women on the Hudson was discussed in court without modesty. Blatant sexual activity was recorded in court cases that contained humiliating terms regarding women and instances of extramarital and/or premarital pregnancy existed. From 1670 to 1685, the Albany courts handled eight cases regarding children born out of wedlock of which three revealed the mother had slept with more than one man around the time of conception.[150]

The rate of premarital sex is documented in a variety of ways in New Netherland. The Old Dutch Church of Kingston recorded its first marriage of Jan Jansen, carpenter from Amersfoort to Catharyn Matthysen on 3 October 1660.[151] Three months later, on 19 December 1660, the records named these two as parents at the baptism of a daughter named Styntje.[152] Apparently, the bride was well into pregnancy on her wedding day because it does not appear to be a premature birth.

During the colonial period, embarrassment about premarital pregnancy was not as shameful as a man unwilling to marry the woman he impregnated. In a case at City Hall on 31 August 1654, plaintiff Grietie Warnaers appeared to prove that William Harck should be condemned to marry her because he had made promises to do so and that she had slept with him, thus requiring him to wed her.[153] Claiming to be pregnant by yet another man, Daniel de Sille, the same woman appeared in court just prior to the admittance of letters proving the first man's intention to marry her.[154] Defendant de Sille acknowledged he had slept with her but did not know if he was the father because he had no knowledge of her other than that, "she ran along the road with a can of wine one evening."[155] The case was taken to the Director General and Clergy for consideration.

Likewise, extramarital affairs occurred repeatedly. In July of 1664, a midwife's testimony was noted regarding the paternity of the child of Hillegont Joris of New Amsterdam. Tryntje Jonas, the midwife claimed that the mother said, "Jan, the pilot, is father of the child," and then later stated, "Laurens Cornelisz is the father of the child."[157] This varied testimony reinforces the multiple sexual activities of the plaintiff or her attempt to establish paternity on any one of her sexual partners. Activity like this was not uncommon. In a hearing 4 November 1659, Adriaan Vincent was accused by Marcus de Sousoy of having another wife with four children.[158] De Sousoy's motivation was for accusing the man is unknown. However, he appeared keenly focused upon revealing the bigamist as such, that he was a plaintiff again that day against Tousein Bryel, who was forced to answer that Vincent did indeed have a wife and children in Amsterdam.[159] De Sousoy tells the court that if the witness was not acceptable, he will send his wife to Holland to collect evidence.[160] The court proceeded to draw up declarations before a notary and witnesses and thus deSousay's wife was given agency to find evidence regarding this case.[161]

Although many men and women were religiously loyal and chaste, when examples of extracurricular sexual activity occurred, Dutch colonial society showed no record of punishment by death as prescribed by law. It was not the case in neighboring Puritan societies. In 1641, a law stated that women found guilty of adultery were punished by death; men received a whipping for the same crime.[162] In New Netherland, judgments were unbalanced between genders as men who fathered illegitimate children were punished for a lack of fiscal responsibility, whereas women were viewed to bring greater harm upon society for birthing an illegitimate child because the action was viewed as a moral offense.[163] Although women's punishment was not fair, the penalty was not death.

Of the many cases involving sex in the courts of New Netherland, surely one of the most disturbing cases was against Nicolaes Hillibrandt, a soldier, accused of attempting to commit sodomy on August 20, 1658.[164] The seven-year-old child victim was recorded as declaring, "he was behind the gardens and said that he saw him pull his mannelyckheyt uyt syn broeck.[165] The boy also declared that the man was assisted by his own mother Elsjen, Hendrick Jochimsen's wife."[166] Though known sodomy cases were few, Roman-Dutch law was clear as to the punishment for such an offense: those found guilty were burned alive to ashes.[167] In this case, there was discussion as to how the child be dealt with because religious beliefs viewed the sodomy victim as having the ability to bring evil upon the community if left to live. The court appeared sympathetic to the boy and rendered the decision. The court's utilization of reason to deal rather than solely religious law, illustrated a society on the path toward a practical humanism.[168]

Motherhood

Another way in which colonial Dutch women were distinct from their colonial peers in North America was in the area of joint child rearing. The shared parenting roles between Dutch men and women demonstrate women's higher social standing. Combined cultural characteristics and borderland life, afforded women the ability to share jointly in child rearing, a practice common to the Netherlands. Though men ultimately held legal control over their children, those tight bonds contributed to assistance for the female in raising a family.

The Dutch were known to be devoted parents focused toward their children to an extent unlike other European cultures of this age. As seen in art of this period, there was a distinction between the portrayal of children in Dutch and English cultures. The representations of families in Dutch pieces suggest affectionate mannerisms similar to a modern historical current. Art reinforces the Dutch view of children and suggests parenting styles. Dutch mothers were depicted as loving and involved in their children's lives. Many examples exist of casual and intimate family affection: One painting by Rembrandt Van Rijn entitled, *A Woman Comforting a Child Frightened by a Dog*, depicts a mother's concern as she calms her child, while another piece by Adrien van de Velde entitled, *A Family in a Landscape*, 1660, portrays a loving family enjoying a relaxed day in the country.[169] The Dutch rendered not only doting parents but also children in children's clothing, doing childlike things, and with youthful expressions. Such characteristics imply a Dutch cultural view of family with lessened expectation of maturity in youth.

Conversely, seventeenth century Puritan art portrayals of mothers and children were quite different from Dutch interpretations. The English illustrated children as little adults with adult-like clothing and stoic facial demeanors such as seen in *The Freake-Gibbs Painters' The Mason Children: David, Johanna and Gabriel, 1670*.[170] Reinforcing this point was the rendering of the boy David. David was actually 8 years old though his portrait seems older; and these depictions suggest English parental attitude as that of detachment as seen in *Clarke Freake and Baby Mary, 1671*.[171]The mother and child were shown as very stiff and lacking in familial relation.

Reinforcing familial warmth, the Dutch practiced apprenticeships like other cultures, but they did not send their children away from home, as did the English.[172] It was their wish to keep children close to their family unit and most apprenticeship records reinforce this point. Tight family bonds contributed to a more positive attitude about women by allowing mothers to have an active role throughout a child's life.

With children at the center of family life, a mother's role was indeed of great importance. Women were expected to be wives and mothers who kept extremely clean homes of the highest standard and artistic representations of pride in such work is evident.[173] Dutch women served as great examples to their children on many levels whether in the ethical, spiritual, or practical. In a common Dutch practice, mothers breastfeed their children often in the view of others.[174] Many women appeared void of modesty and acceptance of breastfeeding likely contributed to that mental disposition. English society often shunned such public displays whereas the Dutch seemed to embrace bonding experiences between mother and child.[175] The perspective regarding breastfeeding is insightful as it presented the action as natural rather than something to be hidden or tied to sexuality. Breastfeeding in public reinforced a women's ability to express her physical womanhood without sexual undertones. What appeared to be minor practices, contributed to the overall openness of society.

Additionally, Dutch mothers were an integral part in the moral development of their children. This development was a direct result of a mother's ability to educate her children, for she herself was educated. Education is often a mechanism for mobility and its strong influence contributed to Dutch women's identity. Dutch females were not exempt from the opportunity to gain an education. Though girls in New Netherland received less education than boys, all children were expected to read and write. Women in this region had literacy levels equal to that of New Englanders and much higher than those in the Chesapeake area.[176] Females gained education from their local church and were taught reading, writing, mathematics and the catechism of the Dutch Reformed Church.[177]

The school day started at 8 in the morning, ended at 4 in the afternoon, with a break at midday. Though girls were not given a secondary education, as were boys, they were afforded a significant education. Though Dutch New Netherlander women were literate, they were neither pen women nor talkers.[178] They did not chat or write letters, as was the custom of many English women.[179] With less time spent for talk, they were much more active in establishing themselves as productive citizens. Though English women toiled very hard, the Dutch cultural dispositions for less chatter allowed them to be involved in more facets of life, except of course in religious avenues.

Though the portrait of New Netherland's women was that of mobility, it cannot be ignored that women were not afforded full rights, as were men in most areas of society. That was clearly demonstrated by women's place in religious life. Records and beliefs illustrate that Dutch females did not find full religious freedom or status within the Dutch Reformed Church. Unlike the Quakers who allowed women to take an active role, the Dutch Reformed Church retained the Biblical principle that males were supreme and assumed all leadership roles.[180] Women were not permitted to enter any ministry of the church because of their strict Calvinistic background that stated, "You shall not exercise any dominion over your husband, but be silent."[181] The church in New Netherland remained a place of oppression for those women who followed its doctrines and a cultural cornerstone of Dutch society well after English takeover.

Although silent in church, women were the moral force of the household as the domestic sphere remained their charge; in the seventeenth century, too, woman's place was in the home. Despite the fact that Dutch women had a reputation for being more independent than their European peers and many lower-class women were forced to work outside the home out of financial necessity, the household remained the woman's domain, as illustrated in the chore of "washing up."[182] In actuality, this circumstance falls contrary to the counter-poetry of the bossy Dutchwoman. From two cues found in poetry and artwork, woman can be viewed as both authoritarian and under the thumb of patriarchy. Such a combination made women a foundation to successful social function.

It has been stated that woman as keepers of the private duties were the center of the "fixed circle" of human history, and thus the lines of men extend from and toward her stationary point.[183] A 1650s saying that states, "Womans the centre and lines are men," suggests that women's power cannot be underestimated and her role stands as the wellspring of family life.[184] Time and again, examples of women appear as foundations of social fluidity; whether in building the household morality, representing her husband's interests or in assistance to the poor.

Conclusion

Women in New Netherland experienced a varied and complicated life that involved in all parts of society. Not solely wedded to the domestic sphere and included in one of the most liberal empires, women were able to undertake many roles typically reserved for men. From traders to businesswomen, from mothers to landowners, New Netherlander women were active participants in society. The combined challenges of borderland life, cultural diversity, business as well as a pliable legal system afforded the weakest in a patriarchal society various rights that contributed to the unique position of women in this Dutch colony. Though subject to their husbands and clearly a part of a male-dominated society, Dutch women exhibited a bold and even officious spirit. Describing the tenacious manner in which Dutch women were viewed, Golden Age Dutch poet Jacob Cats penned,

> *If a glass or porcelain breaks,*
> *The house is soon too small,*
> *So violently does the wife rage,*
> *It seems a he wants to give her maid a thrashing,*
> *Kitchen, parlour, hall and floor,*
> *Everything is in an uproar,*
> *It seems she will go into battle,*
> *With a boy, with a servant,*
> *With her daughter, or her child,*
> *With whomever she finds first,*
> *And, in between the man*
> *Will certainly get his share.*[185]

With their mottled gender roles, driving essence and every so often a fight or two, it was precisely those New Netherland women that were the man's "share." The study of New Netherland and its affect upon American colonization remains important because of its charter group status.[186] As scholarship continues, a fuller picture is coming into focus about the fascinating lives that New Netherlander women lived and their vital place in Seventeenth-Century Dutch imperial growth.

Bibliography
Primary Sources:

Anthology of New Netherland or Translations from the Early Dutch Poets of New York with Memoirs of Their Lives, Edited by Henry C. Murphy. Port Washington, NY: Ira J. Friedman, Inc., 1969. Originally Published in 1865 by the Bradford Club

Baptismal and Marriage Registers of the Old Dutch Church of Kingston, Ulster County, New York, 1660-1809. Edited by Roswell Randall Hoes. Baltimore, MD: Genealogical Publishing Co., Inc., 1997. Originally published 1891

Charters and Freedoms, 1629, as reprinted in New York: A Chronological & Documentary History, 1524-1970. American Cities Chronology Series. Edited by Howard B. Furer. Dobbs Ferry, NY: Oceana Publications, Inc., 1974.

Early Records of the City and County of Albany and Colony of Rensselaerswyck, Notarial Papers I and II, 1660-1696. Vol. 3. Edited by A.J.F. Van Laer. Albany, NY: The University of the State of New York, 1918.

Fort Orange Court Minutes 1652-1660. New Netherland Documents Series. Edited by Charles T. Gehring. Syracuse, NY: Syracuse University Press, 1990.

Fort Orange Records 1656-1678. New Netherland Document Series. Edited by Charles T. Gehring. Syracuse, NY: Syracuse University Press, 2000.

Moryson, Fynes. *An Itinerary: Containing His 10 Yeeres Travell Through the Twelve Dominions of Germany, Bohmerland, Sweitzerland, Netherland, Denmarke, Poland, Italy, Turky, France, England, Scotland & Ireland*. Glascow: James McLehose & Sons, 1908.

New York Historical Manuscripts, Dutch: The Kingston Papers. Kingston Court Records, Volume 1, 1661-1667. Edited by Peter R. Christoph, Kenneth Scott and Kenn Stryker-Rodda. Baltimore, MD: Genealogical Publishing Co., Inc., 1976.

New York Historical Manuscripts, Dutch, Register of the Provincial Secretary, 1638-1647. Edited by Kenneth Scott and Kenn Stryker-Rodda. 2 vols. Baltimore, MD: Genealogical Publishing Co., Inc., 1974.

The Dutch Records of Kingston, Ulster County, NY (Esopus, Wildwyck, Swanenburgh, Kingston) 1658-1681 with some later dates Part I: May 31, 1658-November 18, 1664 Esopus-Wildwyck, Edited by Samuel Oppenheim. New York: New York State Historical Association, 1912.

The Freake-Gibbs Painter. Elizabeth Clarke Freake and Baby Mary, ca. 1671. Worcester Art Museum, Massachusetts.

-------------------------------- *The Mason Children*: David, Johanna and Abigail, 1670. De

Young Museum, San Francisco.

The Records of New Amsterdam from 1653-1674 Anno Domini: Minutes of the Court of Burgomasters and Schepens. Edited by Berthold Fernow. 7 vols. Baltimore, MD: Genealogical Publishing Co., Inc., 1976. Originally published 1897

Ulster County, N.Y. Probate Records Vol. I & II , trans. Gustave Anjou. Rhinebeck, NY: Palatine Transcripts, 1980.

Union of Utrecht, 1629. As reprinted in Selected Documents Illustrating Mediaeval and Modern History, Edited by Emil Reich,London: P.S. King & Son, 1905.

Van de Velde, Adrien. *A Family in a Landscape, 1660.* Rijksmuseum, Amsterdam.

Van Rijn, Rembrandt. *A Woman Comforting a Child Frightened by a Dog, 1636.* Institute Néerlandais.

Vermeer, Johannes. *The Kitchen Maid,* ca.1658. Rijksmuseum, Amsterdam.

Winthrop, John. Winthrop's Journal, 1630-1649, "History of New England." Original Narratives of Early American History. Vol. II, Edited by James K. Hosmer. New York, NY: Charles Schribner's Sons, 1908.

Secondary Sources:

A Beautiful and Fruitful Place, Selected Rensselaerswijck Papers, (New York: New Netherland Publishing, 1991).

"A Brief Outline of the History of New Netherland." n.d. http://www.coins/nd.edu/Col-Coin/ColCoinIntros/NNHistory.html (accessed Dec. 4, 2008). Department of Special Collections, University of Notre Dame.

A Companion to Colonial America. Edited by Daniel Vickers. Malden, MA: Blackwell Publishing, 2003.

Berkin, Carol. *First Generations: Women in Colonial America.* Edited by Eric Foner. New York: Hill and Wang, 1996.

Berlin, Ira, *Many Thousands Gone: The First Two Centuries of Slavery in North America.* Cambridge, MA: The Belknap of Harvard University Press, 1998.

Biemer, Linda Briggs. *Women and Property in Colonial New York: The Transition from Dutch to English Law, 1643-1727.* Studies in American History and Culture. Vol. 38, Edited by Robert Berkhofer. Ann Arbor, MI: UMI Research Press, 1983.

Children in Colonial America, Edited by James Marten, New York: New York University Press,2007.

"Colonial Albany Social History Project." n.d. http://www.nysm.nysed.gov/albany/nnd.html (accessed Oct. 2, 2008).

Colonial Dutch Studies: An Interdisciplinary Approach. Edited by Eric Nooter and Patricia U. Bonomi. New York: New York University Press, 1988.

Craven, Wesley Frank. *White, Red, and Black: The Seventeenth-Century Virginian.* Charlottesville, VA: The University Press of Virginia, 1971.

Fabend, Firth Haring. *A Dutch Family in the Middle Colonies, 1660-1800.* New Brunswick: Rutgers University Press, 1991.

Fiske, John. *The Dutch and Quaker Colonies in America in Two Volumes.* Volume I, Cambridge, UK: Houghton, Mifflin and Company, 1902.

Gaze, Delia. *Concise Dictionary of Women Artists.* London: Fitzroy Dearborn, 2001.

Gherke, Michael E. "Dutch Women in New Netherland and New York in the Seventeenth-Century." PhD diss., College of Arts and Sciences at West Virginia University, 2001.

Goodfriend, Joyce D. *Before the Melting Pot: Society and Culture in Colonial New York City, 1664-1730.* Princeton: Princeton University Press, 1992.

Goodfriend, Joyce D, Benjamin Schmidt, and Annette Stott. *Going Dutch: The Dutch Presence in America, 1609-2009.* Boston, MA: Brill, 2008.

Goodwin, Maud W. *The Dutch and English on the Hudson: A Chronicle of Colonial New York.* New York, NY: Cosimo, Inc., 2005.

Gundersen, Joan R and Gwen Victor Gampel. "Married Women's Legal Status in Eighteenth-Century New York and Virginia." The William and Mary Quarterly 39, no. 1 (1982): 114-134.

Homberger, Eric. *The Historical Atlas of New York City: A Visual Celebration of 400 Years of New York City's History.* New York: Henry Holt & Company, LLC, 1994.

Jacobs, Jaap. *New Netherland: A Dutch Colony in Seventeenth Century America. The Atlantic World: Europe, Africa and the Americas, 1500-1830.* Vol. III, Edited by Wim Klooster and Benjamin Schmidt. Netherlands: Brill, 2005.

Keenan, Jerry. *Encyclopedia of American Indian Wars, 1492-1890.* New York, NY: W.W. Norton & Company, 1997.

Klein, Herbert. Lecture: "African Slavery in Brazil and Comparative Perspectives". State University College at Oneonta, 6 March 2008.

Lives of American Women: A History with Documents. Boston, MA: Brill, 1981.

Matthew Blanchan in Europe and America. Edited by Ruth P. Heidgerd. New Paltz, NY: Dubois Family Association Huguenot Historical Society, 1979.

McCusker, John J and Russell R. Menard. *The Economy of British America, 1607-1789.* Chapel Hill, NC: University of North Carolina Press, 1991.

Mixing Race, Mixing Culture: Inter-American Literary Dialogues. Edited by Monika Kaup and Debra J. Rosenthal. Austin, TX: University of Texas Press, 2002.

Narrett, David E. *Inheritance and Family Life in Colonial New York City.* Ithaca, NY: Cornell University Press, 1992.

Negotiated Empires: Centers and Peripheries in the Americas, 1500-1820. Edited by Christine Daniels and Michael V. Kennedy. New York, NY: Routledge, 2002.

"New Netherland Project." n.d. http://nnp.org/nnp/index.html (accessed Dec. 4, 2008).

Prak, Maarten. *The Dutch Republic in the Seventeenth Century.* Cambridge: Cambridge University Press, 2005.

Price, J. L.. *Culture and Society in the Dutch Republic During the 17th Century.* New York: Charles Scribner's Sons, 1974.

Proceedings of the New York State Historical Association, The Thirteenth Annual Meeting, With Constitution, By-Laws and List of Members, Vol. XI, "Wiltwyck Under the Dutch", Augustus H. Van Buren. New York: New York State Historical Association, 1912.

Revisiting New Netherland: Perspectives on Early Dutch America. Edited by Joyce D. Goodfriend. Leiden and Boston: Brill, 2005

Shattuck, Martha Dickenson. "A Civil Society: Court and Community in Beverwijck,

New Netherland, 1652-1664." PhD diss., Boston University, 1993.

Shaw, Susan Elizabeth. "Building New Netherland: Gender and Family Ties in a Frontier Society." PhD diss., Cornell University, 2000.

Slavery in New York. Edited by Ira Berlin and Leslie M. Harris. New York, NY: The New Press, 2005.

Stangroom, Jeremy and James Garvey. *The Great Philosophers: From Socrates to Foucault.* New York, NY: Barnes & Noble, 2005.

Sullivan, Dennis. T*he Punishment of Crime in Colonial New York: The Dutch Experience in Albany During the Seventeenth Century.* IX History. Vol. 186, New York, NY: Peter Lang, 1997.

Sylvester, Nathaniel Bartlett. *History of Ulster County New York.* Interlaken, NY: Heart of Lakes Publishing, 1994.

The British Atlantic World, 1500-1800. Edited by David Armitage and Michael J. Braddick. New York: Palgrave MacMillian, 2002.

The Creation of the British Atlantic World. Edited by Elizabeth Mancke and Carole Shammas. Baltimore, MD: The Johns Hopkins University Press, 2005.

The Empire State: A History of New York. Edited by Milton M. Klein. Ithaca, NY: Cornell University Press, 2001.

Ulrich, Laurel Thatcher. *Good Wives: Image and Reality in the Lives of Women in Northern New England, 1650-1750.* New York: Vintage Books, 1980.

Van Deursen, A. T.. *Plain Lives in a Golden Age: Popular Culture, Religion and Society in Seventeenth-Century Holland.* Cambridge, UK: Cambridge University Press, 1978.

Venema, Janny. *Beverwijck: A Dutch Village on the American Frontier, 1652-1664.* Albany, NY: Verloren/State University of New York Press, 2003.

----------------- "Poverty and Charity in Seventeenth-Century Beverwijck/Albany, 1652-1700." New York History, Oct. 1999, 369-390. Published by the NYS Historical Association, Cooperstown, NY.

Wagman, Morton. "Corporate Slavery in New Netherland." The Journal of Negro History 65, no. 1 (1980): 34-42.

Woody, Thomas. *A History of Women's Education in the United States.* Vol. 1, New York, NY: Octagon Books, 1974.

Zimmerman, Jean. *The Woman of the House.* NY: Harcourt, 2006.

[1] Thesis title on cover page is taken from, The Tragedy of Sir John van Olden Barnevelt by W.P. Frijlinck as reprinted in A.TH.Van Deursen, *Plain Lives in a Golden Age* (Cambridge: Cambridge University Press, 1978), 83. In Dutch-speaking areas, a schout was a local official appointed to carry out administration, law enforcement and prosecutorial tasks. The office was abolished with the introduction of administrative reforms during the Napoleonic period. *The Dutch Records of Kingston, Ulster County, NY* (Esopus, Wildwyck, Swanenburgh, Kingston) 1658-1681 with some later dates Part I: May 31, 1658-November 18, 1664 Esopus-Wildwyck, ed. Samuel Oppenheim(New York: New York Historical Association, 1912), 83.

[2] The Dutch Records of Kingston, Ulster County, 83.

[3] Ibid, 83.

[4] Ibid, 85.

[5] A caroulus guilder was a Dutch coin of the period equaling one and one-half a guilder.

[6] The English takeover of New Netherland occurred in 1664 when Peter Stuyvesant officially surrendered the city of New Amsterdam on September 8, followed by an oath of allegiance to the English authority by the Dutch officials and residents on October 20. Another attempt by the Dutch to regain New Amsterdam was made in 1673 but failed as the colony was given back to England on 10 November, 1674 and further remaining under full sovereignty of England.

[7] These laws were well known to citizens and though regional control allowed for variation, Dutch-Roman law was at the foundation of legalities. See Fernow, "Court Minutes of December 14, 1654," Records of New Amsterdam, when the burgomasters and schepens, who were not certain about how to dispose of a certain case, said they would have to refer to the "Custom and written law of the fatherland." The Records of New Amsterdam from 1653-1674 Anno Domini. Minutes of the Court of Burgomasters and Schepens ed. Vol.I, 1653-1655, Inclusive, ed. Berthold Fernow, (Baltimore, MD: Geneological Publishing Co., Inc., 1976), 273.

[8] "A Brief Outline of the History of New Netherland", www.coins.nd.edu/ColCoin/ColCoinIntros/NNHistory.html, Department of Special Collections: University of Notre Dame, (accessed 12/4/08).

[9] Historian Wim Klooster suggests, "Since the republic's government continued to be based on provincial assemblies and town councils, power and authority were heavily decentralized. *Negotiated Empires: Centers and Peripheries in the Americas, 1500-1820.*Edited by Christine Daniels and Michael V. Kennedy (New York: Routledge, 2002), 172.

[10] J.L Price, *Culture and Society in the Dutch Republic During the Seventeenth Century* (New York: Charles Scribner's Sons, 1974, 170.

[11] Linda Biemer, "Criminal Law and Women in New Amsterdam and Early New York", *A Beautiful and Fruitful Place*, Selected Rensselaerswijck Seminar Papers, Ed. Nancy Anne McClure Zeller (New York: New Netherland Publishing, 1991), 73. ; And *Children in Colonial America*, Edited by James Marten, New York: New York University Press, 2007, 92.

[12] The extent of women's freedom was not considered important to many scholars, as illustrated the early twentieth century, historians such as John Fiske or Maud Wilder Goodwin wrote with a patriarchal perspective placing women on the margins of society. Both Fiske and Goodwin wrote during the Progressive Era, which was reflected in their grand narratives of "the American story." At a period in which groups were trying to establish the definition of the American character, historians stressed the triumphs of great men of American history. That approach left little room for the study of women, no less giving them significant role in societal establishment beyond supporting males. Goodwin, a female historian, reinforced that methodology by only hinting about gender, society, class and race. Works by historians of the early 20th century include: Goodwin, Maud W. *The Dutch and English on the Hudson: A Chronicle of Colonial New York.* New York, NY: Cosimo, Inc., 2005; Fiske, John. *The Dutch and Quaker Colonies in America in Two Volumes.* Vol. Volume I, Cambridge, UK: Houghton, Mifflin and Company, 1902.

[13] Augustus H. Van Buren, *Wiltwyck Under the Dutch,* Proceedings of the New York State

Historical Association, The 13th Annual Meeting, with Constitution, By-Laws and List of Members, Vol. XI (New York: New York Historical Association, 1912), 135.

[14] Many organizations such as the New Netherland Project, established in 1974 at the New York State Archives in Albany, have worked tirelessly to accurately translate early documents. The New Netherland Project, www.nnp.org/nnp/index.html (accessed on 12/4/08).

[15] Joyce D. Goodfriend has written extensively about New Netherland's history including womens' role in that colonial society. See Joyce D. Goodfriend: *Before the Melting Pot: Society and Culture in Colonial New York City, 1664-1730*.(Princeton, NJ: Princeton University Press), 1992; Chapter II Colonial Dutch Studies: An Interdisciplinary Approach. Edited by Eric Nooter and Patricia U. Bonomi (New York: New York University Press, 1980; *Lives of American Women: A History with Documents* (Boston: Little, Brown, 1981); *Revisiting New Netherland: Perspectives in Early Dutch America* (Boston: Brill, 2005); Going Dutch: The Dutch Presence in America, 1609-2009(Boston: Brill, 2008)

[16] Goodfriend argues that, "Because Dutch culture has traditionally been evaluated by the standards of the Puritans, emphasis has too often fallen on its deficiencies-its failure to produce a literature of note, the crass materialism of its people, and the shallowness of their spiritual concerns," and we can overcome this by "examining Dutch colonial culture on its own terms."
Colonial Dutch Studies: An Interdisciplinary Approach. Edited by Eric Nooter and Patricia U. Bonomi (New York: New York University Press, 1980), 19-20.

[17] Ibid, 6.

[18] Since the 1990s, several young scholars continued historical research focused on 17th century women, revealing the rural aspect of Dutch women's lives and its leveling affect on New Netherland society. Such historians as Martha Dickinson Shattuck, Michael E. Gherke, and Susan Elizabeth Shaw are in the process of revealing a more complete portrait of women and gender roles through their scholarship. Martha Dickinson Shattuck is a scholar with the New Netherland Institute. For additional reading: Shattuck, Martha Dickinson. "A Civil Society: Court and Community in Beverwijck, New Netherland, 1652-1664", PhD Dissertation, Boston University, 1993. Michael E. Gherke is a professor at the University of West Virginia. For additional reading: Gherke, Michael E. "Dutch Women in New Netherland and New York in the Seventeenth-Century", PhD Dissertation, College of Arts and Sciences West Virginia University 2001; Shaw, Susan Elizabeth. "Building New Netherland: Gender and Family Ties in a Frontier Society", PhD Dissertation, Cornell University, 2000.

[19] Goodfriend, *Revisiting New Netherland*, 267.

[20] Ibid, 267.

[21] Maarten Prak, *The Dutch Republic in the Seventeenth Century* (Cambridge: Cambridge University Press, 2005), 113.

[22] Prak, *The Dutch Republic in the Seventeenth Century*, 114.

[23] Ibid, 115: The Dutch first settled in present day Albany in 1624, and in 1626 they acquired the island of Manhatta. Eric Homberger, *The Historical Atlas of New York City: A Visual Celebration of 400 Years of New York City's History* (New York: Henry Holt & Company, LLC, 1994), 17.

[24] Shaw, "Building New Netherland", 243.

[25] *Charter of Freedoms and Exemptions, 1629*, as reprinted in *New York: A Chronological & Documentary History, 1524-1970*, ed. Howard B. Furer (Dobbs Ferry, NY: Oceana Publications, Inc., 1974) 58.

[26] *Charter of Freedoms and Exemptions, 1629*, 58. Kilian Van Rensselaer was the patroon of Rensselaerswijck which comprised almost a million acres of land, approximately the present day counties of Albany and Rensselaer in New York State. See Venema, Janny, *Beverwijck: A Dutch Village on the American Frontier*, 1652-1664(Hilversem, The Netherlands: Verloren, 2003), 14.

[27] http://www.nysm.nysed.gov/albany/nnd.html, (accessed on 10/2/08).

[28] Beverwijck literally means 'beaver district'.

[29] Nathaniel Bartlett Sylvester, *History of Ulster County New York* (Interlaken, NY: Heart of Lakes Publishing, 1994), 34. Esopus is an Algonquin Indian name meaning 'river'.

[30] By 1664, Beverwijck had some 82 families in residence, further demonstrating low populations significantly different than their homeland. Janny Venema, "Poverty and Charity in Seventeenth-Century Beverwijck/Albany, 1652-1700." (Cooperstown, NY: NYS Historical Association) New York History, Oct. 1999, 369-390, 372. The population of Albany County in 1689 was 2016. The reference to Albany County is reflective of the English Authority during the time mentioned; the area's name had been Anglicized, changed to honor the Duke of Albany in England. http://www.nysm.nysed.gov/albany/nnd.html(accessed on 10/2/08).

[31] For a statistical population comparison, McCusker and Menard list New England's population as: 13,700 in 1640, 22,900 in 1650, 33,200 in 1660, and 51,900 in 1670. Interestingly, the population estimates did not change from earlier statistical data. John J. McCusker and Russell R. Menard, The Economy of British America, 1607-1789(Chapel Hill: University of North Carolina Press, 1991), 103.

[32] Venema, "Poverty and Charity in Seventeenth-Century Beverwijck/Albany", 374.

[33] Mixing Race, *Mixing Culture: Inter-American Literary Dialogues*, ed. Monika Kaup and Debra J. Rosenthal (Austin: University of Texas Press, 2002), 143.

[34] New Netherland existed as a borderland because it was an area as defined by the meeting place of Europeans (English to the east, French to the north), in addition to the fusing of such cultures. Native American and African cultures as indicated by nearly half the inhabitants of New Netherland not being Dutch. Though New Netherland assumed aspects of frontier life such as wilderness and relations with Native Americans, it was not a society forging forward for dramatic expansion as often the case in a Frontier society. Additionally, New Netherland could not be defined as a backcountry because although adventurous, its citizens were not searching to escape civilization; rather they continued to set up mini-societies reflecting their homeland, aka Beverwijck. The vague or uncertain conditions that existed in New Netherland reflect what Daniel H. Usner, Jr. describes as, the different circumstances which existed in the borderlands, where colonial politics on the ground were different from what colonial rulers intended. See Chapter 17 of *A Companion to Colonial America,* Edited by Daniel Vickers (Malden, MA: Blackwell Publishing, 2003).

[35] Shaw, 169.

[36] Ibid, 169.

[37] *Negotiated Empires,* 173. New Netherland was comparable to the Dutch republic in its

diverse population. During correlating times in the 17th century, Amsterdam's population was 53.9% Dutchmen; similarly New Netherland's Dutch population was about 51%. For more reading about Atlantic history: *The British Atlantic World, 1500-1800*, ed. David Armitage and Michael J. Braddick (Palgrave MacMilian, 2002): *The Creation of the British Atlantic World*, ed. Elizabeth Mancke and Carole Shammas (The Johns Hopkins University Press, 2005).

[38] Sewant is another name for what was called wampum in the English colonies; strung pieces of shell which varied in worth based on coloration. Six white shells would have equaled one purple shell. Venema, Beverwijck: *A Dutch Village on the American Frontier*, 15.

[39] Jerry Keenan, *Encyclopedia of American Indians, 1492-1890* (New York: W.W. Norton, 1997), s.v. "Dutch-Indian Wars, 1641-1664".

[40] Shaw, 251.

[41] Keenan, *Encyclopedia of American Indians, 1492-1890*, s.v. "Dutch-Indian Wars, 1641-1664".

[42] Ibid, 70.

[43] Ibid, 70.

[44] Ibid, 70.

[45] Ruth P. Heidgard. Matthew Blanchan in Europe and America (New Paltz, NY: Dubois Family Association Huguenot Historical Society, 1979), 4: Sylvester, History of Ulster County New York, 50.

[46] Maria Jans is also referred to as Maria Goosen Jans, wife of Steven Jansz in the records. Spelling variations exist.

[47] *Fort Orange Court Minutes 1652-1660*.New Netherland Documents Series. Edited by Charles T. Gehring (Syracuse, NY: Syracuse University Press, 1990), 194.

[48] In 1658, Peter Stuyvesant and his council renewed two ordinances prohibiting the sale of alcohol to Indians; the penalties for violations were 500 guilders, corporal punishment, and banishment. Another ordinance was enacted in 1654 allowing Indians to testify and their statements would be admissible. Dennis Sullivan, *The Punishment of Crime in Colonial New York: The Dutch Experience in Albany During the Seventeenth Century* (New York: Peter Lang, 1997), 176, 189.

[49] By 1650, the Netherlands was the pre-eminent slave trading empire in the Atlantic. During the Dutch Golden Age, Holland's trade spread across the globe, first with the Dutch East India Company and then the Dutch West India Company. Dutch presence existed in Africa, the Spice Islands, the Caribbean, South America, North America and the Indian Ocean.

[50] When in history economic necessity warranted this attitude of superiority over blacks, societies began to "demonize" blacks as inferior. Ira Berlin demonstrates that slaveholders, "discovered much of value in supremacist ideology," by elaborating on notions of slaves as savages and imbeciles. Ira Berlin, *Many Thousands Gone: The First Two Centuries of Slavery in North America* (Cambridge: The Belknap Press of Harvard University Press, 1998), 363.

[51] Berlin, *Many Thousands Gone*, 8.

[52] Goodfriend, *Before the Melting Pot*, 111.

[53] *Slavery in New York*, ed. Ira Berlin and Leslie M. Harris (New York: The New Press,

2005), 40.

[54] *Slavery in New York*, ed. Berlin and Harris, 38.

[55] Ibid, 38.

[56] Ibid, 37. The Dutch West India Company owned about half of the colony's slaves.

[57] This number may be exaggerated because Dutch shipmaster's were highly engaged with Virginia prior to the first Anglo-Dutch War in 1652, and it is suggested that English slave traders were indifferent to the Virginian market during that period. Wesley Frank Craven, *White, Red, and Black: The Seventeenth-Century Virginian* (Charlottesville, VA: The University Press of Virginia, 1971), 89.

[58] Morton Wagman, "Corporate Slavery in New Netherland", The Journal of Negro History, 65, no.1, (1980): 34.

[59] Historian Ira Berlin refers to these people as Creoles. For more about Creolization, See *Many Thousands Gone: The First Two Centuries of Slavery*. See footnote 52.

[60] Wagman, "Corporate Slavery in New Netherland", 37.

[61] The Dutch Reformed Church included people from all ethnicities. For example, in 1664 New Amsterdam, of the 222 men, 168 (76 percent) were Dutch, 24 (11 percent) were German, 15 (7 percent) were French, and 10 (4.5 percent) were English. The remaining 5 men included three Scandinavians (a Swede, a Norwegian, and a Finn), a Jew, and an Irishman. Goodfriend, Before the Melting Pot, 16.

[62] Herbert Klein, "African Slavery in Brazil and Comparative Perspectives", 6 March 2008, State University College at Oneonta.

[63] Bogardus' real name was Evert Willemszoon. Shaw, 21.

[64] *New York Manuscripts Dutch, Vol. 1 Register of the Provincial Secretary, 1638-1642*, ed. Kenneth Scott and Kenn Stryker-Rodda (Baltimore, MD: Genealogical Publishing Company, Inc., 1974), 67.

[65] It must be noted that the description of the child as brown could possibly be the result of Indian/Dutch relations, as found in other colonial societies. New York Manuscripts Dutch, Vol. 1, Scott and Rodda, 67.

[66] Prak, 121.

[67] *Slavery in New York*, 39.

[68] Shaw, 212.

[69] Steendam was a soldier, slave trader and merchant who eventually went to New Amsterdam. *Slavery in New York*, 50.

[70] Ibid, 50. Jacob Steendam's poem as reprinted in text.

[71] Although certain "policies" were present in the Dutch Empire, such as religious tolerance, the codification of specific practices was not present. This allowed for the variation in the colony, as local courts made determinations about situations that arose. Variations of local groups throughout the Dutch empire and their varied treatment of individual groups can be seen with regards to the treatment of Jews. For example, in New Netherland, Jews were greeted with an unfriendly welcome but were living under favorable conditions in New Holland. *Negotiated Empires*, 184.

[72] *Slavery in New York*, 44.

[73] Shaw, 4.

[74] Ibid, 4.

[75] Shattuck, "A Civil Society", 155.

[76] The relationship between 17th century Dutch women and the Atlantic World is far from explored and necessitates continued scholarship.

[77] A.TH.Van Deursen, Plain Lives in a Golden Age: Popular Culture and Society in Seventeenth-century Holland (Cambridge: Cambridge University Press, 1978, 82-83.

[78] The Tragedy of Sir John van Olden Barnevelt by W.P. Frijlinck as reprinted in A.TH. Van Deursen, Plain Lives in a Golden Age, 83.

[79] Ibid, 83.

[80] Taken from The Little French Lawyer, a Jacobean era stage play, written by John Fletcher and Philip Massinger was initially published in the first Beaumont and Fletcher folio of 1647. Ibid, 83.

[81] The case was heard in New Amsterdam on February 18, 1662. The Records of New Amsterdam from 1653-1674 Anno Domini. Minutes of the Court of Burgomasters and Schepens ed. Vol. IV, Minutes of the Court of Burgomasters and Schepens Jan. 3, 1662 to Dec. 18, 1663, Inclusive, ed. Berthold Fernow (Baltimore, MD: Genealogical Publishing Co., Inc., 1976), 34.

[82] Ibid, 130.

[83] Ibid, 140.

[84] This number does not include cases from 1660-1668 which records were destroyed by fire in 1911. The Records of New Amsterdam from 1653-1674 Anno Domini. Minutes of the Court of Burgomasters and Schepens ed. Vol. I, ed. Berthold Fernow (Baltimore, MD: Genealogical Publishing Co., Inc., 1976), 317.

[85] Linda Briggs Biemer. Women and Property in Colonial New York: The Transition from Dutch to English Law, 1643-1727, Studies in American History and Culture Volume 38(Ann Arbor, MI: UMI Research Press, 1983), 8.

[86] New Amsterdam records from 1653-1674 show that women were only in 28 criminal cases, historians suggest this is due to the fact that Dutch law allowed women to take advantage of opportunities and their was little need for criminal activity. Further, very few women were involved in prostitution which may be explained by the social opportunities coupled with the possible punishment of banishment. Other criminal offences like illegal tapping, operating taverns on Sunday after 9 p.m. or assaulting other people were common. Linda Biemer, "Criminal Law and Women in New Amsterdam and Early New York", 73.

[87] Biemer, "Criminal Law and Women in New Amsterdam and Early New York", 79.

[88] Ibid, 73.

[89] The Dutch Records of Kingston, Ulster County, NY (Esopus, Wildwyck, Swanenburgh, Kingston) 1658-1681 with some later dates Part I: May 31, 1658-November 18, 1664 Esopus-Wildwyck, Ed. Samuel Oppenheim. 36.

[90] Dutch Records of Kingston, Ulster County, NY (Esopus, Wildwyck, Swanenburgh, Kingston)
1658-1681 with some later dates, 37.

[91] Ibid, 40.

[92] Sullivan, The Punishment of Crime in Colonial New York, 136.

[93] For midwifery practices and more information about the function of the midwife in colonial society. See Laurel Thatcher Ulrich, A Midwife's Tale, New York: Vintage Books, 1991.

[94] *Dutch Records of Kingston, Ulster County, NY* (Esopus, Wildwyck, Swanenburgh, Kingston) 1658-1681 with some later dates, 40.

[95] *Fort Orange Court Minutes 1652-1660*.New Netherland Documents Series, 165.

[96] New York Historical Manuscripts, *Dutch: The Kingston Papers. Kingston Court Records, Volume 1, 1661-1667*. Edited by Peter R. Christoph, Kenneth Scott and Kenn Stryker-Rodda.(Baltimore, MD: Genealogical Publishing Co., Inc., 1976), 4, 9. The name Wildwyck eventually fell into disuse following under the authority of the Duke of York and was generally referred to as the Town of Esopus. Kingston Paper, xi-xii., Today Esopus is called Kingston.

[97] Ibid, 9. November 8, 1661

[98] Early Records of the City and County of Albany and Colony of Rensselaerswyck, Notarial Papers I and II, 1660-1696. Vol. 3. Edited by A.J.F. Van Laer (Albany, NY: The University of the State of New York, 1918), 49.

[99] Venema, *Beverwijck: A Dutch Village on the American Frontier,* 373.

[100] *The Records of New Amsterdam from 1653-1674* Anno Domini. Minutes of the Court of Burgomasters and Schepens ed. Vol. V, Minutes of the Court of Burgomasters and Schepens Jan. 8, 1664 to May. 1, 1666, Inclusive. Ed. Berthold Fernow (Baltimore, MD: Genealogical Publishing Co., Inc., 1976), 10.

[101] *The Records of New Amsterdam from 1653-1674* Anno Domini. Minutes of the Court of Burgomasters and Schepens ed. Vol. IV, 95.

[102] Ibid.

[103]In her essay entitled, "Criminal Law and Women in New Amsterdam and Early New York," historian Biemer suggests that it is impossible to fully know whether women appeared in court more often under Dutch rule than following English takeover despite fewer appearances of women in the records. She states, "Although women appeared in court fewer times after English takeover (1664) than before, there was an overall decline in the number of court appearances of both men and women after 1664. The Fernow records, unfortunately, stop in 1674, too soon to prove that the decline in female court appearances continues to be significant." A Beautiful and Fruitful Place, Selected Rensselaerswijck Seminar Papers (Syracuse, NY: Syracuse University Press, 1991) 74.

[104] A Domine was a clergyman who led the Reformed Dutch Church. The church served a great purpose to implement biblical ideals like philanthropic activities in Dutch society and was the chief cultural institution of the Seventeenth Century.

[105] *Netherlands. 1579.* Union of Utrecht, January 29, 1579., 610 as reprinted in Selected Documents Illustrating Mediaeval and Modern History, Edited by Emil Reich(London: P.S. King and Son, 1905). Although the Union of Utrecht had promised religious freedom to all faiths, in fact, the Dutch Reformed Church was the only one which could to publically express its views. Prak, 29.; Although New Netherland allowed other faiths to live within its confines, these faiths were not accepted without prejudice. For instance, Jews were still considered of lowly status and court records show several instances of Dutch citizens insulting each other by calling them a Jew. One such case in the Kingston records states defendant Aitjen Sybrandts calling Mr. Gysbert

van Imbrogh, "a Jew and a sucker. New York Historical Manuscripts, *Dutch: The Kingston Papers*, 62.

[106] Price, *Culture and Society in the Dutch Republic During the Seventeenth Century*, 171.

[107] In Rensselaerswijck, church services were compulsory, but rather than shunning non-Calvinistic Christians, others were included in worship services. Venema, *Beverwick: A Dutch Village*, 372.

[108] *Fort Orange Records 1656-1678*. New Netherland Document Series. Edited by Charles T. Gehring (Syracuse, NY: Syracuse University Press, 2000), 285.

[109] Fort Orange Court Minutes 1652-1660.New Netherland Documents Series, 285.

[110] Ibid, 285.

[111] New York Manuscripts Dutch, Vol. 1, 105,107.

[112] Ibid, 105,107.

[113] New York Historical Manuscripts, *Dutch: The Kingston Papers*, 57.

[114] Ulrich's states that should fate or circumstance prevent the husband from fulfilling his role, the wife may have appropriately stood in his place. She adds that beyond the domestic sphere, many colonial Englishwomen would learn trades associated with their husband's work. She does state that many of the women with the ability to act as an assistant to her husband seemed to have lacked to security to act alone; this appears to be a slight difference in attitude among many Dutch women who through words and actions engage personal authority more confidently. Laurel Thatcher Ulrich, *Good Wives: Image and Reality of Women in Northern New England 1650-1750* (New York: Vintage Books, 1980), 35-36.

[115] New York Historical Manuscripts, *Dutch: The Kingston Papers*, 65.

[116] The age of marriage among women in New Netherland was younger than the average age in Holland of 19.8 years. For this and more information regarding marriage ages see Shattuck, "A Civil Society", 147-148.

[117] Biemer, "Criminal Law and Women in New Amsterdam and Early New York", 73-74.

[118] Ibid, 73-74.

[119] David E. Narrett, *Inheritance and Family Life in Colonial New York City* (Ithaca: Cornell University Press, 1992), 43.

[120] *The Empire State: History of New York*, Ed. Milton M. Klein (Ithaca, NY: Cornell University Press, 2001), 70.

[121] Shattuck, "A Civil Society", 181.

[122] Biemer. *Women and Property in Colonial New York*, 5.

[123] Carol Berkin, *First Generations: Women in Colonial America* (New York: Hill and Wang, 1996), 80.

[124] Biemer. *Women and Property in Colonial New York*, 5.

[125] Berkin, *First Generations: Women in Colonial America*, 80.

[126] Berkin, 83. For more on the life of Margaret Hardenbroeck, read: *The Woman of the House*, by Jean Zimmerman (Harcourt, 2006).

[127]Biemer. Women and Property in Colonial New York, 7.

[128] See Tables 1.3 and 1.4.

[129] See Tables 1.3 and 1.4.

[130]New York Historical Manuscripts, *Dutch: The Kingston Papers,* 142.

[131] Ibid.

[132]Women standing in legal situations stood as an agent for their husband in circumstances when males were not able to be present. Biemer, *Women and Property in Colonial New York*, 8.

[133] Women held the right to do with their property as they saw fit in widowhood or single life. Ibid.

[134] Heidgerd, *Matthew Blanchan in Europe and America*, 17.

[135] Ibid, 17.

[136] New York Manuscripts Dutch Vol. 1 Register of the Provincial Secretary, 1638-1642, 212.

[137] Records indicate a consistent decline in female inheritance following English takeover.

[138] Joan R. Gundersen and Victor Gampel "Married Women's Legal Status in Eighteenth-Century New York and Virginia" in The William and Mary Quarterly 39:1(1982): 118.

[139] Ulster County, N.Y. Probate Records Vol. I & II, trans. Gustave Anjou (Rhinebeck, NY: Palatine Transcripts, 1980), 33.

[140] This case is dated August 17(year not mentioned), written in Dutch. The notation is listed by others in 1676. Ulster County, N.Y. Probate Records Vol. I & II, 32.

[141] Early Records of the City and County of Albany and Colony of Rensselaerswyck, Notarial Papers I and II, 1660-1696. Vol. 3, 48. Dated July 17, 1658.

[142] Early Records of the City and County of Albany and Colony of Rensselaerswyck, 63.

[143] Venema, "Poverty and Charity in Seventeenth-Century Beverwijck/Albany", 390.

[144] Ibid, 375.

[145] Ibid, 376.

[146] Ibid, 376.

[147] Ibid, 380.

[148] Ibid, 377.

[149] Ibid, 378.

[150] Sullivan, 136.

[151] Baptismal and Marriage Registers of the Old Dutch Church on Kingston, Ulster County, New York, 1660-1809 (Baltimore, MD: Genealogical Publishing Co.,Inc.,1997), 1.

[152] Baptismal and Marriage Registers of the Old Dutch Church on Kingston, Ulster County, New York, 1660-1809, 499.

[153] This case occurred on September 7, 1654.The Records of New Amsterdam from 1653-1674 Anno Domini. Minutes of the Court of Burgomasters and Schepens ed. Vol. I, 238.

[154] Ibid.

[155] Ibid, 239.

[156] The New York Historical Manuscripts Dutch, Vol. 2 Register of the Provincial Secretary, 1642-1647, Ed. Kenneth Scott and Kenn Stryker-Rodda (Baltimore, MD: Genealogical Publishing Company Inc., 1974), 234.

[157] The New York Historical Manuscripts Dutch Vol. 2 Register of the Provincial Sec-

retary, 1642-1647, 234.

[158] The Records of New Amsterdam from 1653-1674 Anno Domini. Minutes of the Court of Burgomasters and Schepens ed. Vol. III, Minutes of the Court of Burgomasters and Schepens Sept. 3, 1658 to Dec. 30, 1661, Inclusive. Ed. by Berthold Fernow (Baltimore, MD: Genealogical Publishing Co., Inc., 1976), 70.

[159] The Records of New Amsterdam from 1653-1674 Anno Domini. Minutes of the Court of
Burgomasters and Schepens ed. Vol. III, 70.

[160] Ibid, 70.

[161] No further references to this case have been found in records.

[162] The case described by John Winthrop was of an eighteen year old woman, Mary Latham who was put to death on March 21, 1664 after being found guilty of committing adultery. The sentence was according to the "law formally made and published in print," and the women was said to have died, "very penitently...gave good exhortation to all young maids to be obedient to their parents, and take heed of evil company." John Winthrop, John Winthrop's Journal, 1630-1649, Volume II."History of New England" Reprinted in Original Narratives of Early American History, Edited by James Kendall Hosmer (New York: Charles Schribner's Sons: 1908), 161-163.

[163] Both men and women were punished with whipping in accordance to the intensity of their crime. Sullivan, 143-144.

[164] Early Records of the City and County of Albany and Colony of Rensselaerswyck, 69.

[165] This Dutch phrase has not been translated in the documents. In a personal conversation with Dr. Peter van der Riet, a native Dutch speaker, on December 11, 2008, he revealed that the translation is, "took his manhood out of his pants." Dr. Peter Van der Riet, personal conversation with author, December 11, 2008.

[166] Early Records of the City and County of Albany and Colony of Rensselaerswyck, 70.

[167] Sullivan, 291, nn101. Some convicted were shown mercy by being hung first before being burnt to ashes. In another case involving Jan Quisthout van der Linde, a soldier who had been convicted of sodomy in 1660, his punishment was to be stripped of his arms, his sword broken at his feet and then tied in a sack and cast into the river and drowned.

[168] Humanism is a doctrine, attitude or way of life centered on human interests or values. The Dutch culture displayed aspects of this approach utilizing reason and the personal choice of individuals to choose their own morals. Jeremy Stangroom and James Garvey, The Great Philosophers: From Socrates to Foucault (New York: Barnes & Noble, 2005), 144.

[169] Rembrandt van Rijn, A Woman Comforting a Child Frightened by a Dog, sketch, 1636, Institute Neerlandais, Paris. Adriaen van de Velde, A Family in a Landscape, oil on canvas, 1660, Rijksmuseum, Amsterdam.

[170] The Freake-Gibbs Painter, The Mason Children: David, Joanna, and Abigail, oil on canvas, ca.1670, de Young Museum, San Francisco.

[171] The Freake-Gibbs Painter, Elizabeth Clarke Freake and Baby Mary, oil on canvas, ca. 1671, Worcester Museum, Massachusetts.

[172] The Empire State, 68.

[173] Gaze describes women's pride in their domestic work as represented in pieces by artists like Geertrydt Roghman as busily tending their pursuits as opposed to being under the male gaze. Delia Gaze, *Concise Dictionary of Women Artists* (London: Fitzroy Dearborn, 2001), 577.

[174] The Empire State, 68.

[175] Ibid.

[176] Ibid, 68.

[177] Thomas Woody, *A History of Women's Education in the United States* (NY: Octagon Books, 1974), 196.

[178] Woody, *A History of Women's Education in the United States*, 180.

[179] Ibid.

[180]Ibid, 179.

[181] Ibid, 179-80.

[182] Prak, 144. The cleanliness of the home was a woman's primary responsibility. Portrayals of Dutch women in the domestic sphere are found in numerous artworks of the Golden Age; including pieces by female artists such as Geertruydt Roghman. Roghman was an engraver during the Dutch Golden Age from Amsterdam who worked in her family's print shop and left many depictions of women at work in the domestic sphere. Her pieces are described in contrast to other representations of the "grinning woman" with sexual undertones but rather women dedicated to their domestic work. Gaze. *Concise Dictionary of Women Artists*, 576-577. See, Westermann, Mariët, *A Worldly Art: The Dutch Republic 1585-1718* (New Haven: Yale University Press, 1996).

[183] Ulrich, *Good Wives*, 4.

[184] Ibid, 3.

[185] Jacob Cats, Werken, 31. ('Galathea ofte hardersminneklachte') as reprinted in *Plain Lives in a Golden Age*.

[186]Goodfriend stated, the Dutch institutions, laws, and customary practices, altered the landscape, set the pattern for interaction with native people and imported Africans, and selectively transplanted their culture." Goodfriend, *Before the Melting Pot*, 5.

About the author: Maria Vann, Education Programs Manager at the New York State Historical Association has a BS in history and a MA in History Museum Studies. Her credits include educational materials for the NYS Museum and the D&H Linear Park, international presentations, Native American Interpretation, professional development for teachers, and school programs.

Supporting Good Habits: *The Rockefellers, the Sisters of Mercy, and Higher Education in New York State*

by Eric Martone

On Sunday, May 20, 1962, a collection of New York State and Catholic Church dignitaries made its way to Dobbs Ferry for the dedication ceremony of Mount Mercy-on-the-Hudson, a magnificent new complex comprised of over 80 acres overlooking the Hudson River for the New York province of the Sisters of Mercy. The Sisters had already moved into the unfinished facility during the fall of 1961, but the stress of moving and construction delays had prevented a proper dedication ceremony. That time had finally come, and all of the individuals involved in this massive undertaking now had a moment to bask in the glory of their accomplishments. The complex, which had cost more than $6 million to build at a time when the national average price for a house was less than $20,000, included eight impressive brick buildings "of contemporary architecture": the provincial house, a residence for student Sisters, a faculty residence, a residence for senior Sisters, a chapel, Our Lady of Victory Academy, a parish elementary school, and Mercy College.[1]

Although Francis Spellman, Cardinal and Archbishop of New York, presided over the ceremony and blessed the complex with the assistance of Rev. John Maguire, Vicar General of the Archdiocese of New York and Chancellor of Mercy College, the star of the ceremony was New York Governor (and future vice president of the United States) Nelson Rockefeller. His role in the celebration exceeded his capacity as Governor; he stood as the symbol of the Rockefeller family, whose financial contributions to the Sisters' educational endeavors had culminated in a generous $1.6 million gift to finance part of the complex's construction. Nelson, his father, John D. Rockefeller, Jr., and grandfather, John D. Rockefeller, Sr., had all donated funds to aid the Sisters when they had resided in their previous complex, located in Tarrytown near Kykuit, the main Rockefeller mansion. However, it was Nelson's father who made this especially magnanimous gift on top of his offer to purchase the Sisters' too-small Tarrytown property. Without his financial assistance, the Sisters' dreams of expanding their educational mission, the heart of which was the launching of Mercy College as a four-year institution, could never have materialized. Since he had died in 1960, the Sisters had eagerly been awaiting an opportunity to express publicly their heartfelt expressions of gratitude to his son.[2]

Malcolm Wilson, Lieutenant Governor of New York under Nelson Rockefeller and one-time trustee of Mercy College, later lectured at the College's commencement exercises on how significant the move had been to the development of Mercy College:

> *More than I suspect many of you know, 1827 in Dublin, Ireland marked the beginning of the Sisters of Mercy...The New York Province...was established in 1846 and I was present at the 100th Anniversary in 1946 in St. Patrick's Cathedral, New York City. The Mother House of the New York Province stood in Tarrytown diagonally across the road from the Pocantico Hills estate of the Rockefeller family. As a matter of fact, when I first started going up to see the Governor and later Vice President [Nelson Rockefeller], I entered the grounds by way of what was then known as "the Sisters' Gate." In 1950 a college, not for general registration but for members of the order, provided higher education for the Sisters. By the late 1950s it was very evident that they would have to serve a larger constituency. Not only did Mr. Rockefeller, notably John D. Rockefeller, Jr., purchase the house and all the buildings and grounds but also provided a very generous gift that made it possible to move Mercy College to Dobbs.[3]*

As a result of the Rockefellers' aid, Mercy College was able to thrive and evolve into a multi-campus, co-educational and secular institution. Today, it offers nearly 100 undergraduate and graduate degree programs and its main campus at Dobbs Ferry still consists primarily of the buildings built with Rockefeller assistance.

The Rockefellers' support of the Sisters and the development of Mercy College is an important component of broader New York history.

John D. Rockefeller, Sr., progenitor of the Rockefeller Dynasty, founded Standard Oil Company, one of the largest corporations in its day, and became one of the wealthiest Americans of his time.[4] Rockefeller, Sr. who embraced the "American ideal of responsible stewardship"—the idea that with great wealth "comes the duty to serve the public good and improve the conditions of mankind"—has often been praised as "perhaps the most significant philanthropist the United States has ever produced" and that his philanthropy "distinguished him from most other great industrialists."[5] His son, Rockefeller, Jr., continued his philanthropic work.[6] Although the Rockefellers chose to support a variety of causes, they contributed much in the area of education. From 1911 onward, the Rockefellers developed a complex relationship with the Sisters of Mercy, who then lived in Tarrytown next to the main Rockefeller estate of Kykuit. While the Rockefellers' financial support of the Sisters toward the construction of a new complex in Dobbs Ferry to help develop Mercy College is modest in comparison to the Rockefellers' other philanthropic endeavors in the field of education, such as the family's support of the University of Chicago (a total of $35 million between 1889 and 1910), it represents the most significant support to New York higher education outside of Rockefeller University, which Rockefeller, Sr. founded in 1901 as an institute for medical research.[7] Rockefeller University, however, only offers advanced, specialized graduate-level programs and is neither a comprehensive nor liberal arts college. The relationship between the Rockefellers and the Sisters of Mercy, especially in connection with the development of Mercy College, has received only minimal scholarly attention.[8] This article consequently explores the complex relationship between the Rockefellers and the Sisters of Mercy to illuminate a neglected aspect of Rockefeller philanthropy in their home state of New York.

Tarrytown Neighbors: Rockefellers and the Sisters of Mercy

The Sisters of Mercy, after forming in Ireland in the early nineteenth century, branched out to other parts of the Atlantic world. At a time when most women could not generally own property as individuals because of their subordinate status as wives, Sisters could collectivize wealth, derive business revenue, sign contracts, get loans, and incorporate institutions under female control.[9] The Sisters began their work in New York City during the mid-1800s with an orphanage. They also started an industrial school for young women to teach them skills like sewing and opened up a Select School for Girls, where daughters of wealthier people in the community could get "a proper English education." Later, they spread to other locations, including Pelham Bay and the Bronx. On December 23, 1892, the Sisters expanded to Tarrytown after acquiring the roughly thirty-acre Kingsland estate. The estate took its name from Ambrose Kingsland, a mid-nineteenth century merchant and former mayor of New York City, who had built a mansion on part of this land (which became known as "Wilson Park," after nineteenth-century New York City merchant William Wilson built a large home in the area). The Sisters later discovered remnants of colonial slave quarters on their property's northern end, dating from its Philipsburg Manor days.[10]

The Sisters' move to Tarrytown coincided with the time when the area was becoming a favorite residence for the many prominent industrialists and business figures of the era. Although John D. Rockefeller, Sr., spent his adolescence and early adult years in Ohio, he was born in Richmond, New York in 1839. In 1884, he finally moved back to New York State when he established a residence in New York City. Tarrytown, however, soon became the Rockefellers' New York retreat. In 1893, Rockefeller, Sr. purchased about 400 acres at Pocantico Hills, including Kykuit Hill (a name imposed by Dutch colonists, meaning "lookout") overlooking the majestic Hudson River. He continued to expand this parcel of land. By the early twentieth century, it reached about 2,000 acres.[11] He initially stayed at the Parsons-Wentworth House, near the present-day coach barn, until it burned down in 1902. Rockefeller, Sr. then resided at existing residences on the property.

None of them, however, commanded an impressive view of the Hudson or took advantage of the property's full beauty. Consequently, his son, John D. Rockefeller, Jr., decided to oversee the construction of Kykuit, a home he intended to be "a house appropriate to his [Rockefeller, Sr.'s] stature as one of the country's leading industrialists and philanthropists."[12] The lavish mansion, which became the Rockefeller family's "principal home," was constructed in two phases between 1906 and

1913. Rockefeller, Sr. and his wife, Laura Spelman Rockefeller, spent the fall at Kykuit in 1908. However, the hard-to-please couple was sorely disappointed: the guest rooms were too small, the fireplaces too smoky, and noise from the kitchen area could be heard in the mansion's private quarters. Consequently, Rockefeller, Jr. literally went back to the drawing board to prove himself to his parents. He redesigned and renovated Kykuit during 1911 to 1913.[13] The new Kykuit met Rockefeller, Sr.'s approval and the mansion served as a retreat for him until his death in 1937. It subsequently served as a retreat for Rockefeller, Jr. until his death in 1960, and for his son, Nelson Rockefeller, until his death in 1979.

Shortly after being built, the Rockefellers began to have some unexpected problems with their neighbors, the Sisters of Mercy. Many Sisters, who came predominantly from working-class backgrounds, were amazed by the new "palace" next door. Indeed, it embraced a degree of extravagance that many of them had neither seen nor imagined. The magnificence of Kykuit, especially its gardens, proved to be a local "wonder" that particularly entranced the younger members of the order. Sometimes the Sisters wandered into the garden in amazement and ended up near the main mansion, much to the Rockefellers' disapproval. While the Rockefellers did not necessarily mind their new neighbors' admiration, they felt that the Sisters wandered too close to their private quarters and intruded upon their privacy. A polite, but firm letter was sent to the Sisters' superior.[14]

However, more pressing annoyances emerged. Rockefeller, Sr., while certainly not opposed in principle to the Sisters' not-for-profit business activities, never truly warmed to the occurrence of these endeavors next to his estate. At times, he expressed his view that the Sisters' complex was an eyesore. For example, as tradition has it, Rockefeller Sr. asked the Sisters if he could arrange to have their roof, which he could see from Kykuit, painted from a distracting red to green to better match the landscape.[15] Yet, he also had to deal with his wife's complaints, a bane to any husband's ears. Rockefeller, Sr.'s wife, Laura, who died in 1915, was not in good health during her years at Kykuit. In an uncomfortable state, she especially did not enjoy the noise coming from the Sisters' property, which then housed an orphanage for children committed to the Sisters by the City of New York. As one Rockefeller representative diplomatically phrased it in a 1911 letter, "Mrs. Rockefeller has expressed herself that the noise made by the children at the school was many times heard on their place, and perhaps not always pleasantly."[16] As Rockefeller, Jr. explained more bluntly several years later, the actions on the Sisters' property "detract from our enjoyment of the Kykuit property."[17] As a result, its very existence next to the Rockefeller estate compromised their individual privacy and their property's residential sanctity. In fact, the Rockefellers were so obsessive about the maintenance of this privacy/sanctity that they eventually paid to relocate the noisy New York and Putnam railroad, which they felt traveled too close to their estate. The railroad actually passed through the Sisters' property and made a stop at Pocantico Hills. In 1929, however, Rockefeller, Jr. paid to reroute the New York and Putnam Railroad out

Tarrytown-on-Hudson, N. Y. Sisters of Mercy Home.

This postcard from the Hugh C. Leighton Company, circa 1912, depicts the Tarrytown-on-Hudson, home of the Sisters of Mercy. The property was comprised primarily of two buildings: the Sisters' convent, housed in the former Kingsland mansion (located to the right), and the school building (located to the left).

The Rockefellers had entertained a similar approach to the Sisters, hoping that they could get rid of them by buying their property and helping them move elsewhere. Rockefeller, Sr. approached the Sisters in December 1911 about buying their property, the size of which was estimated at about 33 acres. Negotiations over this possibility ultimately created much ado throughout 1912.[19] The Tarrytown Sisters and their administrators, then located at 1073 Madison Avenue in New York City, were initially surprised at the sudden offer, but nevertheless supported a deal in principle. At the time, the Tarrytown Sisters wanted to be closer to New York City. However, the order needed to locate a suitable replacement location as well as the necessary funds to replicate the Tarrytown facility on this new site. The Sisters also desired approval from the local Church hierarchy, which served as their advisors. In January 1912, after contemplating what to do, the Sisters set a high asking price of $600,000 based on what Mother Rose, the Superior, estimated as the cost to purchase ($300,000) and renovate ($360,000) a 9-acre site on Aqueduct Avenue, near 177th Street, that the order was interested in acquiring as a substitute.[20] Rockefeller, Sr. felt that that price was unreasonable, but the Sisters, prodded by their Church advisors, seemed slow to budge.

In June, at Rockefeller, Sr.'s bequest, three private appraisers naturally assessed the property for much less than the sum of $600,000. The estimates, however, ranged widely from $200,000 to $450,000. The appraiser for the highest estimate based his value on the fact that the "buildings on this property are very well built. They have fire-proof stair casings, extra thick walls all the way through." Despite the variances, the estimates generally corresponded with the amount of $300,000 that the Sisters wanted in order to purchase a replacement property, since their intentionally inflated total sum of $600,000 included the amount necessary to cover additional renovation costs. By August, Eugene Quin, who represented the Sisters in the negotiations, sought to break the impasse by suggesting a sale price of $350,000.[21] Quin knew that Rockefeller, Sr. would grumble at this offer. He consequently sought to frame the price as a cumulative sum for the property and a charitable "gift." As he wrote in a letter to Rockefeller, Sr.: "when I think of the unstinted liberality you have so readily extended to other philanthropic institutions throughout this entire country, I cannot but hope that you may feel inclined to extend the same liberality to the good Sisters whose appreciation would be so deep, and which I am sure would return a reward of a thousand fold in the feelings of satisfaction that would surely come to you for your magnanimity."[22] Rockefeller, Sr. was receptive to the ploy and warmed to the idea of giving the Sisters a donation in addition to a sum for their property. But the crux of the problem was that in his mind the property was only worth about $75,000. He therefore wanted to pay about $125,000, an amount that included a $50,000 "gift." To Rockefeller, Sr., the buildings on the property were utterly worthless; he wanted to demolish them. After all, the purpose for acquiring the property was to buttress his estate to enhance its privacy. In addition, he argued that the New York and Putnam Railroad, which then still cut through the property, greatly reduced its value. Despite all of his money, despite how much he wanted the Sisters to relocate, he refused (in his mind) to overpay.[23] By the end of the summer, negotiations cooled off and the Tarrytown Sisters received some news from their administrators about the future of the site. As Quin revealed in a November 1912 letter to Rockefeller Sr., the Sisters were "preparing to convert their Tarrytown institution into one of a different nature [a school for girls] than now conducted, and that this will involve the withdrawing of the property from further consideration of selling."[24] Nevertheless, negotiations lingered on for years. The Sisters, however, held firm on a high asking price, which still remained at $500,000 in March 1921.[25]

During the late 1920s, discussions to purchase the property regained traction, this time with Rockefeller, Jr.[26] Negotiations followed the same general terms as had existed between the Sisters and his father: a "fair market value" for the property along with a donation to help cover the costs of reconstructing the Tarrytown facility elsewhere. Naturally, problems arose during attempts to set a specific sum for the two components. In 1928, Rockefeller, Jr. finally decided that he was willing to pay an amount closer to what the Sisters desired.[27] But to religious officials, it seemed that he was too late. Mother Mathilde, the Sisters' new Mother Provincial in New York City, supported the sale. However, she did not feel optimistic about its success because "the Sisters [at Tarrytown] did not care to sell." Consequently, Rockefeller, Jr. "would have to wait for a change of administration [there] to get a change of attitude."[28] Church officials were also eager to sanction the transaction. Still, they too revealed their conviction that "sentimental reasons" would delay the Sisters from acquiescing to a deal. By this time, the Sisters had grown accustomed to life in Westchester and no longer wished to relocate out of the county, as they feared religious officials would decree.[29]

Nevertheless, October seemed to be the month of miracles. A deal was nearly struck to purchase the roughly 20-acre property—about nine acres of which had been previously sold—for $100,000, with an additional $200,000 gift based on the condition that the Sisters could secure a suitable new site. Rockefeller, Jr. even offered to let the Sisters remain on "the premises for a period of two years from the date of the deed" to help them with their move.[30] The Sisters, however, were still reluctant and discussions crawled into 1929. In January, the contrary Sisters again set a high price of around $500,000, but began the hunt for a new location.[31] By November, Rockefeller, Jr. began to tire of these negotiations and made the Sisters, who had recently secured permission to re-locate in Westchester County, his "best and last offer" of $600,000: $100,000 for the property and a $500,000 gift. Yet, the Sisters then decided that they wanted Rockefeller, Jr. to cover the full, specific construction costs for relocating to a new site. Consequently, negotiations once again cooled off.[32] During the 1930s, sporadic talk of buying the property occurred, but the Rockefellers had become frustrated with the "Tarrytown situation," as lawyer Franklin Brooks liked to term it.[33]

As the Rockefellers generally abandoned efforts to purchase the Sisters' property, they began to enjoy increased cordial relations with their neighbors, often assisting them financially with their school and maintenance repairs. The Rockefellers generally gave friendly waves and engaged in brief social interactions with the Sisters as they passed each other. Nevertheless, the Rockefellers were not always quite sure of the Sisters' individual names or proper etiquette in terms of how to address the order's superiors for formal matters (such as in a letter). Meanwhile, the Sisters often took advantage of the Rockefeller family's desires to have their property well-maintained to get them to pay for various maintenance and service needs. The Rockefellers thus took various short-term measures to improve the appearance of the complex, often taking the view that if the most offensive objects on the property were out of site, they were out of mind. Over the course of decades, the Rockefellers, somewhat begrudgingly, became one of the Sisters' largest and most consistent benefactors. The Sisters tended to go to them whenever they were soliciting donations or organizing fund raisers for their non-profit business activities. The Rockefellers sent donations, usually modest ones, on a case by case basis. They generally donated simply to maintain good neighborly relations, but avoided sending a response and/or a donation if they felt that they could do so. Nevertheless, the Rockefellers' financial support was both needed and appreciated. Since most Sisters and Catholics of the era hailed from relatively recent immigrant stock, the constituents of Catholic parishes during the nineteenth and early twentieth centuries did not have vast financial resources to fund initiatives in the areas of charity work and education.[34] Sisters faced constant pressure to find revenue to support their order, their institutions, and work. Consequently, money was often tight and the Sisters ironically came to view the (Protestant) Rockefellers as their patrons.

It is interesting to note that each subsequent generation of the Rockefellers that occupied Kykuit developed a more sympathetic attitude toward the Sisters. Nelson Rockefeller, who was born in 1908, grew up with the Sisters as his neighbors. He had a fondness for them that surpassed that of both his father, Rockefeller, Jr., and certainly his grandfather, Rockefeller, Sr. As an adult, Nelson's home, located away from the main Rockefeller estate, was situated directly across from the Sisters' property. As a result, he took a greater interest than his father in taking care of the Sisters' property's maintenance needs. However, his father often reimbursed him in part or in full for expenses incurred on the Sisters' behalf. For example, he was so pleased with the relocation of a playground to reduce noise that he decided to reimburse Nelson in full. In a letter to his son, he wrote: "I am realizing...what a great advantage it is to the entire place. Not only is the view as one drives up the County House Road to the Sisters' Gate much more attractive, but the noise is practically eliminated."[35] Over time, Nelson spent thousands of dollars to cover the costs of improvements for the Sisters' property. During the mid-1930s, for example, he bought them a tractor to replace their horse and helped turn their barn into a gymnasium. In 1939, he paid around $2,000 to pave the driveway running through the Sisters' property. He also frequently paid to have it plowed during the winter. Later, in 1952, Nelson sent "Sister Superior" Mary Gratia Maher 130 shares of stock valued at $5,000 to help cover building renovations.[36]

Establishing Mercy College

By the 1940s, the Sisters of Mercy became involved in the management of various hospitals and schools throughout New York. However, to be qualified to staff these institutions, young Sisters needed an education. They often studied for credit granted from local Catholic colleges. A 1938 "thank you" letter from Sister Mary Gertrude, Supervisor of Schools, to their neighbor, Rockefeller, Jr., for a recent library donation described this arrangement in detail. After explaining that the new books would aid Sisters in training, she informed Rockefeller, Jr.: "It may interest you to know that our future teachers spend at least two and one-half years at Tarrytown. During that time, in addition to their religious training, the potential teachers receive training in secular subjects. Each Sister destined for the schools completes two years of college work. This... includes courses that are usually given at Normal Training Schools. However, the work done here is accredited college work. After leaving Tarrytown, the Sister who continues study does so on the third year level at college."[37] Supplying external educations to all Sisters proved to be a costly commitment. As a result, the Sisters decided to establish their own private junior college to educate their order's younger members. The province's superior ultimately charged Sister Mary Gratia Maher, who was still completing her doctoral dissertation examining religious instruction at women's Catholic colleges, with making this institution a reality. She had substantial educational administrative experience, having been a school teacher as well as a former principal of Saint Catharine Academy in the Bronx.[38] As Sister Mary Agnes Parrell, who worked with Sister Gratia, recalled, "leaders somehow always rise from out [of] their time. In fact, they stand above time. Such a scholar was Sister Mary Gratia," who quickly developed the new college's curriculum, established its organization, and selected its faculty.[39] The Sisters' efforts in New York, however, were not unique. Other Mercy convents across the US faced similar circumstances and a movement developed that placed educating Sisters a priority before sending them into the field. As a result, "Mercy Junior College," as it was initially known, was among the five "Sister Formation Colleges" that opened during the 1950s.[40]

Sister Hilda, librarian, stands in the library at the Sisters' complex in Tarrytown.

Of course, Mercy Junior College needed a state charter in order to have the authority to confer degrees. The Sisters, however, were in a hurry. Time is money, as the adage goes. As a result, they negotiated a temporary credit agreement in August 1950 with the Catholic University of America. The College's first classes began during the following month at the Sisters' site in Tarrytown. In 1952, the New York State Board of Regents finally granted the College a charter authorizing its associate degree programs of studies for members of the Sisters' order. To retain a degree of its former student constituency, many local Catholic colleges, such as Manhattan College and St. John's University, offered Mercy Junior College's seniors scholarships to continue their studies.[41]

Over the course of the 1950s, the Sisters developed plans to expand Mercy Junior College. The expansion of this college came to hold special meaning for the Sisters. Indeed, it came to embody the heart of their mission. During these early years, however, the Rockefellers seem to have been oblivious to the College's existence, likely because it served only Sisters. As a result, they did not notice any additional personnel, students, traffic, or noise. Sometime during the mid-1950s, the Sisters made the monumental decision to expand the College to lay women. Naturally, they petitioned their neighbor, Nelson Rockefeller, in 1956 for a donation to support their efforts. The New York Board of Regents had approved the proposed College "in principle" and gave the Sisters "a time limit," soon to expire, to meet their requirements, one of the most significant of which was an expanded physical facility. Nelson, however, was not interested. [42] When his father heard about the Sisters' plans, he predictably became concerned over his property's privacy and even considered making the Sisters an offer of over $1 million to build the College elsewhere.[43]

At this time, it seems that the Sisters contemplated opening their junior college to women as a way to extend their secondary school programs offered on their Tarrytown site at Our Lady of Victory Academy. Ultimately, the Sisters decided to change course: Mercy College was to be re-launched as a private four-year institution for women. Sister Gratia worked with state officials during the late 1950s to change the College's name to "Mercy College" (accomplished in 1956) as well as to establish the institution as a four-year college. According to Sister Agnes, a member of the founding faculty, the decision to become a four-year college was based on the following factors: 1) the need to equip sister students to teach in Mercy grammar and high schools; 2) the cost of sending all juniors, novices, and postulants to other colleges was too expensive; and 3) a desire to not "impose on local college's generosity" in supplying further scholarships. Furthermore, "as the community was founded to equip young women to take their places in society with the necessary skills and knowledge to be successful persons," the new College decided to admit female lay students.[44] The Board of Regents approved an amendment granting the Sisters' desired changes by 1960.

Sisters studying at "Mercy College" in Tarrytown during the 1950s.

Meanwhile, the Sisters began a serious hunt to find a new location to support their educational initiatives. As Sister Mary Jeanne Ferrier, Provincial of the Mercy Community, conveyed in a private letter, the Sisters recognized that their Tarrytown property was inadequate "because of size, character of land and obsolescence of the buildings. The present structures do not lend themselves to either modernizing or expansion of facilities. There is not enough land available near the present site for further expansion and after investigation we have discovered that economically we could not provide for our needs if we remain here."[45] During 1956 and 1957, the Sisters explored about 10 different options and came close to purchasing sites in Cortlandt and Scarborough.[46]

A Dream Realized

News that the Sisters were finally seeking to relocate reached Rockefeller, Jr. His representatives had never believed that the Rockefellers had fully abandoned the dream of acquiring the Sisters' property and, like faithful watchdogs, had kept an eye on the property's status. Rockefeller, Jr. confirmed to his agent that he was interested in resuming negotiations to purchase the Sisters' Tarrytown property if the opportunity arose. His agent suggested that he make a large gift in excess of the "fair market value" to assure the Sisters' move.[47] Rockefeller, Jr. was, therefore, prepared to revisit the terms of the previous negotiations between his family and the Sisters. He estimated that the current cost for duplicating the Sisters' facility was around $1.5 million. This estimate served as the guide for his "gift."[48]

During the summer of 1957, the Sisters made a successful bid of $350,000 for the 85-acre former estate of Edwin Gould, son of robber baron Jay Gould, in Dobbs Ferry.[49] Despite years of Rockefeller prodding, the Sisters were now finally moving on their own terms. The sale of the Sisters' Tarrytown property was imminent and Rockefeller, Jr. authorized his representatives to negotiate with the Sisters on his behalf. He capped his price at $1.75 million, an amount based on his estimate to reconstruct the Sisters' facility and the property's $150,000 "fair market value." The Sisters, however, were reluctant to let go of their Tarrytown property and felt that they had much to lose if either end of the deal fell through. Consequently, the Sisters wanted Rockefeller, Jr.'s personal commitment before proceeding to purchase the Gould estate.[50] In March 1958, Sister Mary Jeanne wrote him a heartfelt letter:

> *During the years since the Sisters of Mercy have been located on the property at Wilson Park, the organization has grown tremendously. For a long period of time it has been realized that the property is inadequate for our use...Therefore, it is our decision to relocate. We have been searching for a suitable site for over a two-year period, and since the Gould property in Dobbs Ferry appears to meet our requirements, it seems very desirable. In order to pursue this further with a view to negotiating for its purchase, we are appealing to you, our good neighbor of many years, to assist us that we may continue our charitable endeavors for humanity. The expansion program that we are considering will involve a huge expenditure far beyond our normal capacity. The accomplishment of this will not be possible unless we can secure the market sale price for our Tarrytown site and a substantial donation over and above. Aware of your manifold charities and your genuinely sincere interest in education and social welfare agencies, it is with confident hope that I present our needs to you.[51]*

Rockefeller, Jr. drafted several versions of a response, contemplating how much detail to provide in sections concerning the history between the Sisters and his family and his intentions to buy the property. In April, he finally sent Sister Mary Jeanne the following letter of pledge:

I have received your very kind and gracious letter of March 25 relative to the expansion program of the Sisters of Mercy. You say that due to your tremendous growth and the limitations of your present property you have been forced to look elsewhere... and you have found in the Gould property at Dobbs Ferry the suitable site that will answer your requirements. In view of the pleasant and neighborly relations which have existed for so many years between the Sisters and the members of our family, I... am now confirming...[my representative, Mr. William Yates's] verbal commitment to you on my behalf—namely, that on your assurance that you have acquired title to the Gould property...and that you will immediately proceed with the erection thereon of buildings required by your institution, I agree to contribute to the Institution of Mercy securities having a market value of $1,600,000 at the time of delivery.[52]

The Sisters heaved a sigh of relief, but only temporarily. New difficulties emerged on the horizon in 1958 as the result of a dispute between the Catholic Church and the local Board of Education over the Sisters' desired property in Dobbs Ferry. The board was contemplating the erection of a new school to alleviate overcrowding issues and had its eye on the former Edwin Gould estate as the potential site for a new school. The board therefore wanted the Sisters to refrain from purchasing the entire estate to leave room for a school. However, the Sisters had already planned on selling the part of the estate that the board wanted to Sacred Heart Catholic Church for the building of a parochial school. The Sisters intended to use this sum to help offset the costs for acquiring and constructing their new complex in Dobbs Ferry. Cardinal Spellman carried the dispute into the local press, arguing that a parochial school would remedy the overcrowding issue.[53] Rockefeller, Jr.'s counsel suggested that he abort his plans to acquire the Sisters' property if they did not secure the Gould property by the end of the year. However, the Sisters decided that they would not sell their Tarrytown property until they had the property in Dobbs Ferry first. Consequently, Rockefeller, Jr., so close to realizing the Rockefeller acquisition of the Sisters' property after 47 years of effort, paid close personal attention to developments.[54]

For their part, the Sisters quickly grew impatient with the school board, which forced the issue to be resolved through a public referendum. The village had already rezoned the Gould property for the Sisters' use without any objections (although there was one abstention).[55] The Sisters felt that the school board had demonstrated no interest in the Gould property until they wished to acquire it. Nevertheless, the Sisters had decided early on that they would relinquish their expansion plans and allow the district to have the property if the public referendum results supported it. However, after the school board failed to obtain residents' approval in the first referendum, the Sisters felt that there should have been no further interference.[56] Yet, the school board pressed for additional referendums, each time making a claim for why the previous results should be invalidated. The Sisters, in the midst of leading a drive to raise $500,000 for the site, became frustrated with local officials. Apparently, even the patience of Sisters has limits. The executors of the Gould estate had also opposed the school board's plan since they wanted to sell the property en masse. However, all parties involved played along with village officials to avoid the possible usage of eminent domain to seize the property. After four referendums, local residents repeatedly voted against the school board's expansion plan and the matter was put to rest.[57]

The agreement of sale between Rockefeller, Jr. and the Sisters for their Tarrytown property (about ten percent of which technically resided in Sleepy Hollow), was signed in May 1958. The Sisters received 32,200 shares of Standard Oil valued at $1.75 million. Rockefeller, Jr. received the title on August 19, during which time he was in Maine.[58] That same month, the Sisters completed their transaction to acquire the Gould property.[59] However, Rockefeller, Jr. made an unusual request. He asked the Sisters to refrain from publicly announcing his $1.6 million gift until later in the year, in part to help boost Nelson Rockefeller's campaign for governor with positive press.[60] The Sisters, happy to oblige, did not announce the gift until October. The pretense created the public perception that the gift was a purely magnanimous act on the part of the Rockefellers unrelated to the purchasing of the Sisters' Tarrytown property.[61] The ploy worked. Not only did the gift receive wide media coverage, the Rockefellers received several thank you letters from Catholics for supporting the Sisters and their educational pursuits with such a gift, especially since he was not a Catholic.[62] Within the broader context of conflicts between Catholic and Protestant reformers that had plagued the early twentieth century, this act was indeed noteworthy.[63]

That same month, the Sisters, no longer forced to conceal their abundant gratitude, sent their "esteemed benefactor" a framed manuscript as token of their appreciation. The Sisters had long perceived the Rockefellers as their patrons, and this gift was viewed as the culmination of their financial support. As the manuscript said, "Each of the four hundred Sisters of Mercy of the Province of New York, in deep and sincere gratitude, has offered to God one day of Prayer Labor Sacrifice in the spiritual and corporal works of mercy." It concluded with a quote from Ephesians 3:6-19.[64]

Meanwhile, Rockefeller, Jr. and his associates expressed relief that this "long drawn-out and at times very trying transaction" was over.[65] However, they were sadly mistaken, for the drama continued as a bitter and drawn-out tax dispute developed between the village of Tarrytown and Rockefeller, Jr. over the valuation of the property. Rockefeller, Jr.'s gift to the Sisters was tax deductible. As a result, he believed that the property could not be assessed for much higher than the "fair market value" he paid for it: $150,000. Tarrytown, perhaps too eager to have the Sisters' former property back on the tax rolls, since religious property was exempt from civil property tax, estimated its worth at over $250,000. Rockefeller thus sued to lower the valuation.[66]

The Sisters, although they now owned the former Gould estate, could not live there until they finished the construction of their new complex. Rockefeller, Jr. therefore leased to the Sisters their former Tarrytown property for $1. The two-year lease called for the Sisters to acquire insurance to protect two cottages on the property that he wanted to keep. It also contained a provision allowing for an extension on a month-to-month basis, "if, after...due diligence, the tenant is unable to complete the construction of such new buildings."[67] The Sisters continued to seek donations for the Mercy Building Fund and even secured an anonymous $1,000 donation from Nelson Rockefeller.[68] The Sisters even unsuccessfully asked Rockefeller, Jr. if he would grant them a low-interest loan for the remaining amount necessary to complete their Dobbs Ferry complex, Mount Mercy-on-the-Hudson.[69]

In December 1959, the Sisters signed a contract to begin the complex's construction, which was scheduled to be completed in 550 days. Sister Mary Jeanne promptly informed Rockefeller, Jr. that the Sisters intended to move in 1961.[70] As the complex's construction was underway, Sister Mary Jeanne continued to correspond with Rockefeller, Jr. During the negotiations to sell the Sisters' Tarrytown property, she made a favorable impression on Rockefeller, Jr.—who described her in private as "wise, able and gracious"—and with his associates, one of whom perceived her as "quite a business lady."[71] Consequently, she and Rockefeller, Jr. developed a sense of mutual respect. As she confided to him in one letter, "the plans for our new Mount Mercy [complex]... are rapidly approaching completion...Eight buildings present a challenge to one's mental efforts as the endeavor is made to avoid any and all mistakes which might arise from insufficient consideration. This is a tremendous project and we shall always be grateful to you. It embodies our prayers, hopes and dreams for an expansion of our facilities that will enable us to work ever more effectively for...the underprivileged of our country and in particular of our eastern area."[72] In April 1960, shortly before his death, she sent him an Easter card, addressing him as the Sisters' "friend and benefactor," and urging his recovery.[73]

A sketch of Mount Mercy-on-the-Hudson from the program for the December 1959 ground-breaking ceremony.

During the fall of 1961, the Sisters moved from Tarrytown to Mount Mercy. Meanwhile, the main buildings on their former Tarrytown property were razed. During the early twenty-first century, construction companies purchased the site of Mercy College's original campus and, despite local opposition, built luxury homes on the property near the intersection of Wilson Park Drive and County House Road.[74] In 1969, Mercy College became a non-sectarian and co-educational institution. During a period of unprecedented expansion during the 1970s and 1980s, Mercy College began to establish branch campuses and extension centers throughout the New York metropolitan region, diversified its academic programs, and first achieved national recognition as one of the most innovative institutions of higher education in the United States. Mercy College, comprised of only the "College Building" (now Main Hall) in 1961, soon absorbed the other buildings within the Mount Mercy complex into its main campus as the Sisters sold off their Mount Mercy complex. By 2013, it had united six of the eight buildings built with Rockefeller money under its auspices.[75] Throughout its history, Mercy College, literally a "house that the Rockefellers built," has retained a deep commitment to community service and to providing motivated students innovative programs that provide the opportunity to transform their lives through higher education.

Endnotes

[1] Program for the Mount Mercy groundbreaking ceremony, December 12, 1959, Mercy College Library Archives, Dobbs Ferry, NY; "Rockefeller Helps Dedicate a Convent That Father Aided," New York Times, May 21, 1962.

[2] "Rockefeller Helps Dedicate a Convent That Father Aided"; Sister Mary Agnes Parrell, A History of Mercy College, 1950-1982 (Dobbs Ferry, NY: Mercy College, 1985). 8.

[3] Malcolm Wilson, Address, Commencement Exercises, January 1982, in Parrell, Mercy, 65.

[4] Mansel G. Blackford and K. Austin Kerr, Business Enterprise in American History, 3rd ed. (Boston: Houghton Mifflin, 1994), 125-225.

[5] Andras Szanto, ed., Rockefeller Philanthropy: A Selected Guide (Sleepy Hollow, NY: Rockefeller Archive Center, 2011), 8; Henry Joyce with Cynthia Bronson Altman and Susan T. Greenstein, Kykuit: The House and Gardens of the Rockefeller Family, 2nd ed. (Pocantico Hills: Historic Hudson Valley Press, 2005), 7.

[6] Joyce, Kykuit, 7.

[7] Szanto, *Rockefeller Philanthropy*, 40-47.

[8] The topic is addressed briefly in Sister Mary Agnes Parrell's early history of Mercy College, which was limited to 20 spiral-bound copies. See: Parrell, Mercy College, 4, 8.

[9] Maureen Fitzgerald, "Habits of Compassion: Irish American Nuns in New York City," in Women's America: Refocusing the Past, eds. Linda Kerber, Jane Sherron De Hart, and Cornelia Hughes Dayton, 7th ed. (New York: Oxford University Press, 2011), 219.

[10] See: Margaret Vetare, *Philipsburg Manor Upper Mills* (Pocantico Hills: Historic Hudson Valley Press, 2004), 18-22; Edgar Mayhew Bacon, *Chronicles of Tarrytown and Sleepy Hollow* (New York: G.P. Putnam's Sons, 1897); On the slave quarters on the Sisters' Tarrytown property, see: Katherine Burton, His Mercy Endureth Forever (Tarrytown: Sisters of Mercy, 1946).

[11] Joyce, Kykuit, 9.

[12] Ibid.

[13] Ibid., 7, 11-13.

[14] Folder 230, box 35, Educational Interests series, Record Group 2 Office of the Messrs. Rockefeller (OMR), Rockefeller Family Archives, Rockefeller Archive Center, Sleepy Hollow, New York (hereafter designated RAC).

[15] *Daily News* (Tarrytown), August 21, 1958.

[16] George Mackay to Henry Cooper, December 19, 1911, folder 230, box 35, Educational Interests series, RG 2 OMR, Rockefeller Family Archives, RAC.

[17] Letter from John D. Rockefeller Jr., October 24, 1956, folder 233, box 35, Educational Interests series, RG 2 OMR, Rockefeller Family Archives, RAC.

[18] See: Daniel Gallo and Frederick Kramer, *The Putnam Division: New York Central's Bygone Route through Westchester County* (New York: Quadrant Press, 1981).

[19] Folder 230, box 35, Educational Interests series, RG 2 OMR, Rockefeller Family Archives, RAC.

[20] Eugene Quin to George Mackay, February 2, 1912, folder 230, box 35, Educational Interests series, RG 2 OMR, Rockefeller Family Archives, RAC.

[21] Appraisal from Bryan Kennelly, March 12, 1912, folder 230, box 35, Educational Interests series, RG 2 OMR, Rockefeller Family Archives, RAC; Memorandum, January 17, 1928, folder 230, box 35, Educational Interests series, RG 2 OMR, Rockefeller Family Archives, RAC.

[22] Eugene Quin to John D. Rockefeller, Sr., October 17, 1912, folder 230, box 35, Educational Interests series, RG 2 OMR, Rockefeller Family Archives, RAC.

[23] Memo (Charles Heydt), November 29, 1912, folder 230, box 35, Educational Interests series, RG 2 OMR, Rockefeller Family Archives, RAC.

[24] Eugene Quin to John D. Rockefeller, Sr., November 22, 1912, folder 230, box 35, Educational Interests series, RG 2 OMR, Rockefeller Family Archives, RAC.

[25] Memorandum, January 17, 1928, folder 230, box 35, Educational Interests series, RG 2 OMR, Rockefeller Family Archives, RAC.

[26] See: Folder 231, box 35, Educational Interests series, RG 2 OMR, Rockefeller Family Archives, RAC.

[27] Charles Heydt to John D. Rockefeller, Jr., March 5, 1928, folder 231, box 35, Educational Interests series, RG 2 OMR, Rockefeller Family Archives, RAC.

[28] Charles Heydt to John D. Rockefeller, Jr., April 11, 1928, folder 231, box 35, Educational Interests series, RG 2 OMR, Rockefeller Family Archives, RAC.

[29] Letter to John D. Rockefeller, Jr., May 28, 1928, folder 231, box 35, Educational Interests series, RG 2 OMR, Rockefeller Family Archives, RAC.

[30] Charles Heydt to George Gillespie, October 1, 1928, folder 231, box 35, Educational Interests series, RG 2 OMR, Rockefeller Family Archives, RAC.

[31] George Gillespie to Charles Heydt, January 19, 1929, folder 231, box 35, Educational Interests series, RG 2 OMR, Rockefeller Family Archives, RAC.

[32] William Conklin to Charles Heydt, September 23, 1929, folder 231, box 35, Educational Interests series, RG 2 OMR, Rockefeller Family Archives, RAC; Chales Heydt to George Gillespie, November 6, 1929, folder 231, box 35, Educational Interests series, RG 2 OMR, Rockefeller Family Archives, RAC.

[33] Folder 232, box 35, Educational Interests series, RG 2 OMR, Rockefeller Family Archives, RAC.

[34] Fitzgerald, "Habits of Compassion," 217, 220.

[35] John D. Rockefeller Jr. to Nelson Rockefeller, December 19, 1936, folder 233B, box 35, Educational Interests series, RG 2 OMR, Rockefeller Family Archives, RAC.

[36] Sr. M. Immaculata to Nelson Rockefeller, June 15, 1939; Letter from Elizabeth Phillips, June 28, 1939, folder 232, box 35, Educational Interests series, RG 2 OMR, Rockefeller Family Archives, RAC; Dana Creel to Nelson Rockefeller, June 29, 1954, folder 233A, box 35, Educational Interests series, RG 2 OMR, Rockefeller Family Archives, RAC; Jay Downer to Mother Provincial, May 29, 1936 and Nelson Rockefeller to John D. Rockefeller, Jr., December 21, 1936, folder 233B, box 35, Educational Interests series, RG 2 OMR, Rockefeller Family Archives, RAC; Nelson Rockefeller to Sr. Mary Gratia Maher, July 28, 1952, folder 233, box 35, Educational Interests series, RG 2 OMR, Rockefeller Family Archives, RAC.

[37] Sister Mary Gertrude to John D. Rockefeller, Jr., folder 232, box 35, Educational Interests series, RG 2 OMR, Rockefeller Family Archives, RAC.

[38] Although the school is still open today, Sister Gratia was principal when the school was located at a former location.

[39] Parrell, Mercy, 6.

[40] Sister Mary Jeremy Daigler, *Through the Windows: A History of the Work of Higher Education among the Sisters of Mercy of the Americas* (Scranton: University of Scranton Press, 2001), 131; Sister Mary Gratia Maher, The Organization of Religious Instruction in Catholic Colleges for Women (Washington, DC: The Catholic University of America Press, 1951).

[41] Parrell, Mercy, 2-4; Daigler, *Through the Windows*, 132.

[42] Dana Creel to Nelson Rockefeller, February 8, 1956, folder 233, box 35, Educational Interests series, RG 2 OMR, Rockefeller Family Archives, RAC; Public memory also ignores the fact that Mercy College operated on the site. In a 2011, articles cov-

ering local opposition to the construction of luxury homes on the Sisters' former Tarrytown property fail to mention that Mercy College opened and operated there for 10 years, instead focusing on only Our Lady of Victory Academy. See: Elaine Marranzano, "'Mansions' Return to Tarrytown's Wilson Park," Tarrytown-Sleepy Hollow Patch, July 26, 2011. <http://tarrytown.patch.com/articles/mansions-return-to-tarrytowns-wilson-park-but-pale-in-comparison-to-majestic-estates-of-past>

[43] William Yates to John D. Rockefeller Jr., November 19, 1956, folder 233, box 35, Educational Interests series, RG 2 OMR, Rockefeller Family Archives, RAC.

[44] Parrell, 4.

[45] Mother Mary Jeanne Ferrier to John D. Rockefeller Jr., March 25, 1958, folder 233, box 35, Educational Interests series, RG 2 OMR, Rockefeller Family Archives, RAC.

[46] Mother Mary Jeanne Ferrier to William Yates, December 4, 1956, folder 233, box 35, Educational Interests series, RG 2 OMR, Rockefeller Family Archives, RAC; William Yates to John D. Rockefeller Jr., October 22, 1956, folder 233, box 35, Educational Interests series, RG 2 OMR, Rockefeller Family Archives, RAC; William Yates to John D. Rockefeller Jr., May 23, 1957, folder 233, box 35, Educational Interests series, RG 2 OMR, Rockefeller Family Archives, RAC.

[47] William Yates to John D. Rockefeller Jr., February 15, 1956, folder 233, box 35, Educational Interests series, RG 2 OMR, Rockefeller Family Archives, RAC; William Yates to John D. Rockefeller Jr., March 3, 1956, folder 233, box 35, Educational Interests series, RG 2 OMR, Rockefeller Family Archives, RAC; William Yates to John D. Rockefeller Jr., October 22, 1956, folder 233, box 35, Educational Interests series, RG 2 OMR, Rockefeller Family Archives, RAC; Letter from John D. Rockefeller Jr., October 24, 1956, folder 233, box 35, Educational Interests series, RG 2 OMR, Rockefeller Family Archives, RAC.

[48] William Yates to John D. Rockefeller Jr., February 15, 1956, folder 233, box 35, Educational Interests series, RG 2 OMR, Rockefeller Family Archives, RAC; William Yates to John D. Rockefeller Jr., March 3, 1956, folder 233, box 35, Educational Interests series, RG 2 OMR, Rockefeller Family Archives, RAC; William Yates to John D. Rockefeller Jr., October 22, 1956, folder 233, box 35, Educational Interests series, RG 2 OMR, Rockefeller Family Archives, RAC; Letter from John D. Rockefeller Jr., October 24, 1956, folder 233, box 35, Educational Interests series, RG 2 OMR, Rockefeller Family Archives, RAC.

[49] William Yates to John D. Rockefeller Jr., July 15, 1957, folder 233, box 35, Educational Interests series, RG 2 OMR, Rockefeller Family Archives, RAC.

[50] Philip Keebler to John D. Rockefeller Jr., April 8, 1958, folder 233, box 35, Educational Interests series, RG 2 OMR, Rockefeller Family Archives, RAC; William Yates to Philip Keebler, March 28, 1958, folder 233, box 35, Educational Interests series, RG 2 OMR, Rockefeller Family Archives, RAC.

[51] Mother Mary Jeanne Ferrier to John D. Rockefeller Jr., March 25, 1958, folder 233, box 35, Educational Interests series, RG 2 OMR, Rockefeller Family Archives, RAC.

[52] John D. Rockefeller Jr. to Mother Mary Jeanne Ferrier, April 8, 1958, folder 233, box 35, Educational Interests series, RG 2 OMR, Rockefeller Family Archives, RAC.

[53] New York *Times*, June 23, 1958.

[54] Letter to Philip Keebler, April 7, 1958, folder 233, box 35, Educational Interests series, RG 2 OMR, Rockefeller Family Archives, RAC.

[55] William Yates to John D. Rockefeller Jr., June 25, 1958, folder 233, box 35, Educational Interests series, RG 2 OMR, Rockefeller Family Archives, RAC.

[56] William Yates to John D. Rockefeller Jr., November 6, 1957, folder 233, box 35, Educational Interests series, RG 2 OMR, Rockefeller Family Archives, RAC.

[57] *Daily News* (Tarrytown), June 1958; William Yates to John D. Rockefeller Jr., July 19, 1957, folder 233, box 35, Educational Interests series, RG 2 OMR, Rockefeller Family Archives, RAC; William Yates to John D. Rockefeller Jr., March 10, 1958, folder 233, box 35, Educational Interests series, RG 2 OMR, Rockefeller Family Archives, RAC.

[58] Memorandum to Mother Mary Jeanne Ferrier, July 6, 1959, folder 234, box 35, Educational Interests series, RG 2 OMR, Rockefeller Family Archives, RAC; Memorandum to Philip Keebler, August 19, 1958, folder 233, box 35, Educational Interests series, RG 2 OMR, Rockefeller Family Archives, RAC.

[59] Parrell, Mercy, 4; William Yates to Paul Folwell, August 6, 1958, folder 233, box 35, Educational Interests series, RG 2 OMR, Rockefeller Family Archives, RAC.

[60] Philip Keebler to William Yates, July 22, 1958, folder 233, box 35, Educational Interests series, RG 2 OMR, Rockefeller Family Archives, RAC.

[61] The event received wide media coverage. Examples: Catholic News, October 25, 1958; New York Times, October 22, 1958; Daily News (Tarrytown), October 21, 1958.

[62] The letters are contained in: Folder 234, box 35, Educational Interests series, RG 2 OMR, Rockefeller Family Archives, RAC.

[63] Protestant reformers, often from the middle and upper classes, had perceived poverty as a moral problem rooted in particular cultures. Thus, in Protestant logic, it was the immigrant cultures (a part of which was the Catholic religion) that posed the root of the problem. Consequently, Protestant Progressives had generally opposed the formation of Catholic schools, which they perceived as institutions that would perpetuate conditions of dependency. See: Fitzgerald, "Habits of Compassion," 215.

[64] The transcript is contained in: Folder 234, box 35, Educational Interests series, RG 2 OMR, Rockefeller Family Archives, RAC.

[65] William Yates to John D. Rockefeller Jr., August 19, 1958, folder 233, box 35, Educational Interests series, RG 2 OMR, Rockefeller Family Archives, RAC.

[66] William Yates to Philip Keebler, April 1, 1958, folder 233, box 35, Educational Interests series, RG 2 OMR, Rockefeller Family Archives, RAC; Daily News (Tarrytown), August 21, 1958; Daily News (Tarrytown), December 15, 1959.

[67] Philip Keebler to Robert Gumbel, September 4, 1958, folder 233, box 35, Educational Interests series, RG 2 OMR, Rockefeller Family Archives, RAC; Philip Keebler to William Sanders, September 4, 1958, folder 233, box 35, Educational Interests series, RG 2 OMR, Rockefeller Family Archives, RAC.

[68] Vera Goeller to Sister Mary Brendon, December 18, 1958, folder 233, box 35, Educational Interests series, RG 2 OMR, Rockefeller Family Archives, RAC.

[69] William Yates to Philip Keebler, January 29, 1959, folder 234, box 35, Educational Interests series, RG 2 OMR, Rockefeller Family Archives, RAC.

[70] Philip Keebler to John D. Rockefeller Jr., January 5, 1960, folder 233, box 35, Educational Interests series, RG 2 OMR, Rockefeller Family Archives, RAC.

[71] John D. Rockefeller Jr. to William Yates, March 13, 1958, folder 233, box 35, Educational Interests series, RG 2 OMR, Rockefeller Family Archives, RAC; William Yates to John D. Rockefeller Jr., October 22, 1956, folder 233, box 35, Educational Interests series, RG 2 OMR, Rockefeller Family Archives, RAC.

[72] Mother Mary Jeanne Ferrier to John D. Rockefeller Jr., June 28, 1959, folder 234, box 35, Educational Interests series, RG 2 OMR, Rockefeller Family Archives, RAC.

[73] Mother Mary Jeanne to John D. Rockefeller, Jr., 1960, folder 233, box 35, Educational Interests series, RG 2 OMR, Rockefeller Family Archives, RAC.

[74] Marranzano, "'Mansions' Return to Tarrytown's Wilson Park."

[75] The two buildings built with Rockefeller assistance that are not currently part of Mercy College's Dobbs Ferry Campus are the provincial house (also known as Christie Hall), which was demolished during the late 1980s to make room for what became The Landing at Dobbs Ferry, a townhouse development; and the Sacred Heart Catholic Church's parochial school, which is now the Alcott Montessori School.

Eric Martone, who earned his PhD in history from Stony Brook University, is Assistant Professor of History and Social Studies Education at Mercy College. He is the co-author, along with Michael Perrota, of *Mercy College: Yesterday and Today* (The History Press, 2013). The views expressed in this article are those of the author and do not represent the official position of Mercy College.

One Man's Contribution to the War Effort

by Robert E. Yott

As we enter the third year of the sesquicentennial of the Civil War, I feel it appropriate that remember one of the many veterans of Steuben County, whose tireless efforts helped to preserve the Union; Major John Stocum.

John Stocum was born in Pultney, Steuben County, on April 27, 1825. That same year his father drowned in the Conhocton River. Alone and penniless, John moved to Bath in1840. Here he learned the cabinet making and undertaking trade. In February of 1847 Stocum, a member of the First Presbyterian Church married Elizabeth Metcalf of Bath. Together they had at least three children; John L., James D. and daughter, Osie (nicknamed Kate.) When his son John was old enough he joined his father's business. The Directory of 1854 shows Stocum and Son had a warehouse located on the eastern edge of Pioneer Cemetery on West Steuben Street. In 1858 Elizabeth died. Stocum remarried in June of 1860. His new wife Susan B. Townsend of Elmira gave birth to Frank and Ruby.

In 1852, Stocum had joined the local militia, the 60th Regiment, 27th Brigade, New York State Volunteers and served as the orderly sergeant. When its commanding officer, Captain Levi C. Whiting, was promoted to major, Stocum was commissioned captain by New York governor Myron H. Clark. Stocum served in this capacity until 1858. He also served as watchman for the village of Bath from 1853 to 1857.

When the Civil War broke out in early 1861 President Lincoln called for troops. General Robert B. Van Valkenburgh of Bath asked Stocum to recruit members for a new regiment being formed, the First New York Light Artillery. Stocum wasted no time. In just two weeks enough men enlisted from Bath and nearby towns to form Battery E. Stocum was elected its captain.

Mustered into service in Elmira, Battery E departed for Washington, D.C in late October. It was here that the volunteer officers of the regiment would attend the school of instruction in tactics and gunnery.

Like many of the volunteer artillery officers, Captain Stocum failed to qualify. As a result, he was relieved of command and unceremoniously discharged from service. Command of the battery was given to newly promoted Captain Charles C. Wheeler of Bath. In the first week of January, 1862, Stocum returned home. New York Lieutenant-Governor Robert Campbell, also of Bath, wrote the War Department and demanded Stocum be reinstated or at least allowed to re-take the exam.

In February, armed with letters of introductions from Governor Campbell and the Honorable Guy McMasters of Bath, Stocum headed to Washington to meet with General James Wadsworth. The general ordered Stocum to Yorktown, Virginia where Battery E was stationed. Taking a steamer to Fortress Monroe, Stocum arrived in time to watch the "Monitor" and "Merrimac" do battle for the last time. After a three day's march with very little food Stocum was inside Union lines, where he found the boys of Battery E. After a brief and jubilant visit Stocum continued on to the division commander, General William F. Smith. After Stocum stated his business the general abruptly denied him a re-examination. Knowing that argument was futile Stocum returned to the battery.

The next morning saw Battery E heading out for their first battle. Stocum followed and remained 500 yards to the rear as his battery fired the first rounds in the battle for Yorktown. An artillery duel ensued and he watched as his boys knocked out the rebel artillery while taking several near-fatal hits. After the battle Stocum was commended by Colonel Guilford T. Bailey for having the best drilled battery in the regiment.

Stocum turned for home while Battery E, now known as Wheeler's Battery, would serve gallantly throughout the war. Being the first artillery unit to land on the peninsula, it fired the first shots on the Army of the Potomac's advance on Yorktown during the Peninsula Campaign. Although being nearly decimated by a lightning strike while on the peninsula, the battery continued to serve. It saw action at Antietam, Chancellorsville, Gettysburg, the Wilderness, Petersburg and Appomattox.

Disheartened, Stocum returned to Bath but his stay would be temporary. President Lincoln called for an additional 300,000 men in July of 1862 and for any districts unable to meet their quotas, a draft would be instituted. The War Committee, having limited success recruiting for the newly forming 161st New York Volunteer Infantry Regiment decided to call upon Stocum for assistance. Despite his recent experience with the military, Stocum agreed and immediately sprang into action. Again, in two weeks' time, one hundred men from Bath and Howard enlisted into Company F; sparing Bath the draft. Naturally, Stocum was elected captain.

In the last week of October, as the 161st was mustered into service at Elmira, a Typhoid epidemic broke out; claiming the lives of many soldiers there. Captain Stocum was severely affected and, while a majority of his regiment was being transported to the Department of the Gulf, he was ordered to the hospital. After three months, although not fully recovered, Stocum was able to resume command of his unit. He successfully led his company on many daring exploits during the battles of Plain's Store and the siege and surrender of Port Hudson. It was while on picket detail that Captain Stocum fell victim to heatstroke and was once again ordered to the hospital. This time the hope of a full recovery was slim and after two months Captain Stocum was again made to resign and he returned home.

Company F and the 161st fought on with great distinction throughout the war; taking part in Sherman's celebrated March to the Sea. They mustered out of service in November of 1865; suffering over 300 casualties.

Again, Stocum's return home was temporary. Lincoln made one final call for troops during the summer of 1864 and Captain Stocum, now sufficiently recovered, again answer the call. He pitched his tent in the village park in Bath and recruitment was swift. In nine days enough men had signed up to form up Company A of the 189th New York Infantry Regiment. Once again, Stocum was elected captain.

Promotions for senior commanders gave Captain Stocum the opportunity to take charge of the entire regiment which consisted of 10 companies. Here, Stocum displayed his natural leadership abilities. One such occurrence took place in January of 1865 when he marched his men eight miles to recover the body of fellow officer Captain Burrage Rice who was killed by bushwhackers. Entering a set of woods Stocum's men were met by the enemy and a fierce firefight ensued. His men drove off the enemy and the body of Captain Rice was recovered. After witnessing his courage and abilities, the commissioned officers of the 189th petitioned New York governor Reuben E. Fenton for Stocum's promotion to major. In February of 1865, the promotion was granted.

On April 9, 1865, the 189th was positioned around Appomattox Courthouse. It was here that two companies of his regiment had met and driven back the last rebel battery sent out by General Robert E. Lee. By 4:00pm General Lee had surrendered.

The 189th took part in the battles of Hatcher's Run, White Oak Ridge, Five Forks, the fall of Petersburg and the Battle for Appomattox. They had lost eighty enlisted men to combat and disease. After the surrender, the regiment marched from Appomattox to Washington D.C. where they took part in the Grand Review on May 23rd. They mustered out of service on June 1, 1865. Company A returned to Bath and they honored Major Stocum by forming in the village square so that Major Stocum could review his troops one last time and bid them farewell. To the townsfolk the mutual affection between the major and his men was obvious.

With the war over Major Stocum focused on his business. By the mid-1880s Stocum and Son had become the most prominent furniture business in this part of the country and the oldest of its kind in Bath. Stocum eventually bought the lot next to his and built a large addition, 100 feet long, two storied with a full basement, to serve as a showroom divided into five showcases. A majority of its stock; chairs, book cases, sideboard tables, bedroom suites, dressing cases and many other items was manufactured on the premises. They also offered upholstering.

His was the leading undertaking trade the in the county as well and he served as vice-president of the Steuben Country Undertakers Association. The morgue, located at 115 West Morris Street (known as Stocum's Point) provided a large range of caskets, coffins and burglar-proof grave vaults. His son John was a certified embalmer. They owned three hearses; one of which was white, the only one of its kind in this part of the country. Because he offered such a wide variety in both trades his low prices rivaled those found in Elmira and Rochester. Stocum and Son were known to their customers as "...honest, square dealing and energetic men."

When the Grand Army of the Republic Soldiers Home of the State of New York was established here in Bath in 1876, Major Stocum was appointed the official undertaker of the institution. Stocum, according to his obituary, had wished that, "...he might be permitted to bury his comrades at the Home as long as he should live" did so for a nominal fee. In the early 1880s a competitor demanded bids be accepted for the position. Trustees of the Home had no choice but to agree. The competitor submitted a ridiculously low bid which Stocum knew would break any undertaking business. Compelled by loyalty to his comrades, Stocum offered to continue as undertaker for two thirds his competitor's price. He would rather donate the casket with a plaque engraved "Our Comrade" mounted on it than to have his competitor, who did not serve during the war, perform the services. Stocum was retained as undertaker and by the time of his death, he had buried nearly 2,000 veterans at the Home.

Unlike many of his comrades at the time Major Stocum, an ardent Democrat, never dabbled in politics. He became a member of Custer Post No. 81, G.A.R. of Bath on June 28, 1878. On several occasions, Stocum served as Marshall of the Day during the Memorial Day ceremonies in Bath. It was remarked that he "...looked every inch the soldier" as he donned the same uniform he wore in Appomattox when Lee surrendered. When Bath celebrated its centennial in 1893, it was Major Stocum the planning committee asked to record the military history of the town. The Sons of Veterans of Bath also honored Stocum by naming their camp after him.

In November of 1889, he purchased a cottage site along the west shore of Keuka Lake. The following spring he began work on a three-story hotel which he named Ruby Cottage Hotel. Next to it he had built a smaller house called the "Stocum House." Major Stocum hosted several reunions here for the three hundred plus men he recruited for the war. Members of Battery E (now referring to themselves as Stocum's Battery,) Company F and Company A were brought to the hotel from Hammond-sport by Stocum's steamer yacht, the Sally Beekman. In August, 1895, Stocum sold his summer hotel property, to Simeon Rathbone of Elmira who renamed the place "Snug Harbor" and used it as a private residence. The property still goes by that name today.

Major Stocum died February 5, 1905. As the oldest businessman in Bath he enjoyed passing his later years sitting on his porch, reminiscing. His contribution to the war effort and to the community has certainly earned him a place in the annals of Steuben County.

About the author: Robert Yott, author of *From Soldiers' Home to Medical Center* lives in Mitchellsville and is a carpenter by trade. He built his own cannon with limber and his unit represents Wheeler's Battery at Civil War reenactment, parades and educational programs. A portion of his artifacts from the Civil War and Bath Soldiers' Home collection wereon display in 2012 at the New York State Museum in Albany as part of their exhibition commemorating the 150th anniversary of the Civil War.

How the Piarists and the Docent Saved Frank Lloyd Wright's Graycliff

by Paul E. Lubienecki, Ph.D.

"Dear Dar:

I have been-seen-talked to, admired one of nature's noblemen-Mr. Frank Lloyd Wright. He is not a freak-not a crank-highly educated and polished, a straightforward business like man with high ideals.

He would be pleased indeed to design your House. Mr. Wright says he don't want any man to accept his ideas just because they are his-he proposes to furnish a reason for his ideas and wants judgment made solely on the merits.

He will build you the finest, most sensible house in Buffalo. You will be the envy of every rich man in Buffalo, it will be published in all the Buffalo papers, it will be talked about all over the East. You will never grow tired of his work, and what more can you ask? He is pure gold."[i]

This letter, dated October 22, 1902, from Chicago businessman William E. Martin to his brother Darwin, would forever alter the architectural landscape of Buffalo, New York and establish a strong and enduring friendship between Frank Lloyd Wright and the Martins. Through the years, the distances and the personal and professional tumults, Darwin Martin and Wright remained steadfast in their mutual admiration. In his autobiography, Wright states "I would like to tell...especially of the lifelong interest and loyalty of Darwin D. Martin and the building of several houses for him..."[ii]

In 1904 Darwin Martin commissioned Wright to construct a house for him on a lot at Jewett Parkway in Buffalo. This house became the epitome of the Prairie Style home. It was the image of the Midwest prairie: a broad, flat, horizontal plain that meets the horizon. To translate this into architecture, Wright designed a horizontal building that was low to the ground as if it was growing from the soil. The architectural features of the Prairie Style incorporated horizontal rather than vertical lines. The roof was cantilevered to symbolize the branches of a tree. Usually the structure was two stories with a one story wing or porch. There were bands of casement windows and the other windows designed with colored patterns. But this created dark interiors which did not suit Darwin's wife Isabelle. Belle, as she was lovingly called, enjoyed the brightness and colors of the outdoors and the amount of light entering the new house proved to be insufficient for her.

Due to sound investments, and a substantial salary as an executive at the Larkin Company, Darwin was a millionaire by 1907. When he retired on September 1,1925, his estimated net worth was close to $2,500,000. The couple planned to enjoy their retirement years and spent the summers at the Lake Placid Club in the Adirondack Mountains. But Belle's health and eye condition made travel more inconvenient for them.

The Summer House

There was no direct indication who wanted a summer home. The Martins had purchased property in 1909 in Bay Beach, Canada along the Lake Erie shoreline. Wright was initially commissioned to design a summer home there, but it was never built and the property later sold.[iii] In mid-April 1926, Darwin purchased an eight acre lot in Derby, New York, just twenty-two miles from their Jewett Parkway home, for the construction of the summer house. It was Belle's impaired vision that contributed to her continuing unhappiness with the "darkness" of the house at Jewett Parkway designed for her husband and she wanted something bright and airy. Aside from its shadows that plagued her, the house also failed to provide bedrooms of a size she preferred, and it lacked ample closets.[iv] By the mid-1920's, with Mrs. Martin's health inhibiting her vacation travel to Lake Placid, the decision was made to build a summer home closer to Buffalo. It would be the antidote to the Jewett Parkway house.

The ideal location was at the top of a fifty foot cliff on the shores of Lake Erie in Derby, New York. Darwin knew of the location from the

Larkin Family when he was a guest, in the 1880's, at their nearby camp site known as Idlewood.[v] Darwin purchased eight acres from Dexter Rumsey, who owned a neighboring estate. This lot extended from Lake Shore Road to the cliff and was two hundred fifty feet in width.[vi] It would come to be affectionately known as Graycliff.[vii]

Wright encounters Isabelle

At this time, Isabelle wrote to Frank Lloyd Wright requesting: "Are you entirely free and fully disposed to design severely simple two story house for lake shore for Martin Family for early construction and occupancy. Specifications not important. No superintendent required..."[viii]

Wright was embroiled in his own personal difficulties at this time which consumed his energies and the letter went unanswered.

A few weeks later Darwin wrote to him requesting a reply. Wright responded: "Free and fully disposed to serve you to the best of my ability, terms regular."[ix] He invited them to Taliesin but Darwin telegrammed back:

"Your client is Mrs. Martin. She is unable to travel and everything must be made as easy as possible for her."[x]

He reminded Wright that in 1910 the architect had made a sketch for a proposed summer home, on the Canadian shores of Lake Erie, which was never constructed. That design might suffice for the summer home they now planned, except that Isabelle wanted bedrooms on the second floor. Darwin requested that a "black crayon on white paper sketch" for the design be sent as soon as possible for Mrs. Martin's inspection.[xi]

Several different design sketches were presented and either altered or rejected, not so much by Darwin but by Isabelle. Belle became fully involved in the planning and design of the summer estate at Graycliff. It was to be her house. While Darwin was in near worship of Wright, Belle was not as enamored of the architect. The continuous alterations made this a test of wills. In the frenetic correspondence between Martin and Wright, Darwin often had to remind the architect who he worked for: "Your client is Mrs. Martin. If a house is built it is only for her pleasure and we must make a joy to her of the very planning and building."[xii]

The original plans featured a two-story living room on the lake side of the house, characteristic of Wright's own home in Wisconsin: Taliesin.[xiii] As architectural historian Henry-Russell Hitchcock bemoaned, Graycliff has the same "vocabulary as Taliesin but as is it was unsupervised (by the architect) it is not one of Wright's really satisfactory houses."[xiv]

The two-story living room plan was dismissed because of Isabelle's declining health and heating concerns. More importantly, the Martins wanted a view of Lake Erie: "no two story living room, entrance hall wider and must have a vista to the lake."[xv] Darwin advised that this was to be only a summer residence, and he would relay his wife's revisions to the noted architect. Letters continued, nearly everyday in June and July, concerning alterations and adjustments. Belle's letter to Wright of June 29, 1926 was most detailed and, in a somewhat aggravated tone, requested that the architect: "move the maid's bathroom"; "what is the cost of the flooring material"; "stair may turn at right angle not winding"; "what is the cost of the copper pipe"; "move the south wall further out"; "all windows on the first floor are to open out"[xvi] Basically, these were the same questions that any homeowner asks the architect or contractor when they are designing a custom home.

A woman who knew her own mind was the kind of client Wright emphatically did not want unless she was a special kind of enlightened woman who wanted the kind of house he wanted.[xvii] Belle taunted the architect about her continued list of revisions writing " with all the realm of architectural design at your command your unparalleled genius surely will not balk at this small problem."[xviii] Not wanting to offend this patron and loose the commission, especially at a time of personal financial difficulties, Wright wryly replied that Isabelle does not appear to understand what is involved in the design process and that "I will do my damnedest, as she seems to be doing, 'Angels can do no more.'"[xix] The experience of designing Graycliff would prove to be a joyless experience for everyone concerned.[xx] However her confidence in him slowly increased. By 1928, after her first summer in the house, Belle wrote to Wright proclaiming that "We can't proceed a step without you."[xxi]

The Grammar of Graycliff

Wright eventually developed the specifications for the lake house property. The house would be parallel to the lake with a garden wall connecting it to the garage and therefore forming an L shape. He connected the element of water to the house by placement of a pool in the center of the driveway circle. The L shape is repeated throughout and is the architectural shape-relationship or "grammar" of the house. Wright purposely set the house back from the cliff's edge the same distance as the height of the cliff's wall creating an L.[xxii] Wright believed that a house "should be a grammatical expression of an organic integrity"; it should be a complete design.[xxiii] By "grammar" Wright was expressing a relationship of the natural elements to the entirety of the structure. Wright observed:

> "Every house worth considering as a work of art must have a grammar of its own. 'Grammar' in this sense means the same thing in any construction - whether it be of words or of stone or wood. It is the shape-relationship between the various elements that enter into the construction of the thing. The 'grammar' of the house is its manifest articulation of all its parts. Your limitations of feeling... your choice of materials for the doing (and your budget of course) determine largely what grammar your building will use."[xxiv]

Driving onto the property through two stone piers, the visitor views Lake Erie and the horizon before any buildings are encountered. Wright developed a diagonal axis across the property aligning it with the setting sun to conform with the geology of the site.[xxv] The architect followed form in his use of natural light for the summer house:

> "The best way to light a house is God's way - the natural way, as nearly as possible in the daytime and at night as nearly like the day as may

be, or better. The sun is the great luminary of all life. It should serve as such in the building of any house."[xxvi]

Wright's personal dictum "out of the ground and into the light" refered to the organic process of building and, because of its nature, a structure is never finished.[xxvii]

Graycliff filled this descriptive pattern. After all the revisions, proposed additions and alterations, building started in 1926 and concluded in the early 1930's. At this time, Wright's life was an entanglement of personal crises (with his soon-to-be former wife) and financial difficulties (a pending foreclosure on Taliesin). On September 18, 1926, John Lloyd Wright, the architect's son, sent a letter to Darwin stating that he would be supervising the project "Have been requested to continue architectural services, trust I may be allowed to inspire your confidence in my ability to serve you in this matter."[xxviii] An agitated Darwin insisted that Frank Lloyd Wright be available to handle the construction of Graycliff personally "I hope you will understand and perhaps agree with me when I say there is only one Frank Lloyd Wright and no one can substitute for him. I hope Mr. Wright's retreat is not so remote that he cannot give us the cooperation promised."[xxix] John sheepishly replied "I am not trying to impersonate Frank Lloyd Wright, I am simply trying to help him, his work and you at this time."[xxx]

Wright originally designed the main house as two houses joined by a second story bridge, further defining the view of the lake. It would be a screen between the land and the lake. At the front of the house the porte cochere[xxxi] extends over its stone pier supports and continues over a stone basin from which water flows into a pool.[xxxii] Originally, the Martins requested that the architect "eliminate the porte-cochere and substitute glass awning as was verbally asked when you were here."[xxxiii] That request was ignored by the architect. Wright's vision was to create the natural impression of the lake flowing through the house; he later revisited this concept with his design of the Kaufmann House, better known as Fallingwater.[xxxiv]

As with any custom built home, there will always be a degree of disconnect between the Client and the Architect. The Martins were continually altering the house designs and these changes exasperated Wright. Ultimately, Wright knew that his friend and client, Darwin Martin, would get the house that Belle wanted. However, this was not the summer cottage that was first envisioned by the Martins. They received a different type of summer house unlike anything ever conceived by Wright. He submitted designs that favored a hip roof, which the Martin's approved. Above the porte cochere, on the second floor, is a diamond shaped window. This configuration is repeated in the roof to the left and at the end of the porte cochere. This window is set in tichenor limestone, located ten to twelve feet below the surface of the property and also on the cliff face.[xxxv]

Wright built on the "human scale". He designed the house, and its corresponding objects, to appear of normal size. He understood that people responded to differing scales and experienced space and form by way of empathic experience. A hulking fireplace with a low mantle combined with low ceilings made occupants feel taller and more in command of the space and vistas.[xxxvi] By doing this doors, windows, stairs, placement of handles and switches fell within the range of familiar experience.[xxxvii] It was the continuous presence of the organic in the details and an observed trait at Graycliff.

Isabelle, renowned for her floral arrangements, was at home in her garden, and Wright designed Graycliff to fulfill her needs with gardens at the front and rear of the house. The home was filled with her bouquets from the flower beds, and guests would leave with baskets of vegetables from the other gardens.[xxxviii] Eventually, the Martins hired landscape architect Ellen Biddle Shipman to reconstitute and revise Wright's landscaping scheme, including the removal of the pond in the circle.[xxxix]

Even though Wright designed the house it was understood, by all, that the summer house had always been Belle's concept. The Martin family enjoyed the summers there with Isabelle entertaining or holding afternoon teas. There was a genuine grace and charm to the residence because of Isabelle. By opening up the house, it allowed for nature and light to enter and bring the family together and make living more relaxed, certainly as it should be at a summer house.[xl] Wright planned this building to be in harmony with the bounty of the natural surroundings. It was a positive influence on the living patterns of the family. This truly mystical, if not spiritual, experience was only enjoyed for several more years.

The End of Belle's Summer House

The stock market crash of 1929 and an adverse tax decision in 1933 eroded the Martin's fortune and likely contributed to Darwin's declining health.[xli] Starting in 1929, Darwin sustained a series of mild strokes and a more serious episode, on December 17, 1935, resulted in his death. It was reported that upon hearing of Darwin's death, Wright stated he had lost his best friend and most influential patron. "I only wish I had been less taking and more giving where he was concerned" lamented Wright.[xlii] Over the years, Darwin loaned or gave Wright approximately $70,000. None of it was ever repaid.

With Darwin's death, Belle was unable to cope with the financial difficulties. She attempted to sell the home and furniture on Jewett Parkway and even Graycliff, but there were no buyers. In 1937, Isabelle effectively abandoned the main residence in Buffalo, not even bothering to lock the door behind her. She moved into an apartment, owned by her son, located at 800 West Ferry Street in the city.[xliii]

In 1940, Belle, with her aide Cora Herrick, moved in with daughter Dorothy. She continued to summer at Graycliff until 1943 but stayed in the former chauffeur's apartment since she could not afford to open the main house.[xliv] Bedridden the last two years of her life, this gentle and gracious lady died on February 22, 1945 at the age of seventy-five.[xlv]

The summers at Graycliff were warmly recalled by Margaret Reidpath Foster, the granddaughter of Isabelle and Darwin Martin, on her visit to the estate in August, 2005. Her thoughts were of the house filled with sunlight, abundant flowers and refreshing breezes from the lake. change [xlvi] Margaret remembered the enjoyment of splashing in the fountain by the porte cohere and of sitting on the terrace and looking through the house to see Lake Erie. "We'd open all the windows in the music room and Aunt Polly would play the piano, and I would sing. Then the birds outside would sing. It was a harmonious place. Joyful. There was no sadness."[xlvii]

The Martin's grandson, Darwin Foster, also has fond memories of the summer house. He remembers limousines lining the drive when Belle entertained or held afternoon tea.[xlviii] Flowers could be found in the gardens and bouquets throughout the residence. Croquet on the front lawn or a house filled with over night guests was reminiscent of the civility and tranquility of the summer estate.

These pleasant times would not long endure. Just prior to 1929's "Black Friday" Darwin, in failing health, established the Buffalo Phoenix Corporation as an investment and insurance company for his son, Darwin R. Martin, to operate and manage the family wealth.[xlix] Due to under performing investments, the Great Depression eroded the Martins' fortune. During this time, both estates were owned and maintained by the Buffalo Phoenix Corporation. In 1946, the City of Buffalo took possession of the city property for back taxes, while the summer house remained vacant.[l]

Scholarum Piarum

In 1949 a priest of the Buffalo Diocese, Father Julius Szabo, petitioned Bishop O'Hara to introduce a religious order of men from Hungary into the diocese as they were accomplished in their education skills.[li] The Scholarum Piarum (of the Pious schools) or Piarist Fathers, were founded by St. Joseph Calasanctius in 1617. Moved by the misery of the poor children of Rome, he opened a free school for them in 1597, which was available to all children regardless of religion, and is considered to be the first modern public elementary school.[lii] The hallmark of this religious order would be the education of youth, especially the underprivileged, providing them with the highest quality of instruction.

As do many other religious communities, members of the Piarist Order, profess vows of poverty, chastity and obedience. In addition, the members of this order also profess a fourth vow to dedicate their lives to the education of youth. In 1948, Pope Pius XII named St. Joseph Calasanctius the "Patron of all Christian Schools."[liii]

With these prominent credentials, several Piarist fathers traveled from the provincial house in Devon, Pennsylvania to Buffalo, New York in 1949. Upon their arrival, the Fathers began searching for a property that could become a local foundation for a school, a residence for the priests and also to be utilized for other religious functions.[liv] The priests, mostly of Hungarian descent, became a welcomed addition for the ethnic Hungarians in western New York, southern Ontario and northern Ohio, receiving donations and assistance from this community. [lv]

The Piarists at Graycliff

In 1951, the Fathers decided upon the former Martin Family estate in Derby, New York and purchased the property from the Buffalo Phoenix Corporation for $50,000.[lvi] It became a focal point for education and Hungarian culture in the area. The main residence and other buildings were suitable and would need some alterations to accommodate the needs of these unassuming and humble priests.

Initially, Mass was celebrated in the living room, but it was soon apparent that a chapel was needed for formal worship. The garage was considered but there were other future plans for that building. Consideration was given to building a separate structure, but the costs were prohibitive.[lvii] It was decided to enclose the south terrace and convert the space into a chapel. The work was done by a local contractor and volunteer members of the local Hungarian community.[lviii] The workers filled in the sunken garden area with concrete to bring it even with the stone terrace. An outer wall was constructed on top of the stone wall and the interior doors were moved to that wall to serve as windows. The clear glass was replaced by colored, opaque glass to simulate stained glass windows. The roof was extended from the cantilevered second floor corridor to cover the new structure.[lix]

St. Michael's Chapel was a small, modest sacred space that could accommodate approximately fifty worshipers. Naturally, it was the raison d'etre, the life of this small religious community. After the pronouncements of the Second Vatican Council in 1965, the altar and tabernacle were moved away from the back wall; this was the only significant alteration to the chapel during the Piarist ownership.[lx] Flowers that decorated the altar and house came from the flower beds in front and along side of the main house. These were the same gardens that Isabelle tended.[lxi]

Prayer is central to the life of the priest and the community of faith and as such, daily Mass was celebrated as was the recitation of the Liturgy of the Hours.[lxii] The Chapel was also the central focus for special occasions. Christmas and New Year's Day Mass were particularly well attended by the local community with an overflow crowd into the living room and dining area. The holidays were fondly remembered by all the guests and visitors to the house. Traditional old world decorations framed the celebration, and there was the singing of Hungarian Christmas Carols. This was followed by a feast of Hungarian specialties shared by all.[lxiii]

The Piarist Fathers continued with their adjustments to the main building. An aluminum frame and glass enclosure was added to part of the second floor north terrace.[lxiv] This was the area facing the lake off of Mrs. Martin's room. The roof shingles were replaced in the late 1950's, as some minor leaking was discovered. The winters were brutality cold, with the lake winds penetrating the house designed as a summer residence. In the mid to late 1960's, a forced air natural gas heat system was added, which entailed alterations to the walls and the addition of duct work. The priests were told this would make the house warmer but it did not have a great impact so some areas of the house were closed off.[lxv]

The "heat hut" was later utilized as a wine cellar, but it was seldom used. It held sacramental wines and homemade wines given as gifts. It became a source of local folklore for all the wines that were not stored there. The priests were more proud of the homemade honey from the hives on the property that was also stored in the hut.[lxvi]

Father Stephen Gerencser, Sch.P. was the influential leader of the initial group of priests to settle at what the Fathers would simply call "the Derby House".[lxvii] He knew of the legacy of Frank Lloyd Wright and that the Order was fortunate to live in this special place. The mission of Fr. Gerencser was to start a school for gifted children from pre-kindergarten through high school, and so he began the Calasanctius School in Buffalo soon after the Piarists arrived.

In 1955, near the main entrance to the Graycliff property, a two story concrete block school building was erected. This building originally was used as a school, but by the early 1960's was converted to a boarding house for students attending Calasanctius High School.[lxviii] The high school was located on Windsor Avenue in Buffalo, and ironically was only a few blocks from Darwin Martin's home on Jewett Parkway. Due to financial difficulties the school closed in 1991.[lxix]

At the Derby House, the garage and apartments were also enlarged into living space to accommodate a novitiate.[lxx] The first novices arrived in 1966 and the novitiate program lasted until it was transferred to Florida in 1982. Duties for a young novice consisted of cutting the grass, painting where needed, general maintenance and shoveling snow.[lxxi] Afterward this building, the former residence of Isabelle's daughter, was eventually used for religious retreats. During the course of the Hungarian Revolution of 1956, refugees were temporarily housed at Graycliff while they sought asylum or were in transition.[lxxii] Additionally, the Fathers constructed a gym at the south end of the property in 1957.

By the late 1980's, enrollment at Calasanctius High School was declining and the number of Piarist Fathers who could staff the school was dwindling. To continue in the spirit of the order, the Evans Pre-School Center was opened at the site of the former school building in 1979.[lxxiii] Later, St. Michael's School, a Catholic elementary institution, was formed in 1987. Both schools unfortunately did not remain open for extended periods.[lxxiv]

The number of Piarist Fathers occupying the residence, not including novices, varied from as many as nine to the final two in 1999. The estate was always lively and filled with people- either novices, those on a spiritual retreat or guests.[lxxv] Every May, there was the May Crowning of the Virgin Mary. In July, the Piarist Guild conducted a Lawn Fete to raise money for the school and in August, the Fathers would hold a Garden Party to raise money for the upkeep of the property, which was in need of repairs.[lxxvi] These events were well attended and anxiously anticipated by the participants.

Wright Returns

Of the many guests to visit Graycliff, the most notable was its designer: Frank Lloyd Wright. He first visited the site in April 1927 one year after the land was purchased and several months into the construction of the structures. He made a few other visits to the summer house, having dinner with the Martins in the Summer of 1929 and attempting to dissuade Darwin from a third floor addition to the main house.

In the Spring of 1936, several months after Darwin had died, Wright and some of his students were traveling from Buffalo to Pittsburgh. En route to Pittsburgh, they stopped by Graycliff to pay their respects to Isabelle who was not at the summer house. Upon entering the main house, Wright directed the group to remove the furniture covers, and the noted architect began to rearrange the furniture. After that, he instructed the students to get knives from the kitchen and cut some flowers which were placed in vases in the living room. Wright left a note for the Martins: "Stopped by to visit you, FLLW, your architect."[lxxvii]

But the most notable visitation, one that has taken on mythical proportions, was the architect's last visit to Graycliff in October 1958 just months before his death in April of 1959. The ninety-one year old Wright made a surprise visit to the property. He surveyed the changes to the main house: the addition of the chapel at the south terrace, the new school building, and the overgrown gardens. According to then rector, Fr. Alphonse Vereck, the agitated architect emerged from his car and, shaking his cane at the house, clamored: "Who did this? Who made these changes? This is not my work!"[lxxviii] The priest explained to the noted architect that as a religious community of priests they needed a chapel. Wright replied in disgust: "Well, I guess if you need it."[lxxix]

The Sgraffito

Not all of the treasures at the Derby House can be credited to Frank Lloyd Wright. In 1967, noted Polish artist Josef Slawinski created a mural of St. Joseph Calasanctius in commemoration of the 350th anniversary of the founding of the Piarist Order. The large 12x18 foot mural graced the side of the school building erected by the Order. It portrays the Saint on a panoramic view of Rome surrounded by the children he sought to educate.[lxxx]

The mural is a sgraffito. This is a very labor intensive technique in which the artist applies four layers of pigmented cement to a wall surface. The first one is black, the second red, then yellow and finally white while all the cement layers are still wet. Then, the wet layers of cement are carefully scraped away to create the image.[lxxxi]

In 2001, the Polish Arts Club of Buffalo was contacted about preserving the mural as this building was to be demolished. Through the efforts of this cultural organization, the mural was saved and restored. In November, 2005, it was placed in a special wall structure on the north side of the E. H. Butler Library at Buffalo State College, Buffalo, New York.

The Fathers Prepare to Leave

In 1991, Calasanctius High School closed its doors, and only three priests remained in residence at Graycliff. Their primary duties were to minister to the local Hungarian community and assist the Church where needed. These clerics were in their late seventies, and so housekeeping and maintenance of the buildings and grounds was nearly impossible. The main use of the Derby House was as a private retreat center. The complex was nearing the end of its intended purpose. The buildings were showing signs of age and neglect. The roof, chimney, windows and driveway all needed to be replaced; there was a broken gas pipeline that had to be repaired. Heating costs proved to be a drain on the meager financial resources of the community.[lxxxii]

During the 1995 annual visit by the Provincial, a dialogue began concerning the future health of the priests, their limited duties and the financial burden of maintaining the Derby House. The possibility of selling the property was realized. The priests were reluctant to leave their home. It had become a place of contemplative prayer and beauty for them. Their mission was to minister to the faith community and conduct retreats, but their ability to continue was dwindling.[lxxxiii] Through the first half of 1996, the discussions continued and it was decided that the property would be sold and the remaining priests transferred to a small Hungarian parish, the Assumption of the Blessed Virgin Mary, in Lackawanna, New York.[lxxxiv]

During the years, the Piarist Fathers recognized that their house was significant because of the design and the architect. Fr. Miskolczy contacted the Frank Lloyd Wright Building Conservancy in Chicago for an assessment of the buildings and the current fair market value.[lxxxv] They responded that the estate was worth $1.1 million dollars, but that was dependent upon the condition of the property. The estate, worn and weathered, tattered and torn could not justify the estimated value. The initial asking price was $500,000 based on the recommendation of the real estate agency and Father Provincial.[lxxxvi] The "For Sale" sign was posted on July 12, 1996. While several potential buyers expressed interest, there were no serious offers to purchase the former Martin estate. The local government, residents and Frank Lloyd Wright devotees were concerned that the property would be sold to a developer and the buildings demolished to be replaced by lake side condominiums. But the Piarist Fathers were determined that this valuable Wright property remained intact.

The Docent

The Darwin Martin House in Buffalo, was in the midst of a renovation and rehabilitation of the property in the 1990's. It was the more well known of the Wright structures in western New York and so it received the lion's share of attention and funding. It was here that the seeds of salvation for Graycliff were planted. A volunteer docent at the Martin House, Carol Bronnenkant, and others were discussing the sale of Graycliff in December, 1996. It was assumed that a developer would purchase the site, demolish the buildings and construct high valued condominiums, as was done at the former Dexter Rumsey Estate.[lxxxvii]

This docent, with a thirst for preserving architectural history, was interested in viewing the interior of the house before its presumed destruction. In discussing Graycliff with her husband, it was decided to contact the realtor and visit the estate under the alias as a potential buyer.[lxxxviii] The family toured the house the following month and realized that the structures were in need of a major renovation. However, walking through the structures and absorbing the vistas of Lake Erie, Bronnenkant received her avocation at that moment. She was determined that the estate should be saved and not be a part of local architectural infamy like Wright's other significant structure in Buffalo, the Larkin Administration Building, which was demolished in the 1950's.

The Graycliff Conservancy

Bronnenkant realized that this was a movement that she alone would foster. A call to action meeting was scheduled on March 18, 1997 at the Buffalo and Erie County Historical Society. It attracted over one hundred and twenty Wright enthusiasts. From this, a core of thirty formed the nucleus of what ultimately became the Graycliff Conservancy Incorporated.[lxxxix] Their venture was profoundly simple: purchase and restore Graycliff to its elemental beauty. The final goal was to return the estate to the 1930's as if Belle was still there, somewhere on the property, anticipating the arrival of her guests for afternoon tea.

To do this, funding was needed to first secure ownership and then preserve the property. The money came from grants, fund raising efforts and corporate support. However, the Conservancy's first task was to secure enough money to take an option on the property for $20,000 by December 1, 1997.[xc] The Conservancy had bid $420,000 for the estate, which was $30,000 less than the selling price. They still needed to raise the additional amount within nine months. There were more than fifty interested parties and better offers, but the Conservancy appeared to have had a more "workable" plan for the purchase.[xci]

Bronnenkant was pleased that the Piarist Order supported the Conservancy's bid as she stated: "I view it as a sign of trust from the Piarist Fathers. It shows that they still care about the property. Our conservancy feels like we've been entrusted with this property and entrusted to preserve the area's architectural heritage." The priests who still resided at Graycliff realized the value of the property from an historical and aesthetical perspective. Their personal feelings, as well as those of the Piarist Order, was to save and preserve the property as a museum type of structure for the enjoyment of future generations. [xcii]

Fund raising events continued which included arranging for the Martins' granddaughter as a speaker and black tie gala functions brought in enough money to meet the option deadline. Obtaining the additional funds was an equally daunting task, and due to foresight, extensions were negotiated into the sales contract. This enabled the Conservancy to gain extra time to find the necessary supplemental revenue streams and also allowed for some creative methods to raise awareness of the project.[xciii]

While the Piarist Fathers were still in residence, tours were offered of the Derby House. It was an arrangement that suited all parties. For Bronnenkant, the numbers were staggering. Four thousand people toured the estate in the first year (1998) and and many became paid supporting members of the Conservancy.[xciv] The Piarist Fathers were very supportive and welcoming of their guests. The priests believed that the tours were good for helping the Conservancy buy the house and it was an opportunity to show the visitors who the Piarists were. It was hoped by seeing the Chapel, that some would be reminded of "who is the real Creator of this place." [xcv] However, money was still an issue.

In late 1998, the Baird Foundation became a viable partner in the efforts to save Graycliff by agreeing to underwrite the purchase of the property by the Conservancy. The Foundation's manager, Catherine Schweitzer, stated that the "purchase and restoration of Graycliff will benefit the entire community."[xcvi] The Foundation provided a $200,000 cash grant with a guaranteed $450,000 bank mortgage for the acquisition of Belle's summer house. With the newly acquired funds, the Conservancy was able to commission an historic structures report on the cost to restore the property and determine how the complex should be utilized.[xcvii] On April 5, 1999, the Graycliff Conservancy took formal possession of the property from the Piarist Order; the estate had been rescued.

The journal entry in the *Historia Domus* for April 5, 1999 begins:

> *"The day of doom for Derby House; the selling has been effectuated this day, Our Motherhouse gone!"[xcviii] For the humble, elderly priests, it was a sad day to leave their home. The Mass that day was somber as that of a funeral liturgy. It was followed by a procession around the grounds with incense in thanksgiving for what had been and as a blessing for those past, present and future guests to this sacred place.[xcix]*

Items from the chapel were donated to a local retreat house and others either given away or taken to the new Piarist residence in Lackawanna, New York. Naturally, the priests were dismayed at leaving. This now closed the door on the Derby House, which had been the Piarist Father's home for nearly fifty years.

It also was the end of Graycliff as a family dwelling and residence, originally for the Martins and then the Piarist community. This space is one of beauty, that melds the elements of nature to the structure. At Graycliff, the visitor senses the gentleness of the surroundings and realizes that it is actually Isabelle's lingering presence: a warm and genuine welcome for her guests. This space, one that was sacred first in an earthy and then a religious way, would now begin a rebirth, returning it to the essence of what was originally Belle's summer house.

Endnotes:

[i] Letter from William Martin to Darwin Martin of October 2, 1902. Darwin Martin papers, MS 22.8, Box 1, Folder 1. (University Archives, University at Buffalo).

[ii] *Frank Lloyd Wright, An Autobiography.* (New York: Duell, Sloan and Pearce, 1943), p. 253.

[iii] Ibid., p. 6.

[iv] Ramona Pando Whitaker. "The Belle of Graycliff", Buffalo as an Architectural Museum website. HTTP: //ah.phpwebhosting.com/a/DERBY/belle/index.html.

[v] Patrick J. Mahoney, "Frank Lloyd Wright, Unexecuted Designs for Western New York." Western New York Heritage, Spring 1999 Vol 3, No, 1, p. 38.

[vi] Docent handbook material from Graycliff Tour, 2005, p. 5.

[vii] In September 1928, a house guest Paul A. Harsh, suggested the name of the residence be called "Graycliff" in honor of its location at the top of the bluff and the gray hues of the surrounding rocks. From Darwin Martin papers, MS 22.8, p. 6. (University Archives, University at Buffalo).

[viii] Darwin Martin papers, MS 22.8, Box 4, Folder 4-23. (University Archives, University at Buffalo).

[ix] Anita L. Mitchell. *Darwin D. and Isabelle R. Martin.* Docent material from Graycliff, January 2005, p. 6.

[x] Darwin Martin papers, MS 22.8, Box 4, Folder 4-23. (University Archives, University at Buffalo).

[xi] Darwin Martin papers, MS 22.8, Box 4, Folder 4-23. (University Archives, University at Buffalo).

[xii] Darwin Martin papers, MS 22.8, Box 4, Folder 4-24. (University Archives, University at Buffalo).

[xiii] Mahoney, "Frank Lloyd Wright, Unexecuted Designs for Western New York", p. 39.

[xiv] Henry-Russell Hitchcock, *In The Nature of Materials, The Buildings of Frank Lloyd Wright: 1887-1941.* (New York: Da Capo Press, 1942) p. 79.

[xv] Letter of Darwin Martin to FLW of May 5, 1926. Darwin Martin papers, MS 22.8, Box 4, Folder 4-23. (University Archives, University at Buffalo).

[xvi] Darwin Martin papers, MS 22.8, Box 4, Folder 4-24. (University Archives, University at Buffalo).

[xvii] Meryle Secrest, *Frank Lloyd Wright, A Biography.* (New York: Alfred Knopf, 1992), p. 236.

[xviii] Anita Mitchell, "The Belle of Buffalo, The Life & Love of Isabelle Reidpath, Mrs. Darwin Martin". Western New York Heritage, Summer 2005, Vol. 8, No. 2, p. 13.

[xix] Ibid., p. 13.

[xx] Brendan Gill. Many Masks, A Life of Frank Lloyd Wright. (New York: Da Capo Press, 1987), p. 320.

[xxi] Mitchell, "The Belle of Graycliff", p. 13.

[xxii] Docent material from Graycliff Tour, 2005, p. 4.

[xxiii] Robert C. Twombly, *Frank Lloyd Wright, His Life and His Architecture.* (New York: John Wiley & Sons, Inc., 1979), p. 108.

[xxiv] Gail Satler, *Frank Lloyd Wright's Living Space.* (DeKalb: Northern Illinois University Press, 1999), p. 46.

[xxv] Patrick Mahoney, "An Architect's Descriptive History of Graycliff", Graycliff website http://graycliff.bfn.org/pathistory.html.

[xxvi] *Frank Lloyd Wright, The Natural House.* (New York: Bramhall House, 1954), p. 154.

[xxvii] Ibid., p. 13.

[xxviii] Darwin Martin papers, MS 22.8, Box 4, Folder 4-26 (University Archives, University at Buffalo).

[xxix] Letter of Darwin Martin to John Wright of September 21, 1926. Darwin Martin papers, MS 22.8, Box 4, Folder 4-27. (University Archives, University at Buffalo).

[xxx] Letter of John Wright to Darwin Martin, dated simply September 1926. Darwin Martin papers, MS 22.8, Box 4, Folder 4-27.

[xxxi] A porch roof projecting over a driveway at the entrance to a building providing shelter for those getting out of a vehicle. *The American Heritage Dictionary of the English Language.* (New York: American Heritage Publishing Co., 1969), p. 1021.

[xxxii] Docent material from Graycliff Tour, 2005, p. 6.

[xxxiii] Letter of Darwin Martin to FLW dated July 21, 1926. Darwin Martin papers, MS 22.8, Box 4, Folder 4-25. (University Archives, University at Buffalo).

[xxxiv] Norris Kelly Smith, *Frank Lloyd Wright, A Study in Architectural Content,* (Englewood Cliffs: Prentice-Hall, Inc., 1966)., pp. 128-129.

[xxxv] A stratum of hard bluish gray limestone 10 to 14 inches thick at all exposures from Onondaga county to Lake Erie, showing little variation in character. Likely to contain mineral additives such as quartz or oxides. D.D. Luther, "Geology of the Auburn-Geneoa Quadrangles", New York State Museum, Museum Bulletin 137 (1909), p. 23.

[xxxvi] McCarter, ed., *On and By Frank Lloyd Wright.* A Primer of Architectural Principles, p. 304.

[xxxvii] Edgar Tafel, *Apprentice to Genius, Years with Frank Lloyd Wright.* (New York: McGraw-Hill Book Co., 1979),p. 50.

[xxxviii] Mitchell, "The Belle of Buffalo', p. 14.

[xxxix] Shipman was a contemporary of FLW and considered the "Dean of America Women Landscape Architects." She utilized geometric organization contrasted with lush flower plantings. Her work was uniquely American and meant to augment existing archi-

tectural styles. She designed private gardens for Ford and Rockefeller and locally, worked with the Knox family, the Schoellkopfs and other prominent Buffalo area families. In April 1929, Darwin had purchased 50 assorted pines in addition to the 220 he previously bought from John D. Larkin, Jr. for the summer house.(Darwin Martin Papers, MS 22.8, Box 4, Folder 5-19, University Archives, University at Buffalo).

[xl] Tafel, *Apprentice to Genius*, p. 51.

[xli] Mitchell, Darwin D. and Isabelle R. Martin, p. 9.

[xlii] Letter of FLW to Isabelle Martin, December 1935. Darwin Martin papers, MS 22.8, Box 6. (University Archives, University at Buffalo).

[xliii] Mitchell, Darwin D. and Isabelle R. Martin, p. 9.

[xliv] Mitchell, "The Belle of Buffalo", p. 15.

[xlv] Isabelle and Darwin Martin are buried in an unmarked plot at Forest Lawn Cemetery, Buffalo, NY.

[xlvi] John Conlin, "Graycliff". Buffalo Spree Magazine September 1997, p. 56.

[xlvii] Tom Beckman, "Martin kin sheds light on creation of Wright house." Buffalo News, July 9, 1997 no pagination.

[xlviii] Anita Mitchell, "Belle of Buffalo, The Life & Love of Isabelle Reidpath, Mrs. Darwin Martin." Western New York Heritage, Vol. 8, No.2, (Summer 2005), p.14.

[xlix] Leona M. Ketterl, "Graycliff, A Proposal for the Rehabilitation of a Master Work." May 1997, without pagination. Darwin Martin papers, MS 22.2, University at Buffalo Archives.

[l] Ada Louise Huxtable, *Frank Lloyd Wright*, (New York: Penguin Group/Viking Press, 2004), p. 98.

[li] Historia Domus, p. 66. This is the official record and journal maintained by the Piarist fathers during their ownership of Graycliff. Entries were recorded by the rector of the house several times weekly and contain information about significant events or the mundane daily routine that would affect this religious community.

[lii] Fr. Calasanz Bau, Sch. P., Saint Joseph Calasanctius. (Madrid: ICCE Publications, 1976), p. 145.

[liii] Ibid., p. 402.

[liv] *Historia Domus*, p. 70.

[lv] Oral history interview of Fr. Kalman Miskolczy SchP. and Fr. Nicholas Fodor, SchP. on May 16, 2006. These two Piarist priests were the last residents at Graycliff and had resided there during irregularly extended intervals since the 1950's until 1998.

[lvi] Ketterl, "Graycliff, A Proposal for the Rehabilitation of a Master Work", without pagination.

[lvii] Oral history interview of Fr. Kalman Miskolczy SchP. and Fr. Nicholas Fodor, SchP.

[lviii] Fr. Miskolczy indicated that many of the volunteers had experience as carpenters and builders and documents show a "Mr. Lee" as a hired contractor. The project was completed within several weeks.

[lix] Docent handbook material from Graycliff Tour, 2005, p. 7.

[lx] Interview of Fr. Fodor.

[lxi] The priests were pleased to know that they utilized the same space as the previous

owners for gardening. Different priests would plant flowers and vegetables for their use.

[lxii] The official daily prayers of the Catholic clergy.

[lxiii] Interview of Fr. Miskolczy and Fr. Fodor.

[lxiv] Ketterl, "Graycliff, A Proposal for the Rehabilitation of a Master Work", without pagination.

[lxv] Interview of Fr. Miskolczy and Fr. Fodor.

[lxvi] Ibid.

[lxvii] *Historia Domus*, p. 117.

[lxviii] Interview of Fr. Miskolczy and Fr. Fodor.

[lxix] Diocese of Buffalo Archives, Calasanctius High School folder.

[lxx] A novitiate program is an intense year or two of introspection and development of a religious candidate preparing him for the priesthood. This is usually done during theological studies.

[lxxi] *Historia Domus*, p. 136. "There always seemed to be a lot of snow!" per Fr. Fodor.

[lxxii] For related information refer to Buffalo News article of February 3, 1999 by Tom Beckman, "Former Refugee Recalls Role of Piarist Fathers in Preserving Graycliff." Fathers Miskolczy and Fodor confirmed that refugees were on site but would not elaborate.

[lxxiii] *Historia Domus*, p. 118.

[lxxiv] Interview of Fr. Miskolczy and Fr. Fodor.

[lxxv] Both priests stated that sometimes a visitor would stop by as they were interested in seeing this particular work by Wright.

[lxxvi] Ibid. The *Historia Domus* indicates that the 1979 money went to repair a broken water main on the property.

[lxxvii] Edgar Tafel, *Apprentice To Genius, Years with Frank Lloyd Wright,* (New York: McGraw-Hill Book Co.,1979), p. 93.

[lxxviii] John H. Conlin, "Frank Lloyd Wright's Last Visit to Graycliff", The Graycliff Conservancy Newsletter, 2000, 2nd Edition, no pagination.

[lxxix] Fr. Fodor recalls Fr. Vereck telling them of this incident that evening at dinner. The priests could not fully understand why the architect was upset over the addition of the chapel and thought it a bit amusing at the time.

[lxxx] Polish Arts Club of Buffalo website: http//pacb.bfn.org/projects/graycliff/.

[lxxxi] Ibid.

[lxxxii] Interview of Fr. Miskolczy and Fr. Fodor, and the Historia Domus.

[lxxxiii] Ibid.

[lxxxiv] *Historia Domus*, p. 108.

[lxxxv] *Hisoria Domus*, p. 177.

[lxxxvi] Document entitled: "Our 'Mother house' in Derby, NY " by Fr. Miskolczy detailing the selling of the property in 1996. Fr. Miskolczy believed the offering price was too low for such a significant property.

[lxxxvii] This property is located on Old Lake Shore Road next to the Graycliff property. It was sold in the 1980's and housing was erected on the site.

[lxxxviii] Christina Abt, "Doing the 'Wright' Thing." EVE Magazine, Winter 2001.

[lxxxix] Author not listed, "Restoring the Legacy-Graycliff Restoration", Frank Lloyd Wright Quarterly, Spring 2005, Vol. 16, No. 2, p. 20.

[xc] James Fink, "Preservationists take option on Wright's Derby complex," Buffalo Business First, November 17, 1997.

[xci] Ibid.

[xcii] Ibid. From the oral history interview of Fr. Miskolczy and Fr. Fodor and the *Historia Domus*.

[xciii] Christina Abt, "Doing the 'Wright' Thing". EVE Magazine, Winter 2001.

[xciv] Ibid.

[xcv] Fr. Miskolczy interview.

[xcvi] Tom Beckman, "Foundation Will back Acquisition of Graycliff," Buffalo News, November 15, 1998.

[xcvii] Ibid.

[xcviii] *Historia Domus*, p. 118.

[xcix] *Historia Domus*, p. 122.

About the author: Paul Lubienecki is a Doctor of Philosopy of History at Case Western Reserve University.

"Raise My Voice Against Intolerance." The Anti-Nazi Rally in Madison Square Garden, March 27, 1933, and the American Public's Outrage over the Nazi Persecution of Jews

by Dr. Robert G. Waite

"I have come to Madison Square Garden many times, mostly to speak on behalf of the political party to which I belong," explained Alfred E. Smith, former governor of New York State and 1928 presidential candidate, to the 23,000 plus listeners crowded into the arena on the evening of March 27, 1933. Another 35,000 had massed on the streets outside, listening to the words of Governor Smith and each of the other speakers broadcast over a public address system. "But I don't believe I ever came into it with greater satisfactions than I feel tonight to raise my voice against intolerance, bigotry and against the suppression of freedom of speech and the press and the abridgement of the right of public assembly."[1] Governor Smith was joined on the podium by a group of prominent figures, including New York City mayor James P. O'Brien, president of the American Federation of Labor William Green, Senator Robert Wagner, distinguished members of the clergy, and Rabbi Stephen Wise, president of the American Jewish Congress and the organizer of this mass protest against recent measures taken by the Hitler regime in Germany against its Jewish citizens. "This protest is not against the German people whom we love and revere," Rabbi Wise assured the audience when he came to the podium. "It is not against the political program for Germany is master within its own household, but solely against the present anti-Jewish policy of the Nazi government." Similar rallies were held in more than 65 cities in 25 states as a wave of outrage swept across America. An estimated one million were expected to join the protest meetings.[2]

The rally in Madison Square Garden grew out of a far-reaching and deep-seated anxiety in America over the Nazi treatment of the Jews and the regime's assault on organized labor and political opponents. As reports of mistreatment and discrimination were published in newspapers throughout the nation, Jewish communities, political figures, religious leaders, and rank and file labor became alarmed and they added their voices to the protest which percolated into a steady stream of letters to German consulates in the US and into rallies in cities throughout the nation. The rejection of Nazi policies was widespread, deeply felt, and sincere. The responses showed how much Hitler's repression had touched a raw-nerve among the American people and not simply its Jewish citizens. Rarely have so many American from such diverse backgrounds, from such differing religious and political beliefs, come together in common cause to voice their outrage over persecution and repressive policies. The rally in Madison Square Garden culminated this spontaneous protest movement and sent a powerful message to political leaders in the United States and in Germany. Its impact was, however, mixed.

Concern about the repressive policies of the new government that came to power on January 30, 1933, in Germany had mounted steadily across the US as Nazi pressure on political opponents, labor unions and Jews intensified in the ensuing weeks. Reports of arrests, beatings, abuse, and rampant discrimination came regularly out of Germany. As early as 1930 American Jews viewed with some anxiety the anti-Semitic outbursts of Nazis troops.[3] Following Hitler's appointment as Reich Chancellor troublesome reports came repeatedly from Germany and "the news of these events shocked the outside world."[4] On March 3, for example, the Chicago Tribune's correspondent in Berlin, Sigrid Schultz, reported the arrest of some 3,500 alleged communists and the political unrest in the capital city that had led to the death of at least three persons. The newly established auxiliary police, comprised largely of members of the Nazi paramilitary unit the SA, had occupied the offices of the leading Jewish organization. As these accounts spread across America, concern mounted. In St. Louis, a group of "prominent Jewish citizens" went in mid-March to the German consulate there "to protest the alleged persecution of Jews."[5]

Widely cited in the press was an article in the London *Daily Her-ald* that asserted "plans are completed for an anti-Jewish pogrom...on a scale as terrible as nay instance of Jewish persecution in 2,000 years."[6] High ranking Nazi officials moved, however, to calm fears abroad, show-ing a remarkable sensitivity to world opinion. On March 14 the New York *Times* reporter in Berlin summarized a broadcast by Hitler "commanding the Nazi storm troops to put an immediate stop to acts of political terror, personal persecutions and interference with private business." The result was, he wrote, "a visible relaxation of political tension throughout Ger-many."[7] Writing from Berlin, Sigrid Schulz reported in mid-March that Hitler had ordered the arrest of three Nazis in Cologne who had broken into the home of a Jewish merchant and robbed him. "The arrests are the direct result of Chancellor Hitler's order to his followers to cease acts of terrorism and to refrain from interfering with the business life of the na-tion," she observed. Similar accounts came from other German cities.[8]

The respite from Nazi inspired violence was short-lived, however, and before long actions on the streets of German revealed the regime's intentions, its aggressive mistreatment of political opponents and Jews, and the Nazi leaders' inability, actually their unwillingness, to curb radi-cals within their ranks. Throughout early March newspapers in Germany reported Nazi aggression and violence against Jews and Jewish owned businesses. Boycotts of Jewish stores grew more common and ominous with SA troops, thugs sporting the ominous brown uniform, blocking ac-cess to shops. On March 10 the *Jüdischen Rundschau* reported that "in a number of cities...numerous department stores and Jewish businesses were closed" as the result of such actions. SA men stood at the entrances with signs reading "Germans, buy in German shops." Rumors of more closings spread when on March 11 "several uniformed SA people" barred access to the Karstadt department store in Hamburg. Department stores through-out Germany, even Woolworths which Nazi leaders quickly identified to their henchmen as American and not Jewish owned, were the subject to SA attacks.[9]

Throughout America, voices of protest rose during the month of March, the most vocal often coming from prominent figures in the Chris-tian communities. The Reverend Dr. S. Parkes, a leader of the Protestant church, released a statement that called on Christians to unite against anti-

Semitism. In Louisville, Kentucky, more than 150 residents met at the urging of the Louisville Council of Churches and adopted a resolution "appealing for the cessation of alleged persecution of Jews in Germany and asking President Roosevelt and the Department of State to convey the message to the German government." Across New York City clergymen condemned Nazi oppression of Jews from the pulpits of churches during the services that preceded the Madison Square Garden rally. The rector of the French Church du Saint-Esprit on East 78th Street called Hitler's policy a "recrudescence of medieval barbarism." The congregation of the Community Church on West 43rd Street adopted a resolution calling upon President Roosevelt to "investigate the persecutions." Views among the city's rabbis were mixed, however. Rabbi William Rosenblum, Temple Beth Israel on West 91st Street called for a boycott of German goods. At Temple Emau-El the rabbi warned that protests might further imperil Germany's Jewish communities. Representatives of New Jersey's Jewish congregations met and adopted a resolution urging the State Department to take "suitable...action."[10] On March 20, the American Jewish Committee and the B'nai B'rith made public that they had asked the government "to make proper representations to the government of Germany" against the anti-Jewish policies of the Hitler regime.[11] Even the editor of New York City's German language newspaper, the *Staats-Zeitung*, joined the protest against what he termed the "insane persecution of the Jews." Its publisher, Bernard Ridder, added in comments directed toward Nazi Germany: "Any regime founded upon the basis of religious or racial persecution must inevitably meet the united moral opposition of the civilized world."[12]

Other prominent individuals and organizations joined the call for protests against the Nazi persecution of Germany's Jews and political opponents. The editor of the influential magazine The Nation called the "official pronouncements and behavior" of the Hitler regime "barbarism without parallel since the Middle Ages."[13] In late March the American League for Human Rights adopted a resolution stating that it viewed "with abhorrence the persecutions and discriminations that have taken place in Germany," and it strongly urged the US government to call upon the Hitler government "to put an effective stop to such abuses and to guarantee the exercise of essential rights to all within its borders." The

President of Princeton University called Hitlerism a threat to world peace. Some prominent figures advocated opening the doors for Jews and others fleeing Nazi oppression. "The Administration in Washington should adopt the most liberal and most humane interpretation possible under our statues, facilitate the grating of visas, and consider even a brief modification of the law, if necessary, to permit the entry of the German victims of political persecution," argued an editor of The Nation.[14]

Governors, state legislators and members of Congress spoke out, too, adding their voices to the mounting wave of protest. The governors of South Dakota, Montana, Arizona, and California sent telegrams to the American Jewish Congress on the eve of the New York City rally voicing their concerns over Nazi policies and support for the protest rally.[15] State legislatures issued resolutions urging the members of Congress representing these districts, the President, and Secretary of State to, as the New York Assembly stated, use their "best diplomatic efforts in an attempt to persuade the German Government to desist from any further outrages and persecution."[16] More states joined the protest against Nazi persecutions. In late March the Assembly of the state of Rhode Island passed a resolution protesting "against the atrocious demand of Adolf Hitler for the political and economic extermination of the Jewish people in Germany." It termed "this anti-Semitic hatred, not truly representative of the German spirit,... an insult not only to the Jews of Germany but to the world as well." The Rhode Island resolution called the policy of the Hitler regime "one of the most tragic events in the long history of Jewish martyrdom."[17] The General Court of Massachusetts adopted a resolution condemning "all acts of persecution reported to be committed against the members of the Jewish faith in Germany and urges the President and the Congress of the United States to present these sentiments to the German Government."[18] New York City Alderman James Kiernan added his voice to the growing outcry. On March 23 he released to the press a resolution he planned to introduce that called upon the city "to petition the Government of the United States to make vigorous and proper representations to the German Government to put an immediate stop to these barbaric persecutions and to restore to German Jewry its civil and religious rights and the protection of the laws of the Reich."[19]

Congressmen also spoke out forcefully. Already on March 9, Representative Emanuel Celler (D-NY) introduced a lengthy resolution that identified the "serious antisemtic [sic] outbreaks," the "oppressions and proscriptions of Jews," the "denial of the fundamental rights of every human being" in Nazi Germany, and which called upon the State Department "to make known to the German Government that it does not view with favor the cunning cruelties, outrages, and insults now practiced against... Jews." Congressman Celler termed Nazi policy "a sort of cold pogrom" and asserted that "unless there are changes for the better in Germany...we shall be compelled to use every weapon in the legislative arsenal to help put an end to the acts of these cowards and cravens."[20] On March 22, Representative Joseph A. Gavagan (D-NY) told his colleagues in the House: "The recent news of persecution and proscription against the Jew, coming out of Germany, saddens the heart and soul of the lovers of justice the world over." And he added, "once again humanity is aroused from its lethargy by the persecution of a member race of the human family." Several other Congressmen introduced concurrent resolutions condemning the persecution and calling upon the President to speak out strongly. "Whereas the present Hitler regime in Germany has taken measures to suppress and persecute certain groups within its borders, and has singled out for particular attack, according to press reports, Jews of that country," wrote Congressman John Douglass (Democrat, Massachusetts) in a resolution submitted on March 22. It "authorized and directed" the President to make clear to the Nazi regime that this nation "view[s] with concern the tyrannical methods employed" and strongly urged "a more humane policy." Two other resolutions passed that same day called upon the State Department to "make known to the German Government" its acute displeasure with the "cunning cruelties, outrages, and insults" directed against Jews.[21] Concurrent with the final plans for the Madison Square Garden rally concern mounted across the nation and calls for the State Department to lodge protests grew.

As reports of Nazi oppressive measures and violence against Jews and political opponents continued to spread, plans for a series of anti-Nazi rallies across the US began to emerge. On March 12, the national executive committee of the American Jewish Congress met at New York's Hotel Commodore to consider a range of economic and organizational issues as well as the recent events in Germany. The "turbulent three-hour session," a reporter for the New York *Times* wrote, quickly focused exclusively on "the anti-Semitism of Adolf Hitler and his party." Those in attendance united in their call for "widespread protest" and a show of unity in opposition. The meeting concluded with plans for a "mass meeting" in Madison Square Garden, as originally suggested by Dr. Samuel Margoshes, editor of *The Day.* Simultaneous meetings to "bring the matter before Congress" were planned for a host of other cities across the nation.[22]

In New York City, prominent business leaders went to the head of the German consulate "as representatives of their government to voice the most serious concern" with the planned Nazi boycott of Jewish businesses. Although American protests had subsided, the consular official telegrammed Berlin that the recent measures have prompted a "new sense of urgency" in America which "threatens to go to such an extent as to seriously threaten German-American relations."[23] The steadily mounting pressure on the Jews of Germany led in the US to the planning for a "nation-wide expression of indignation against the anti-Semitism of Adolf Hitler." Rallies were scheduled in more than 80 cities. The American Jewish Congress took the lead and met at New York City's Hotel Astor once again on March 19th to "formulate plans," the New York Times reported. Emotions at the meeting ran high as some 1,500 representatives of various Jewish organizations sought entry. The session ran for more than four hours. Proposed resolutions called for designating a day in the near future for "mass meetings...in every Jewish community" to protest Nazi policy directed against Jews and for a mass rally in Madison Square Garden. Bernard Deutsch, president of the American Jewish Congress, told those in attendance that his offices were "flooded with messages from all over the country demanding protest action." Jews across the nation were, he added, "unanimous" in their desire to express the "horror and indignation against the reign of terror to which our brethren are subjected in Germany." The issue of a boycott of German goods was raised and vigorously debated.[24]

While plans for the rally at Madison Square Garden were being discussed, some opposition groups took to the streets in protests and marches. By March 12 demonstrations and mass meetings against Nazi violence had been organized in more than 20 cities in 18 different nations, from Buenos Aires and Rio de Janiero to Sydney and from Tunis to Istanbul. Most were called for by inter-denominational coalitions and some were, a reporter for the *American Jewish Year Book* observed, "held entirely under non-Jewish auspices." The "most notable" demonstrations came later, in New York City on March 27, in Paris on May 10 and London on June 27.[25]

Already on March 23, an estimated 2,000 Jewish veterans paraded to City Hall in New York in a protest of Nazi repressive policies. The marchers walked quietly through the streets, from Cooper Square, down Lafayette Street to City Hall, organized in columns of four and carrying no placards. Some walked with the banners of the veteran organizations they represented, such as the Veterans of Foreign Wars, the Disabled American Veterans, and the American Legion. More than 10,000 spectators lined the route.[26] In a strong show of support, New York's Mayor Patrick O'Brien came out of his office and walked to the front steps of City Hall. He stood there for 25 minutes, watching the vets and their supporters march by carrying only American and Jewish flags. The mayor addressed the veterans and spoke out forcefully against the oppressive actions of the Nazi government. "Any regime that has for its basis religious or racial intolerance or persecution is bound to meet the moral opposition of the entire world," O'Brien explained. He received from the leaders of the parade resolutions calling for a boycott of German goods and urging the US government to submit a formal diplomatic protest. The mayor assured the group's leaders of his support and told them to wait until Monday to hear his words at the rally scheduled to take place in Madison Square Garden.[27]

Several days before the big New York City rally the American Jewish Committee issued a strong statement of protest of the Nazi regime's policies toward the Jews of Germany and asserted that "Every proper step must be taken to remedy these injustices." The call was made for a "day of national protest against the mistreatment of Jews in Germany." Rabbi Stephen Wise was more frank in his comments. "The time for caution and prudence is past," he told an attentive audience. "What is happening in Germany today may happen tomorrow in any other land on earth unless it is challenged and rebuked."[28] Prominent Christians and religious organizations such as the Catholic Truth Society spoke out against what its president, the Reverend Edward Lodge Curran, termed in a protest sent to the State Department "the unjust, unchristian and barbarous anti-Semitic activities of the Hitler regime." Reverend Curran urged the State Department to lodge a formal protest because, he wrote, "A protest from the United States Government may be the means of awakening the great bulk of the German people to the folly of being represented by a former Austrian citizen whose path has already been marked by blood."[29] The American Jewish Committee and the B'nai B'rith formally asked the US government on March 20 "to make proper representations to the government of Germany" condemning the persecution of Jews. "The events of the past few weeks in Germany have filled with indignation not only American Jews, but also Americans of every other faith," the statement read. "The conscience of the civilized world is aroused against this reversion to medieval barbarism." Prominent leaders of Christian faiths joined the protest against Nazi policies.[30]

Local political organizations in communities across the nation raised their voices in protest. On March 25, Brooklyn's Pallex Democratic Club forwarded to the German Embassy in Washington a resolution it adopted, a "solemn PROTEST against the appalling injustice of which German Jews have become the victims, and utter our deep sense of pain and resentment against the persecution and tortures inflicted upon the Jewish people of Germany." The Pallex Club resolved to "ask the USofA in the name of Justice and humane mankind that they intercede in behalf of the tortured and persecuted people of Germany." The German Embassy reported other actions, including, for example, a meeting on March 25 in Chicago of an estimated 200 workers "to protest fascist terror in Germany."[31]

Throughout March leaders of the Jewish communities continued to meet in New York City to plan their course of action. They were "swamped with communications and telegrams of support," the New York Times reported, as they discussed calls for a boycott of German goods and other measures.[32] While meeting at the offices of the American Jewish Congress Rabbi Wise and other leaders finalized plans for a massive rally in Madison Square Garden. The American Jewish Congress assembled a group of prominent and well-respected Americans for the New York City rally, including former Governor Alfred E. Smith, Senator Robert F. Wagner, New York Mayor Patrick O'Brien, Bishop Francis J. McConnell, former president of the Federal Council of Churches, Bishop William T. Manning, officials of the Greater New York Federation of Churches and the Interfaith Committee. On March 23 New York's Governor Lehman sent word that he too would join the speakers at Madison Square Garden, if work in Albany permitted. Organizers announced that similar inter-denominational protests were to be held in some 80 cities across the nation in a powerful statement of concern and opposition to the Nazi regime's anti-Jewish policies and actions.[33]

The roster of speakers for the Madison Square Garden rally included some highly respected political, civic and religious leaders. Already on March 23 the American Jewish Congress announced that Governor Alfred E. Smith would be one of the featured speakers.[34] That same day, William Green, President of the American Federation of Labor, made public his agreement to speak at the rally. Organized labor throughout the country had repeatedly petitioned against Nazi repression and Green told Rabbi Wise that he would be happy to appear and to express "the protest and indignation of the masses of organized American workers of all faiths against the outrages being committed by the Fascist regime in Germany against the Jews and all forward-looking movements in Germany." His organization, the AFL, represented some three million Americans.[35]

Crowds began to assemble outside the doors of Madison Square Garden already by 2:30 in the afternoon of March 27. Over the next several hours subways and elevated trains continued to bring more men and women to "the already overcrowded area," the New York *Times* reported. Shortly before six o'clock in the evening the doors swung open. Within half an hour the balconies filled with attendees and before long all of the Garden's 23,000 seats were taken. An estimated 35,000 people "were unable to gain admittance." Newspapers across the nation reported that tens of thousands had turned out to protest.[36] Many assembled on the streets outside to listen to the speeches over a public address system. Telegrams from governors and members of Congress condemning the Nazi persecution of Jews and expressing solidarity with the aims of the rally organizers arrived.[37]

Shortly after 8PM former Representative Nathan Perlman came to the podium and introduced Bernard Deutsch, president of the American Jewish Congress and chair of the rally. Deutsch set the tone for the evening, telling the audience that the protests meant no "feeling of un-friendliness or ill will toward the German nation." Rather, he continued, "The time has come when the civilized nations of the world should be concerned not only for the safety and protection of their nationals abroad, but should be keenly interested in the preservation of human rights of all minorities wherever they may be." Rabbi Stephen Wise, an outspoken leader in the broadening protest against Nazi violence against Jews, struck a similar tone. It would be a grave wrong "to make German Jews scape-goats because Germany has grievances against the nations," Rabbi Wise explained as he called upon the world to accept Germany's position in the world. But the "elementary maxims of civilization" also demanded "the immediate cessation of anti-Semitic activities and propaganda in Germa-ny."[38]

The speeches of Alfred Smith, William Green, President of the American Federation of Labor, Senator Robert Wagner, and Mayor Pat-rick O'Brien and the others who addressed the rally were broadcast by the Columbia Broadcast System across the nation. Stations in cities as distant as Los Angeles carried the addresses live. They were published too, each in its entirety, the next day in the New York *Times*.[39] "It is a privilege to be here this evening and to be able, in the name of the people of the City of New York, embracing as it does men and women of many races or creeds, to join in a protest against religious and racial persecution" in Germany, Mayor Patrick O'Brien told the audience. The reports from Germany on the mistreatment of Jews have been "so shocking as to seem well-nigh incredible." The mayor continued, summarizing the outstanding contri-butions of Jews to German culture and intellectual life and insisting that the anti-Jewish measures were the work of the extremists in power. He found comfort, however, in the "assurance...from high German officials that resolute action will be taken in Germany to prevent the possibility of any further persecution of Jews in that country."[40]

As Governor Alfred Smith walked to the podium he pulled out three envelopes upon which he had written notes for his speech, the main points he wished to address.[41] Smith explained that prior to the rally he had received "all kinds of telegrams and all kinds of cablegrams" insisting that "there wasn't any reason for a meeting," that reports from Germany had distorted the events there. He did not accept such arguments, telling the audience "where this is a good deal of smoke there must be some fire." The only course of action, the only way to deal with such abusive and growing discrimination was "to drag it into the open sunlight and give it the same treatment that we gave the Ku Klux Klan." Smith turned next to the Hitler regime and the violence in the streets directed against Jews. "Now there is one thing that we are all sure about and that is the platform of the ruling party," he explained. And that platform was anti-Semitic. Those who ran on it had "the avowed purpose...to separate the Jews from the life of Germany." He noted the violence directed against Jews and stated, "This fact, however, remains: That up to the present moment, if we look at the record, the responsible head of the German Government has said nothing in denunciation of this conduct." The best way to combat the violence, he asserted, "is by the expression of public opinion in a meeting such as this one." His speech, the New York *Times* reported the next day in a front page article, "brought the otherwise solemn audience to its feet."[42]

"As I read the reports of the occurrences in Germany that are responsible for this meeting," Senator Robert Wagner told the audience in Madison Square Garden, "of the manifestations of intolerance, discrimination, and even violence, I am filled with horror and dismay," echoing the theme raised by other speakers. Senator Wagner spoke of the economic hardships that men and women had dealt with "in a spirit of kindliness and cooperation." Now, his voice rising, "a new shadow has been cast upon us," he explained. "The black shadow of intolerance...laden with prejudice, heavy with discrimination, is deepening the darkness in which humanity has been groping in the effort to reach the light of a better day." He condemned bigotry in all shapes, particularly that at work in Germany. "Our concern is not limited by the common kinship of our Jewish citizens with the Jews of Germany," he added. "We have assembled under the common flag of civilization." Senator Wagner concluded with these words: "Our purpose tonight is to give expression of our loyalty to the ideal of the nobility of man—regardless of race or creed—an ideal which, when attacked, will find its defenders under every flag, for upon it depends the progress of mankind and the happiness of generations to come."[43]

A number of governors and members of Congress not in attendance sent letters to the organizers of the rally and many were read to the audience. New York's Governor Herbert Lehman remained, however, close to his office in Albany where he did address a mass rally at the Capitol Theatre that same evening. Stating that most Germans were opposed to the Hitler regime's discrimination of Jews, he continued: "The truth must in time allay the passions aroused by appeals to bigotry. All right thinking people, regardless of race, creed or nationality, must unite in the effort to hasten that time." The Albany rally, with speakers representing the three major religious faiths, adopted a resolution calling upon "the Government of the United States to continue its vigilant and vigorous representations in order to secure for the Jews of Germany their civil and religious rights." The same evening, more than 800 persons crowded into a Schenectady high school to voice their outrage, and they too adopted a resolution urging the State Department to lodge a formal protest with Hitler. A similar meeting was held in Troy.[44]

Organized labor had been forceful in its condemnation of Nazi policies, and its leader, William Green, President of the AFL-CIO, told the audience at Madison Square Garden "I come tonight in the name of Labor protesting, in its sacred name, against the atrocities which are being perpetrated upon the Jewish population of Germany." Voicing deep sympathy for them and for German trade unionists, Green said: "Labor in American wishes them to know that it is not unmindful of the suffering to which all of them are being subjected and that it fully appreciates the difficulty and the distressing experience through which they are now passing." And, he added, "We pledge to them our moral and economic support."[45]

Bishop John Dunn of New York's Catholic Archdiocese had agreed to speak but he withdrew at the last moment, basing his decision on a State Department announcement that it had been "assured that the mistreatment of Jews in Germany had been stopped." Other prominent religious leaders did address the rally. Bishop William Manning denounced "the tyrannical and cruel persecution carried on against those representing all religious faiths and the brutal attempt to stamp out all religion" in the Soviet Union and Nazi Germany. "Race prejudice, oppression, religious persecution have no right to exist anywhere in this world," he concluded. Bishop Francis McConnell called for Germany to regain its place among nations, to be respected and treated fairly. He urged that the protests against anti-Semitism continue because "if there is no protest at all against so completely out-of-date a thing as the anti-Semitic movement at the present time, then we will come to a place after a while where the situation becomes intolerable, and then we resort to force." Charles H. Tuttle, president of the inter-denominational Interfaith Committee appealed to the Germany people "not to permit within their borders continuance or resumption of the acts of aggression and injustice against the Jews, lest prejudice and hate overrun the world and civilization lose all that it has gained for tolerance and understanding since the Dark Ages."[46] Other speakers included John Haynes Holmes, Church of the Messiah NYC, Dr. Joseph Tenenbaum, chairman of the executive committee of the American Jewish Congress, Dr. Samuel Margoshes, editor of The Jewish Day, Morris Rothenberg, president of the Zionist Organization of America, James N. Rosenberg, Mrs. Rebecca Kohut, president of the World Congress of Jewish Women, Abraham Cahan, editor of The Jewish Daily Forward, Chaim Greenberg, leader of the Zionist Laborites, Alexander Kahn, president of the People's Relief, and Abraham Goldberg, a prominent Zionist.[47]

Just one day after the rally in Madison Square Garden the New York City Board of Aldermen adopted unanimously a stern condemnation of Nazi policies. The resolution, introduced by Aldermen James F. Kiernan and Joseph Reich, both of Brooklyn, contained numerous grounds for blasting the German government. "Reports from Germany bring to America harrowing tidings of incessant atrocities perpetuated against Jews in Germany," it began. The resolution then gave reasons for its scathing tone. "This persecution and intimidation of peaceful and law abiding people does not accord with the modern enlightened spirit of tolerance and is shocking to the conscience of civilized humanity," and the "outrages" were directed against "a helpless religious minority." They universalized the Nazi attacks, calling the persecutions "a most cowardly, inhuman and un-Christian assault upon every precept of civilized living," and "in direct opposition to the spirit and traditions of American freedom of conscience and religious belief." The sense of outrage extended across religious groups and a number of secular organizations had "raised their voices in protest against these Nazi outrages." Having stated their argument, the two Aldermen turned to the other Board members and together they raised their "voice[s] in solemn protest." The Board unanimously adopted the resolution that was directed squarely at the US government. Its stated aim was to move the Roosevelt to action, to at the very least "make vigorous and proper representations to the German government to put an immediate stop to these barbaric persecutions and to restore to German Jewry its civil and religious rights and the protection of the Laws of the Reich."[48]

Other political figures came forward, adding their voices to the mounting outcry. The New Jersey Legislature adopted unanimously a resolution "protesting against persecution of Jews in Germany." In Detroit, 10,000 protested Nazi oppression of Jews.[49] In the House of Representatives, William J. Sirovich (D-NY) took the floor and told his colleagues that "my purpose in taking the floor of the House this afternoon is to boldly, fearlessly, and courageously protest against the foul, iniquitous, and brutal treatment of the nations of Jewish extraction in Germany by the cowardly, sadistic, paranoiac madman of modern Germany, Adolf Hitler." Not mincing his words, Representative Sirovich called Hitler's chancellorship "an insult to the great men who have graced that position in the past." Hitler's "official robes," he added, "have been bathed in the innocent blood of Jewish people." Sirovich called upon Secretary of State Cordell Hull to "protest against this infamous treatment by Hitler and his associates of innocent men and women who have committed no crime outside of being born Jews."[50]

During March and continuing into April the American Jewish Committee and other Jewish organizations called for Secretary of State Cordell Hull to register with the Hitler regime the Roosevelt administration's interest in the welfare of Jews in Germany. Hull declined to act. In a March 26 telegram to the President of the American Jewish Committee, Hull explained that he had directed the American Embassy in Berlin "to investigate the situation and to submit a report."[51] The Embassy replied that "whereas there was for a short time considerable physical mistreatment of Jews this phase may be considered virtually terminated." It concluded that "stabilization appears to have been reached," and "there are indications that in other phases the situation is improving. I feel hopeful in view of the reported attitude of high German officials and the evidence of amelioration already indicated that the situation which has caused such widespread concern throughout this country will soon revert to normal."

A New York *Times* reporter in Berlin concurred. "The German rulers, under the pressure of world opinion, seem to be making a sincere effort to reduce physical persecution and place their regime in a better light before the world," noted Frederick Birchall in the March 27 edition.[52] The presidents of the American Jewish Committee and the B'nai B'rith maintained their pressure, however, and sent Hull a memorandum on April 9 urging that the US government intercede on behalf of the Jewish minority in Germany. On April 28 Hull assured Jewish leaders that he was "continuing to watch the situation confronting the Jews in Germany with careful and sympathetic interest." The State Department, he added, would "do everything within diplomatic usage to be of assistance."[53]

The mounting protests across the nation and the rally in Madison Square Garden gained the attention of prominent Nazis. "Reports of agitation in the United States on behalf of German Jews is hotly resented in the National Socialist newspapers, which regard it as unjustifiable interference with German affairs and propaganda calculated to arouse hostility toward Germany and the new regime," a reporter for the New York *Times* cabled from Berlin. The German government issued a statement calling for "drastic measures" against foreign correspondents "guilty of spreading atrocity reports." The Nazi Party threatened, "well-informed circles" in Berlin told another journalist, to organize a counter movement against Jews.[54] Hitler termed the accounts of anti-Jewish measures "dirty lies" in a trans-Atlantic interview conducted on March 23 by Joseph Connelly, vice-president of the International News Service in New York City. During the 15 minute conversation, Hitler, sitting in his office at Munich's Nazi Party headquarters, the Braun Haus, stated: "There has been no discrimination between Jews and Christians" and he went on to assert, "As a matter of fact, our storm troops have in many cases under the risk of their own lives protected life and property of political opponents, among whom may have been some Jews."[55] The phone call from Munich was clearly intended to assuage the out roar coming from abroad, especially America, against Nazi persecution. It did not take long, however, for the Hitler regime to show its true intentions. A day later, on March 24 the Nazi Party newspaper *Völkischer Beobachter* carried an article on the march to New York City Hall by Jewish veterans and the rally planned for Madison Square Garden, identifying each as part of the "all Jewish hate and atrocity campaign against Germany." The center of this "anti-German propaganda" was New York City whose newspapers "publish articles daily about the alleged incidents in Germany," the Nazi Party organ announced. In an article headlined "The Jewish Power-Struggle Against Germany" the newspaper summarized the protests in New York City, framing them as foreign attacks on Nazi Germany.[56] Other newspapers in Germany moved to fuel the already "strong body of home opinion against the charges abroad of atrocities in this country," reported the New York *Times* on March 26. In a special cable the *Times*' correspondent in Berlin wrote that the reports in the American press are "hotly resented in the National Socialist newspapers, which regard it as unjustifiable interference with German affairs and propaganda calculated to arouse hostility toward Germany and the new regime." Berlin's moderate *Vossische Zeitung* wrote in a front page article of the "defense against the anti-German hate-propaganda."[57] That same day, Hitler issued a "call to all Party organizations to boycott against the Jews" and a host of other anti-Jewish actions. Minister of Propaganda Joseph Goebbels warned, the New York *Times* reported, that his agency would take "sharp countermeasures" against those who had launched "the atrocity campaign."[58] Hitler and Goebbels began to discuss a boycott of Jewish businesses. "Counter-Attack against the Jewish Atrocity Propaganda" is how a front page headline in the *Völkischer Beobachter* termed the planned boycott.[59] Propaganda minister Goebbels in the days leading up to the Madison Square Garden rally prepared an article for an English newspaper, the *Sunday Express*, what he called a "very factual and objective essay against the atrocity propaganda." Over the next couple of days Goebbels remained occupied with the New York City rally and what he referred to as the "atrocity propaganda" coming from America. He met with Hitler and they decided that "we will only be effective against the foreign hatred only when we force out its originators or at least the beneficiaries, namely the Jews living in Germany who have remained here untouched." The pair called for a major boycott of all Jewish shops in Germany. A day later, Goebbels dictated yet another "biting essay" against the "atrocity propaganda of the Jews." The boycott was to begin on April 1 in Germany.[60]

Other members of the Hitler government joined the fray. Foreign Minister Konstantin von Neurath sent a cable on March 28 to Cardinal O'Connell of Boston, attempting to reassure and assuage the American public. "According to newspaper reports, representatives of the Roman Catholic clergy will take part in large protest meetings at Madison Square Garden in New York, and elsewhere, tonight against alleged pogroms against German Jews," Neurath wrote. "Such allegations are devoid of all foundation," and the "national revolution" which aimed at stamping out "the Communist danger and cleansing the public life of Marxist elements, has proceeded with exemplary order." He added further assertions, also devoid of truth. For example, Neurath insisted that "Hundreds of thousands of Jews carry on their lives throughout Germany as usual," and that "thousands of Jewish stores are open every day," as if little had changed following the Nazi takeover in January 1933. Neurath concluded that these stories of discrimination "evidently emanate from sources which desire to poison the friendly relations between Germany and the United States, and to discredit the new National Government of Germany."[61]

While the US Secretary of State moved cautiously and did not issue a formal protest to the Nazi regime, the German diplomatic mission in Washington kept track of the mounting opposition. The information it sent to the Foreign Office in Berlin was extensive and included a 17-page chronology of protests from labor organizations against Nazi measures as well as numerous letters of protest from across the nation.[62] Already on March 17, a telegram from the New York City consular office to Berlin described a recent speech by Albert Einstein calling for protests against Hitler as filled with "anti-German sentiment" which "dominated New York with Jews heavily dominating the press." The slogan "'persecution of Jews' is similar to the Belgium atrocity propaganda [of the First World War] and is used as part of a broader, anti-German campaign."[63] On March 26 the embassy telegrammed Berlin its appraisal of the upcoming rally in Madison Square Garden: "The attacks, to be expected at the assembly on Monday in New York, appear to be based on the following points: 1) anti-Semitic agitation in Germany; 2) the discrimination of Jews, also in economic matters; 3) the lack of legal safeguards and personal protection in the constitution; 4) measures against foreign or non-local Jews, especially the East-Jews [Ostjuden]." The German mission in New York City also provided the home office in Berlin a steady stream of material on reactions to the oppressive measures, such as the

April 1 boycott. The New York office feared that the scheduled visit by the German ambassador would be used by "New York Jews" to "demonstrate" their hostility to Nazi policy. The Foreign Office in Berlin assembled an entire folder of materials for "combating the hate- and atrocity campaign." Increasingly the tone of these cables within the Foreign Ministry mirrored that of the Nazi press and leadership – xenophobic and viciously anti-Semitic.[64]

Groups continued to speak out against Nazi persecution and the organized boycott, and a few observers noted rather optimistically at the time that the wave of protest across America might have tempered Hitler's and Goebbels' ambitions. A Berlin correspondent for the Universal Service, a distributer of news articles, wrote that the Foreign Office had indeed taken notice of the protests and was in fact "greatly disturbed." He added that when vice-chancellor von Papen received a cable from friends in America describing the mounting hostility to Nazi German von Papen he went directly to Hitler.[65] "The power of public opinion against the brown-shirt bestialities has been demonstrated," stated an editorial in The Nation. "Before the expressed sense of outrage throughout the world, the Nazi head devils have pulled in their horns."[66]

Protests continued to be registered in the weeks following the Madison Square Garden rally. Throughout New York City members of the clergy condemned from the pulpit the "persecution of Jews by the Hitler government and the Nazi legions." The pastor of the Union Methodist Church went so far to urge the US government to "lift the bars of immigration to allow the persecuted Jews and others who are discriminated against to enter this country." The American League for Human Rights and the Church Peace Union sent messages to President Roosevelt urging his administration to intervene "against the recent outrages committed in Germany." On April 17 the Federal Bar Association of New York, Connecticut, and New Jersey adopted unanimously a resolution condemning the new restrictions on members of the German legal profession of the Jewish faith, "that many of our brother lawyers in Germany are being grievously persecuted" and forced from their positions and their occupation. "We hereby call upon all believers in human justice throughout the world to publicly condemn the indefensible course that has so far been taken toward those members of our profession, and other professions, by the present administration of the Government of Germany."[67]

When the situation in Germany failed to improve and it actually worsened, calls for a strong statement against Nazi policy continued to be registered during the mid-1930s. Prominent Jewish organizations argued that oppressive measures would be soon directed against Protestants and Catholics as well. More protest rallies were held. A rally in Madison Square Garden on March 7, 1934, featured 23 speakers representing Protestant and Catholic churches, trade unions, political figures, and the American Legion. New York's mayor Fiorello LaGuardia addressed the audience. Organizers called the rally "the case of civilization against Hitlerism."[68] Several years later, on March 15, 1937, another rally was held in Madison Square Garden. Organizers now called Hitler "a menace to world peace" and concluded that his regime's destruction of "all vestiges of democracy and human and civilized procedure in Germany" was but the first step in "an onslaught upon democratic society everywhere." A resolution adopted at the rally concluded that "Hitlerism constitutes the gravest threat to peace, civilization and democracy."[69] Once more resolutions were adopted and forwarded to the State Department and Roosevelt administration; once more they declined to act.

Major newspapers showed a remarkable reluctance to criticize or discuss at length Nazi policies through at least the mid-1930s.[70] Furthermore, not only the top political leaders but also the Jewish community in America was divided on what actions to take, on their appraisal of Hitler and his anti-Semitic policies. Rabbi Stephen Wise and the American Jewish Congress called, on the one hand, for decisive action and had already organized a conference of Jewish organizations that met on April 19, 1933, in New York City to build on the momentum of the Madison Square Garden rally. "Never before has the situation of the Jews required a greater concerted effort of American Jewry than today," the announcement for the meeting read. "The German Government gives assurances that the wave of atrocities is at an end. However the so-called dry-pogrom is being carried on by the authorities of the Reich with shocking vigor." Within Germany large numbers of Jewish professionals continued to be "forcibly thrown out of their positions."[71] The American Jewish Committee, another prominent organization, concluded in 1933, on the other hand, that "The anti-Semitic campaign is but a phase of the intense national flame the Fascists have kindled. The greatest danger in the German situation is not just its anti-Jewish propaganda, unjust and inhuman as this is, but the nationalism that is blazing throughout the land."[72] Across the nation hundreds of thousands of individuals from different religions, followers of differing political parties, men and women from big cities and small towns and from a variety of social backgrounds raised their voices in early 1933 to protest the intolerance, discrimination, and persecution of Jews in Nazi Germany. This massive outcry culminated in the March 27 rally. A huge success by any standard, the Madison Square Garden rally and the massive public outcry against the Nazi regime's repression of Jews failed to move the President or the State Department to act decisively. While the executive branch did take notice of the rally and the State Department received letters and cables from individuals, religious and human rights organizations as well as members of Congress, little was done. There were no formal protests to the German government coming from Washington, no open condemnation of Nazi persecution, no threat of economic sanctions, no hint at the severance of diplomatic relations. "I feel hopeful, in view of the reported attitude of high German officials and the evidences of amelioration already indicated," Secretary Hull wrote in a cable to Berlin, "that the situation, which has caused such widespread concern throughout this country, will soon revert to normal."[73] Without forceful action from the President and the Secretary of State little hope for change in Nazi policy could be expected. Although official statements of concern and protest might have not moved Hitler and his lead henchmen to moderate their persecution of Jews, the reactions in Berlin to the Madison Square Garden rally and the 80 plus rallies held across America that same evening did indeed show that they were listening as the voices of protest across the nation grew louder.

Endnotes

[1] Quoted in "Smith Likens Nazis to Klan," Daily Boston *Globe* (March 28, 1933). "60,000 New York City Jews Protest Action in Germany," Chicago *Daily Tribune* (March 28, 1933).

[2] "Thousands Hear Al Smith Condemn Jews' Persecution," Atlanta *Constitution* (March 28, 1933). "Monday Set Aside By Jews to Protest Against Persecution," Chicago *Daily*

Tribune (March 23, 1933). The estimate of one million protestors comes from The New York *Times;* see "250,000 Jews Here To Protest Today. More Than 1,000,000 in All Parts of the Nation Also Will Assail Hitler Policies," (March 27, 1933). Harry Schneiderman, in "Review of the Year 5693," American Jewish Year Book 35 (1933-1934), 43. Melvin I. Urofsky, A Voice That Spoke for Justice. *The Life and Times of Stephen S. Wise* (Albany: State University of New York Press, 1982), 260-269. Adam Wolfson, "The Boston Jewish Community and the Rise of Nazism, 1933-1939," Jewish Social Studies 48 (Summer-Autumn 1986), 308-309.

[3] See, for example, "Review of the Year 5692," American Jewish Year Book 34 (1932-1933), 27.

[4] Schneiderman, "Review of the Year 5693," 26-31; quote is from page 31.

[5] Sigrid Schultz, "Nazi Terrorism Grows," Chicago *Daily Tribune* (March 9, 1933). St. Louis, Mo., March 13, 1933, Bericht Nr. 23B, Politische Archive Auswärtiges Amt (hereafter PAAA) (Berlin) R98444. See the editorials, "Terrorism Rules Germany," The Nation 136 (March 29, 1933); "World Wrath at Hitler's Attack on German Jews," *The Christian Century L* (April 5, 1933); and "Back to Barbarism," The Nation 136 (April 12, 1933), 388.

[6] "Hitler Cabinet Revives Spirit of Kaiser's Days," Chicago *Daily Tribune* (March 3, 1933). "Anti-Semitism in Germany," Chicago *Daily Tribune* (March 13, 1933). "Charge Reign of Terror," Chicago *Daily Tribune* (March 15, 1933).

[7] "Jews Promised Safety by Hitler," *Atlantic Constitution* (March 11, 1933); and Guido Enderis, "Violence in Reich Subsides on Order," New York *Times* (March 14, 1933).

[8] Sigrid Schulz, "Jail Hitlerites for Terrorizing Jewish Family," Chicago *Daily Tribune* (March 15, 1933). Frederick T. Birchall, "Nazis Combing Out the Storm Troopers," New York *Times* (March 27, 1933). "Editorial. World Wrath at Hitler's Attack on German Jews," *The Christian Century L* (April 5, 1933).

[9] Das Schwarzbuch. Tatsachen und Dokumente. Die Lage der Juden in Deutschland 1933 (Paris: Comité des Délégations Juives, 1934, reprinted 1983, Berlin, Ullstein Verlag), 284-291; quotes are from pages 286, 288 and 291. "Terrorism Rules Germany," *The Nation* 136 (March 29, 1933), 332. Hannah Ahlheim, 'Deutsche kauft nicht bei Juden!' Antisemitismus und politischer Boykott in Deutschland 1924 bis 1935 (Göttingen: Wallstein Verlag, 2011), 243-246.

[10] Schneiderman, "Review of the Year 5693," 45. "Louis, Ky.," New York *Times* (March 27, 1933). "Attacks on Jews Scored in Pulpits," New York *Times* (March 27, 1933). "Jews in Jersey Protest," New York *Times* (March 27, 1933). "Protest on Hitler Growing in Nation," New York *Times* (March 23, 1933).

[11] "Jews Here Demand Washington Action."

[12] Quoted in "German Paper Here Scores Hitler Rule," New York *Times* (March 23, 1933).

[13] "Back to Barbarism," *The Nation* 136(April 12, 1933), 388.

[14] "Roosevelt Urged to Plead for Jews," New York *Times* (March 27, 1933). Schneiderman, "Review of the Year 5693," 45. "Attacks on Jews Scored in Pulpits." "Nazis Against the World," *The Nation* 136 (April 5, 1933), 360-361.

[15] "Roosevelt Urged to Plead for Jews."

[16] Congressional Record. Proceedings and Debates of the First Session of the Seventy-

Third Congress, Volume 77, Part 1 (March 27, 1933), 856.

[17] "Persecution of the Jews in Germany," Congressional Record, Volume 77, Part 2 (April 7, 1933), 1379.

[18] "Petitions and Memorials, March 31, 1933, Congressional Record, Volume 77, Part 2 (April 6, 1933), 1322.

[19] Quoted in "City Protest Urged Over Nazi Policies," New York Times (March 24, 1933)

[20] Congressional Record, Volume 77, Part 1 (April 20, 1933), 2019.

[21] Congressional Record, Volume 77, Part 1 (March 22, 1933), 771. H.CON.RES.7, 73d Congress 1st Session, March 22, 1933. H.RES.75, 73d Congress 1st Session, March 27, 1933. See also, H.CON.RES 11, 73d Congress 1st Session, March 27, 1933; and "Ask House To Order a Protest to Reich," New York Times (March 23, 1933).

[22] "Nation-Wide Protest on Hitler Demanded," New York Times (March 13, 1933). A mass protest rally at Madison Square Garden rally was first called for by Dr. Samuel Margoshes, editor of the newspaper The Day. Moshe Gottlieb, "The Anti-Nazi Boycott Movement in the United States: An Ideological and Sociological Appreciation," Jewish Social Studies 35 (July-October 1973), 198-199, 211. "Monday Set Aside By Jews to Protest Against Persecution," Chicago Daily Tribune (March 23, 1933).

[23] Telegram aus New York, March 22, 1933, PAAA, R98444, Bl. 522075.

[24] "City Protest Urged Over Nazi Policies." "Nazi Foes Here Calmed by Police," New York Times (March 20, 1933). "Jews to Stage Nazi Protests in Many Cities," Times Union (March 26, 1933).

[25] Schneiderman, "Review of the Year 5693," 43-46. On the plans for a rally in London, see "Equality for Jews in Reich Demanded," New York Times (March 27, 1933).

[26] "Protest on Hitler Growing in Nation," New York Times (March 23, 1933). "10,000 March in Jewish Protest," Daily Boston Globe (March 24, 1933).

[27] "O'Brien Reviews 4,000 Hitler Foes. Tells Jewish Veterans at City Hall World Will Oppose Nazis' Intolerance," New York Times (March 24, 1933). Gottlieb, "Anti-Nazi Boycott Movement in the United States," 198-199, 201-202. "Protest on Hitler Growing in Nation."

[28] "Jews Here Demand Washington Action," New York Times (March 21, 1933).

[29] "Protest on Hitler Growing in Nation." "Jews Here Demand Washington Action."

[30] "Jews Here Demand Washington Action," New York Times (March 21, 1933).

[31] Pallex Democratic Club, 1840 Douglass Street, Brooklyn, NY, PAAA, R287849, Bl. 152; "Proteste aus Arbeiterkreisen," PAAA, R287849, Bl. 16.

[32] "Protest on Hitler Growing in Nation," New York Times (March 23, 1933). See, "The Boycott Question," in The American Jewish Committee Twenty-Seventh Annual Report; and "The Anti-German Boycott. A Statement of the Position of the American Jewish Committee," www.ajcarchives.org.

[33] "Al Smith to Speak at Jewish Protest," Daily Boston Globe (March 23, 1933). "Jews Here Demand Washington Action." "Protest on Hitler Growing in Nation." On Governor Lehman, see "City Protest Urged Over Nazi Policies," and "Lehman Appeals To German People," New York Times (March 28, 1933).

[34] "Al Smith to Speak at Jewish Protest."

[35] See, for example, "Proteste aus Arbeiterkreisen," a file of letters and protest resolutions sent to German consulates and the Embassy in Washington from labor groups in a number of American cities, PAAA, R287849. "Protest on Hitler Growing in Nation." 36 "35,000 Jam Streets Outside the Garden," New York Times (March 28, 1933). "Thousands Hear Al Smith Condemn Jews' Persecution," Atlanta Constitution (March 28, 1933). "Rabbis Denounce Hitler in Sermons," New York Times (March 26, 1933). "60,000 New Yorker City Jews Protest Action in Germany," Chicago Daily Tribune (March 28, 1933). "250,000 Jews Here To Protest Today." See the photograph, "Overflow crowds listening to speeches at an anti-Nazi rally at Madison Square Garden," Larry Gordon photographer, Territorial Photographic Collection, RG 120, United States 238, YIVO Institute for Jewish Research (NYC).

[37] "Leaders of Nation Send in Protests," New York *Times* (March 28, 1933).

[38] "Other Faiths Join In. Crowd Overflowing the Garden Hears Leaders Assail Persecution," New York *Times* (March 28, 1933). "250,000 Jews Here to Protest Today." Rabbi Wise announced that following the rally the American Jewish Congress would present the German Ambassador with "four vital demands," including the "immediate cessation of all anti-Semitic activities," the "abandonment of the policy of racial discrimination... and economic exclusion of Jews," "the protection of Jewish life and property," and "no expulsion of 'Ost-Juden' Jews who have come into Germany since 1914;" quoted in "250,000 Jews Here To Protest Today."

[39] "Radio Programs Scheduled for Broadcast This Week," New York *Times* (March 26, 1933). "Jewish Protest to Be Broadcast," Los Angeles *Times* (March 27, 1933). "City Leaders of All Faiths Voice Indignation," New York *Times* (March 28, 1933).

[40] The speech was reprinted in the New York *Times*, see "O'Brien Pays Tribute to Jewish Contribution to German Culture," New York *Times* (March 28, 1933).

[41] These hand-written notes are in the A.E. Smith Private Papers, New York State Library Manuscripts & Special Collections (Albany, NY), Box 33, folder 384.

[42] For the text of Smith's speech see "Smith Calls for a World-Wide Fight on Religious Bigotry," New York Times (March 28, 1933). "Other Faiths Join In."

[43] The text of the speech was printed in the New York *Times*; see "Human Tolerance, Not Judaism, Is the Issue, Wagner Declares (March 28, 1933).

[44] "Leaders of Nation Send in Protests," New York Times (March 28, 1933. "Lehman Appeals To German People," New York *Times* (March 28, 1933); this article contains the Governor's entire speech. "Albany Plans Protest Meeting," *Times Union* (Albany, NY) (March 23, 1933). "Albany Jewry Protests Nazi Excesses Tonight," *Times Union* (March 27, 1933). The front page headline of the *Times Union* read on March 28th, "1,200 Albanians Protest Jewish Persecutions By Hitler." "Gov. Lehman Addresses Meeting in City," *Times Union* (March 28, 1933).

[45] "Other Faiths Join In." "Protest on Hitler Growing in Nation," New York *Times* (March 23, 1933). See the 1933 publication of the American Jewish Committee, "The Voice of Religion."

[46] "Other Faiths Join In.

[47] Ibid.

[48] "No. 752. Resolution Petitioning the Government of the United States to Make Vig-

orous and Proper Representations to the German Government to Put an Immediate Stop to These Barbaric Persecutions and to Restore to German Jewry Its Civil and Religious Rights and the Protection of the Laws of the Reich," March 28, 1933, in Proceedings of the Board of Aldermen and Municipal Assembly, The City of New York, Volume I, Library of the City of New York.

[49] "Suburban Groups Decry Nazi Raids," New York *Times* (March 28, 1933). "10,000 Detroit Jews Meet to Protest," Detroit Free Press (March 30, 1933).

[50] Congressional Record, Volume 77, Part 1 (March 27, 1933), 884. "Urges Congress Act in Interest of German Jews. Sirovich Has Resolution of Protest," Chicago *Daily Tribune* (March 28, 1933).

[51] "Hull Obtains Consuls' Data on Jews' Cases," Chicago *Daily Tribune* (March 26, 1933). "Nazis End Attacks on Jews in Reich, Our Embassy Finds," New York *Times* (March 27, 1933). "Embassy Sees Trouble Ended," Daily Boston *Globe* (March 27, 1933).

[52] F.G. Vosburgh, "Hull Tells Jews Inquiry Proves Violence Ended." Atlanta Constitution (March 27, 1933). Frederick T. Birchall, "Nazi Combing Out the Storm Troopers," New York *Times* (March 23, 1933).

[53] Quoted in "The American Jewish Committee. Twenty-Seventh Annual Report 1933," American Jewish Year Book 36 (1934-1935), 435-436.

[54] "Nazis Resentful At Agitation Here," and "Reich Warns Correspondents Not to Send Atrocity Reports," New York *Times* (March 24, 1933). "Jewish Protests From Abroad Rouse Ire of Hitler's Party," Christian Science Monitor (March 27, 1933). See the column by Claude G. Bowers, "Hitler Can Stop Attacks on Jews," *Times Union* (March 28, 1933).

[55] Albany's *Times Union* newspaper ran front page headline reading: "Hitler, In Trans-Ocean Phone Talk, Brands Jewish Persecution Stories 'Dirty Lies'," *Times Union* (March 24, 1933).

[56] "Jüdische Boykottbestrebungen gegen deutsche Waren," *Völkischer Beobachter* (March 24, 1933). "Der jüdische Machtkampf gegen Deutschland," *Völkischer Beobachter* (March 28, 1933).

[57] "Germans Aroused By Attacks Abroad; Deny Wide Violence," New York *Times* (March 27, 1933). "Anti-American Feeling Grows," *Times Union* (March 23, 1933). "Nazis Resentful At Agitation Here," New York *Times* (March 24, 1933). "Abwehr" and "Auslandshetze flaut ab. Erfolge der deutschen Gegenaktion," Vossische Zeitung Nr. 147 (March 28, 1933).

[58] "Goebbels Warns of Action," New York *Times* (March 28, 1933).

[59] The full text of his speech is in Max Domarus, Hitler. Reden und Proklamationen 1932-1945, Volume I (Wiesbaden: R. Löwit, 1965), 248-251. See the front-page article, "Gegenschlag gegen die jüdische Greuel-Propaganda," *Völkischer Beobachter*, Nr. 83 (March 25, 1933). "Ban on Jews Spreads. Hitler's Party Prepares Boycott in Revenge for 'Atrocity Tales'," New York *Times* (March 28, 1933). "Gegenschlag gegen die jüdische Greuel-Propaganda," *Völkischer Beobachter*, Nr. 87 (March 28, 1933). *Das Schwarzbuch. Die Lage der Juden in Deutschland* 1933, 292ff.

[60] "24. März 1933," "26. März 1933," and "27. März 1933," in *Elke Fröhlich*, editor, Die Tagebücher von Joseph Goebbels, Teil I, Band 2 (Munich: K.G. Saur, 1987), 397-399.

On the April 1st boycott, see Ahlheim "Deutsche kauft nicht bei Juden!," 247-262; and, for example, the front page article "Nach dem Boycott," Vossische Zeitung Nr. 157 (Berlin, April 2, 1933). "Boycott zunächst nur heute," Vossische Zeitung, Nr. 155(April 1, 1933).

[61] "Cable to Cardinal Denies Any Pogrom," *Daily Boston Globe* (March 28, 1933). "Neurath Denies Rumors," New York *Times* (March 27, 1933). "Erfolg der Abwehr-Propaganda," Vossische Zeitung, Nr. 149(March 29, 1933). On the Nazi efforts to link Jews to the Bolsheviks, see Zosa Szajkowski, "A Note on the American-Jewish Struggle against Nazism and Communism in the 1930's," American Jewish Historical Quarterly 53 (March 1970), 272-274. Urofsky, *The Life and Times of Stephen S. Wise,* 266; "Nazis Against the World," The Nation Vol. 136 (April 5, 1933), 36; and American Jewish Year Book Vol. 35(1933-1934), 31-32.

[62] "Protest aus Arbeiterkreisen," March 22-29, 1933, PAAA, in Anlagen zu III A 1814/33, R287849, Bl. 155-172.

[63] Telegram, New York, March 17, 1933, Nr. 20, PAAA, R80307.

[64] Telegram. Deutsche Botschaft Washington, March 26, 1933, Nr. 155, Bl. 522106. See the file, Abteilung III Akten Betriffend: Bekämpfung der Hetz- und Gruelpropaganda sowie Boykottabewhr, vom März 1933 bis Juli 1933, Bd. 2, PAAA, R9844. Consuleramt New York, Telegram, Nr. 34 vom 5. April 1933, PAAA, K31853.

[65] Karl H. Von Weigands, "Anti-German Feeling Grows," *Times Union* (March 23, 1933).

[66] Edwin L. James, "The Nazis Begin to Dodge Anti-Semitic Boomerang. Hitlerites Weaken on Jewish Boycott in Face of World-Wide Protests and Peril to German Trade," New York *Times* (April 2, 1933). "Nazis Against the World," The Nation Vol. 136 (April 5, 1933), 360.

[67] "Attacks on Jews Scored in Pulpits," New York *Times* (March 27, 1933). "Roosevelt Urged to Plead for Jews," New York Times (March 27, 1933). "Persecution of the Jews in Germany" (April 17, 1933), Congressional Record, Volume 77, Part 3 (1933), 2655-2656.

[68] The Case of Civilization against Hitlerism Presented under the Auspices of the American Jewish Congress at Madison Square Garden New York, March 7, 1934 (New York: Robert O. Ballour Publisher, 1934).

[69] Hitler a Menace to World Peace. Addresses and Messages Delivered at the Peace and Democracy Rally at Madison Square Garden March 15th, 1937 (New York: Joint Boycott Committee of the American Jewish Committee and Jewish Labor Committee, 1937), 117-119.

[70] Frederick A. Lazin, "The Response of the American Jewish Committee to the Crisis of German Jewry, 1933-1939," American Jewish History 68 (March 1979), 286-288. Gottlieb, "Anti-Nazi Boycott Movement in the United States," 221-222. Margaret K. Norden, "American Editorial Response to the Rise of Adolf Hitler: A Preliminary Consideration," American Jewish Historical Quarterly 59 (March 1970), 289-293, 296. Szajkowski, "A Note on the American-Jewish Struggle against Nazism and Communism in the 1930's," 272-273. Wolfson, "The Boston Jewish Community and the Rise of Nazism," 305-309.

[71] Urofsky, *The Life and Times of Stephen S. Wise,* 265, 269-270. Schneiderman, in "Re-

view of the Year 5693, 54-56. "New Protest Called by Jewish Congress," New York *Times* (April 15, 1933).

[72] American Jewish Committee, "The Voice of Religion. The Views of Christian Religious Leaders on the Persecution of the Jews in Germany by the National Socialists," (New York: the American Jewish Committee, 1933), 31, www.ajcarchives.org. See "German-Jewish Controversy, June 5, 1934," reprinted in Szajkowski, "A Note on the American-Jewish Struggle against Nazism and Communism in the 1930's," 282-289.

[73] Reprinted in "Nazis End Attacks on Jews in Reich," New York *Times* (March 27, 1933). "A Need for Light, Not Heat," The Christian Century Volume L (April 5, 1933). On the actions of FDR, see See Richard Breitman and Allan J. Lichtman, FDR and the Jews (Cambridge: Harvard University Press, 2013).

About the author: Dr. Robert G. Waite is a historian at the German Resistance Memorial Center in Berlin. When back in the States he resides in Shushan, New York.

Call for New York State History Writers

New York History Review greatly appreciates your willingness to contribute an article to our magazine. Your donation of time and effort reflects both on your knowledge of the field and passion for its growth.

Please visit our submission page on our website for details: NewYorkHistoryReview.com/